JACKSON RISING

The Struggle for Economic Democracy and Black Self-Determination in Jackson, Mississippi

Kali Akuno and Ajamu Nangwaya

Cooperation Jackson

Daraja Press

Published by Daraja Press

http://darajapress.com

© Corporation Jackson 2017

Cover and graphics: Catherine McDonnell

Editorial management: Firoze Manji

Library and Archives Canada Cataloguing in Publication

Jackson rising : the struggle for economic democracy and black self-
determination in Jackson, Mississippi / edited by Cooperation Jackson
(Kali Akuno, Sacajawea Hall, and Brandon King) and Ajamu Nangwaya.

Includes bibliographical references.
Issued in print and electronic formats.
ISBN 978-0-9953474-5-8 (softcover).–ISBN 978-0-9953474-6-5 (ebook)

1. African Americans–Mississippi–Jackson–Economic conditions–
21st century. 2. African Americans–Mississippi–Jackson–Social
conditions–21st century. 3. Jackson (Miss.)–Economic conditions–21st
century. 4. Jackson (Miss.)–Social conditions–21st century. I. Cooperation
Jackson, editor II. Nangwaya, Ajamu, editor

F349.J13J33 2017   976.2'51   C2017-901090-5

C2017-901091-3

Contents

Part III. BUILDING SUBSTANCE

Part IV. CRITICAL EXAMINATIONS

Part V. GOING FORWARD

Part VI. AFTERWORD

Acknowledgements

We would like to thank each and every author who made a contribution to this publication.

We would like to give thanks to Hakima Abbas, Ajamu Baraka, Thandisizwe Chimurenga, Kamau Franklin, Sacajawea "Saki" Hall, Rukia Lumumba, Ajamu Nangwaya, Jessica Gordan Nembhard, Max Rameau, and Makani Themba for your new works and contributions developed specifically for this volume.

Further, we would like to than all of the authors and publications that allowed us to reprint their works in this volume. Thank you for your contributions and support. We would like to acknowledge all of the journals and contributions to bring them to everyone's full attention and to also give these authors and publications their just due and support. Please note the following contributions:

1. Kamau Franklin's *"The New Southern Strategy: The Politics of Self-Determination in the South"* is a compilation of two works in the following journals a) *Grassroots Thinking*, Kamau Franklin's personal blog found at https://grassrootsthinking.com/2009/09/29/the-new-southern-strategy-%E2%80%93-the-politics-of-self-determination-in-the-south/ and b) Organizing Upgrade at http://www.organizingupgrade.com/index.php/modules-menu/community-organizing/item/46-kamau-franklin-the-new-southern-strategy.

2. Kali Akuno's *"The Jackson-Kush Plan: The Struggle for Black Self-Determination and Economic Democracy"* was first published on two sites, the *Malcolm X Grassroots Movement* website as the Jackson Plan at https://mxgm.org/2012/07/07/the-jackson-plan-a-struggle-for-self-determination-participatory-democracy-and-economic-justice/ and in full on Kali's personal blog, *Navigating the Storm* at http://navigatingthestorm.blogspot.com/2012/05/the-jackson-kush-plan-and-struggle-for.html.

3. Kali Akuno's *"The People's Assembly Overview: The Jackson People's Assembly Model"* was first published on two sites, the *Malcolm X Grassroots Movement* website at https://mxgm.org/2014/11/28/peoples-assemblys-overview-the-jackson-peoples-assembly-model/ and on Kali's personal blog, *Navigating the Storm* at http://navigatingthestorm.blogspot.com/2014/11/peoples-assemblys-overview-jackson.html.

4. *"The Jackson Rising Statement: Building the City of the Future Today"*, which was written by Kali Akuno for the Administration of the late Mayor Chokwe Lumumba was first published on the *Jackson Rising: New Economy Conference* website at https://jacksonrising.wordpress.com/local/jackson-rising-statement/.

5. Ajamu Nangwaya's *"Seek Ye First the Worker Self-Management Kingdom: Toward the Solidarity Economy in Jackson, MS"* was first published by *Pambazuka News* at https://www.pambazuka.org/governance/seek-ye-first-worker-self-management-kingdom.

6. Bhaskar Sunkara's *"Free the Land: An Interview with Chokwe Lumumba"* was originally published in *Jacobin Magazine* at https://www.jacobinmag.com/2014/06/free-the-land.

7. Carl Davidson's *"Jackson Rising: An Electoral Battle unleashes a merger of Black Power, the Solidarity Economy and wider democracy"* was first published on *RIPESS the Intercontinental Network for the Promotion of Social Solidarity Economy* at http://www.ripess.org/jackson-rising-an-electoral-battle-unleashes-a-merger-of-black-power-the-solidarity-economy-and-wider-democracy-2/?lang=en.

8. Bruce Dixon's *"Jackson Rising: Black Millionaires won't lift us up, but Cooperation and the Solidarity Economy Will"* was first published in the *Black Agenda Report* at https://www.blackagendareport.com/content/jackson-rising%C2%A0black-millionaires-wont-lift-us-cooperation-solidarity-economy-might.

9. Michael Siegel's *"Why the Left should look to Jackson, Mississippi"* was first published in *Common Dreams* at https://www.commondreams.org/views/2014/05/22/why-left-should-look-jackson-mississippi.

10. Laura Flanders "After death of radical Mayor, Mississippi's capitol wrestles with his economic vision" was first published in *Yes Magazine!* at http://www.yesmagazine.org/commonomics/mississippi-capital-jackson-wrestles-economic-vision.

11. Sara Bernard's *"A Green Utopia in Mississippi?"* was first published in *Grist Magazine* at http://grist.org/cities/a-green-utopia-deep-in-mississippi-this-guy-has-a-game-plan/.

12. Kali Akuno's *"Casting Shadows: Chokwe Lumumba and the Struggle for Racial Justice and Economic Democracy in Jackson, Mississippi "* was first published as a study of the *Rosa Luxemburg Stiftung—New York Office* at http://www.rosalux-nyc.org/casting-shadows/.

13. Katie Gilbert's *"The Socialist Experiment: A New-Society vision in Jackson, Mississippi"* was first published in the Fall 2017 issue of the

Oxford American, with support from the Economic Hardship Reporting Project at https://mail.google.com/mail/u/0/#search/ katie.elizabeth.gilbert%40gmail.com/ 15e3e7ff52ac158f?compose=15e55337bf5fa7a3.

We also have to acknowledge the many contributions of the membership and staff of Cooperation Jackson towards the completion of this work. And lastly, we have to acknowledge the historic contributions of the people of Jackson, Mississippi, without whom this experiment in radical social transformation would not be possible.

Foreword: All Roads Lead to Jackson

Rukia Lumumba

It was March of 1971 when my father first came to the state of Mississippi. It was several months after the unarmed Black students at Jackson State University had been murdered on campus by law enforcement. They were shot in cold blood as they were socializing with their friends outside of the girls' dormitory. My father had come with the Provisional Government of the Republic of New Afrika (hereinafter referred to as PGRNA). Their mission was to establish a new community called El Hajj Malik.[1] The idea was pursuant to the PGRNA's goal of creating a *new society* built with no color, class, gender and physical ability discrimination. The ultimate goal was to create a new community where everybody would be treated at the highest standards of human rights. Their idea was to access funds made available by the Congressional legislation called the "New Communities Act". "The New Communities Act" had been created by the United States Congress to supply loads of funds to Florida for the development of new communities in underdeveloped areas. My father, along with other memmbers of the PGRNA, recognized the urgent need for a similar plan in Mississippi. At this time, in the early 1970s, Black people had made their case against racism, but were still suffering under White Supremacy and White inflicted terror. Even though some doors, some restaurants and some public accommodations had opened to provide Black people with access, this state of affairs did not mean control. The lack of control over resources, governmental systems, laws and basic accommodations meant lower levels of income, a lack of ownership of businesses and social infrastructures and the inability for Black people to create laws and practices that protected them from state and civil society violence. Violence in the form of lynching, police shootings of unarmed Black youth, state ignored beatings and rape of Black women by White men, government led mass incarceration of poor Black people, and state sanctioned theft of Black owned property. It was an invidious violence called racism that was adequately and dramatically portrayed in the photo posted in Jet Magazine of Emmet Till, a 14 year old Black child who was beaten beyond recognition and killed by racist White Mississippians.

As a consequence of this violence, the PGRNA desired to find a spot on earth where they could purchase land and develop a self-sustained community. These new communities would set a standard and pace in which people worldwide could see how Black people could rescue themselves from the depths of White Supremacy. These communities would first be formed in Mississippi, where some of the most horrible oppressions had occurred and where Black people had engaged in the staunchest resistance to White inflicted terror.[2] The Mississippi Freedom struggle was the linchpin of the Civil Rights Movement. The cruelty occurring in Mississippi was a clear sign of the brutality that would be spread and allowed to permeate cities across the South. The Terror imposed on Black MS was unparalleled to the violence against Black people occurring in any other state in the nation. The physical and mental torture inflicted on Black people in Mississippi was exceptional, second to none, incomparably high, incomparable cruelty. Between 1882 and 1940, 534 Black Mississippians were lynched—the highest total in the United States during that period. The federal government ignored terrorism waged against Black people. Congress and the president took no action to prevent lynching and the federal government did not prosecute the perpetrators even when the event was publicized at least a day in advance. With no other available recourse, this predatory violence permeated their souls and produced a fear so great that only resistance, fighting back could cure. So Black Mississippians big and small stood up, and fought back.

With the vision of a new society in mind, in 1971, the PGRNA purchased land outside of Bolden and Edwards, Mississippi to create this new community. On a bright sunny day in March of that year, a group of 500 women, men, children and elders went to celebrate on their newly purchased land. As they approached the land, they were confronted by a blockade. The blockade was led by the same chief law enforcement officer who was responsible for the murders of the two Jackson State students earlier that year. The officer stood in the middle of the road and said, "Niggers, were not going to have a land celebration today." Along with the officer stood the Mississippi Highway Patrol, the FBI and the Ku Klux Klan. But my father and the PGRNA, embraced the strength of Mississippi freedom fighters like Fannie Lou Hamer and Medgar Evers. They stood strong. They had already purchased the land and they were not turning back. My father often told me this story about their resistance on that day:

> This was a different day that was about to break and even though we sometimes start our days somewhat recklessly it was definitely going to break. So it was 500 of us, and we said we come in peace but we come prepared. So those 500 of us went down that road toward that roadblock, and we had old people, young people, we had babies, we had everybody, and we were praying. We were hardcore revolutionaries driven back to prayer. We were praying to God wherever we can find him, because it was serious. Because we knew a few things that we weren't going to tolerate that day. We knew we would not be disrespected; we weren't going to do the dog thing again like in Birmingham; we weren't going to do the waterholes thing; and we weren't in the turning the other cheek mode of things either. Because just as they had their stuff showing we had our stuff showing, and it was a near calamity. I know it's hard for you to believe but it was just like in the Bible, that road blocked opened up just like the Red Sea and we went through there. And when we got through that blockade and got to that land base, people started eating the dirt and that's where that slogan came from—*Free The Land*.

I started this article with this story, because it makes plain the vision for a more just society—a society that is rooted in shared governance, collective stewardship and use of resources, and unity in diversity. Most importantly, it embodies the understanding that critical to people's ability to exercise human rights, is their ability to exercise self-determination and governance of territory. Self-determination as defined by Fannie Lou Hamer is "the process by which a person controls their own life." It is this understanding of self-determination and vision of a better society that led my father to move back to Mississippi in 1989; to join the City Council in 2008, to serve as Mayor in 2013-2014, and is the root cause for the development of Cooperation Jackson and this *Jackson Rising* book.

Cooperation Jackson and the *Jackson Rising* book seeks to continue my father's life's work and the work of great Mississippi freedom fighters who came before him. Like my father, the ongoing organizing and institution building currently taking place in Jackson, Mississippi, is rooted in the desire to realize a new society, a new way of thinking, a new way of engineering and governing in which everyone is treated with dignity. I am honored to continue lifting up the slogan my father championed, "How're we gonna make Jackson rise? Educate, Motivate, Organize!" and introduce this important *Jackson Rising* book.

Jackson Rising documents the history and intersectionality of the Cooperative Movement and the Mississippi Freedom Movement. Most importantly, *Jackson Rising* provides a current and concrete example of what it looks like to build systems that address the unmet needs of people – be they producers, workers, consumers, or purchasers—and to provide them with the goods, services, cultural engagement, democratic rights, and political autonomy needed to live fully empowered lives. Quoting organizer and legal strategist Larry Stafford, "*Jackson* Rising is important because it teaches us how to build and sustain community power; it does not just tell us what we should oppose. It provides a micro cosmic model of what community power should look like." Most importantly, *Jackson Rising* is pivotal because it moves us from talking theory to actualizing theory…taking the steps, putting in the physical work, to make human rights for all a reality.

Through theoretical development and physical labor the *Jackson Rising* movement has seen many gains. We achieved the election of my father, Chokwe Lumumba as Mayor of Jackson, which is the capital and largest populated city in the state of Mississippi. Through Mayor Lumumba's Administration, we initiated Mississippi's first engagement in participatory democracy in which Jackson residents contributed to determining how the City's budget was spent. The best example of this participatory democracy was the people's passage of the 1% Sales Tax to aid the City in fixing its poor physical infrastructure. We championed the State's first Human Rights Charter and Commission that will help the City of Jackson better confront many of the social ills that confront our society, such as the abuse of state power, police brutality, and inhumane policies that lead to the discrimination, inequality, and gross inequities experienced by Blacks, Latinos, Indigenous peoples, immigrants, workers, Muslims and other religious minorities, the homeless and members of the LGBTQI community amongst others.

Following the legacy of Mississippians that came before us, we have contributed to the reemergence of cooperatives by establishing Cooperation Jackson, Jackson's first diverse cooperative that includes urban farming, compost and recycling, arts and culture and policy initiatives. We opened the Lumumba Center which serves as hub for local and international forums and events. We established the Community LandTrust (CLT). Land purchased by the LCT we will be used to provide cooperative housing alternatives to Jackson residents, especially those most impacted by economic injustice, people who are homeless and the working poor. We launched our international climate justice campaign *the Freedom Road from Jackson to Paris and Beyond*. Through this campaign we offer our voice, needs and solutions to the movement for climate control. Finally, we continue to facilitate the operation of People's Assemblies which are mass meetings for and by Jackson residents to address essential social issues, develop solutions, strategies, action plans, and timelines to change various socio-economic conditions in a manner desired by residents.

Though *Jackson Rising* efforts have resulted in several successes, the gains we have made are in serious jeopardy of being destroyed. The Mississippi State Government as well as governing municipalities surrounding Jackson are attempting a takeover. Similar to what we have seen happen in predominantely Black municipalities across the United States, the Governor and the overwhelmingly white Mississippi State Legislature is attempting to enact legislation to remove local control from the hands of the largely Black city council of Jackson. The State Legislative Body and Governor have reallocated monies collected through the 1% sales tax to fund State initiatives. The State Senate has introduced "the Airport Takeover Bill", SB 2162, to relinquish Jackson's control of the airport and all commerce derived therefrom. The State Senate has introduced the "Downtown Annexation Bill", SB 2525, to give business owners outside of Jackson the right to determine the development of Downton Jackson. The State Senate has introduced the "Racial Profiling/ Immigrant Targeting Bill", SB2306, to authorize police officers to arrest people based on skin color and culturally suspicious behavior, as well as authorize police officers to arrest people based on the officer's perception of a person's immigrant status. The State Senate passed "the Religious Freedom Bill" to criminalize members of the LGBTQI community; and to add insult to pain, Mississippi Governor Phil Bryant has enacted law establishing April as Confederate Heritage Month. The actions of the Governor and Mississippi State Legislature are blatant and direct attacks on the Human Rights afforded all people of color and the LGBTQI community. Inherently, these legislative efforts devalue Black governance and explicitly evidenced the paternalistic and racist intentions of the white power structure in Mississippi to control the lives and land upon which Black and non-white Mississippians reside. The aforementioned bills virtually condone and even promote Mississippi's historical and deeply rooted legacy of white supremacy.

Mississippi is not alone in the recent introduction and enactment of laws that are tantamount to the promotion of hatred. States across the U.S. are enacting similar laws. That is why the work we are doing in Jackson, Mississippi, is so important. In this *Jackson Rising* book we offer historical examples and current concrete solutions to address the struggles we face. I hope you find this book inspirational and find ways to engage in our work in Jackson. Like my father, I see Jackson, Mississippi, as a start When Jackson rises, WE all rise!

> I just can't give up now
> I've come too far from where I started from
> Nobody told me, the road would be easy
> But I don't believe he brought me this far to leave me.[3]
>   We will rise!

♦

This article is dedicated to my parents, Nubia and Chokwe Lumumba, Harriet Tubman, Fannie Lou Hamer, Ella Baker and all the women, men, children and gender self-identifying people of Mississippi who directly and indirectly sacrificed their lives to protect the Black body and Black joy. FREE THE LAND!

Notes

1. El Hajjwas the name given to the land purchased by members of the Republic of New Afrika. El Hajj Malik El Shabazz was the free name given to Malcolm X upon his return from his Haj in Mecca. The name was given to the land in honor of Malcolm X and his teaching of the right to self-determination.

2. Dr. Akinyele Omowale Umoja, *We Will Shoot Back: Armed Resistance in the Mississippi Freedom Struggle,* (New York and London, New York University Press, 2013).

3. *I Just Can't Give Up Now.* Artist: Mary Mary. Album: Thankful. Released: 2000

I

GROUNDINGS

1.

Build and Fight: The Program and Strategy of Cooperation Jackson

Kali Akuno

The fundamental program and strategy of Cooperation Jackson is anchored in the vision and macro-strategy of the Jackson-Kush Plan[1]. The Jackson-Kush Plan, as you will read later in this book, was formulated by the New Afrikan People's Organization (NAPO) and the Malcolm X Grassroots Movement (MXGM) between 2004 and 2010, to advance the development of the New Afrikan Independence Movement and hasten the socialist transformation of the territories currently claimed by the United States settler-colonial state. And as noted in several articles throughout the book, Cooperation Jackson is a vehicle specifically created to advance a key component of the Jackson-Kush Plan, namely the development of the solidarity economy in Jackson, Mississippi, to advance the struggle for economic democracy as a prelude towards the democratic transition to eco-socialism.

Although Cooperation Jackson is rooted in an ideological framework, vision and macro-strategy, it is not a static organization. Like any dynamic organization we do our best to center our practice on addressing the concrete conditions of our space, time and conditions and to align our theory with our practice. As such, our program and strategy are constantly adapting and evolving to address new challenges and seize new opportunities. And it will continue to do so.

End pursuits

The fundamental program and strategy of Cooperation Jackson is intended to accomplish *four fundamental ends*:

1. To place the ownership and control over the primary means of production directly in the hands of the Black working class of Jackson;

2. To build and advance the development of the ecologically regenerative forces of production in Jackson, Mississippi;

3. To democratically transform the political economy of the city of

Jackson, the state of Mississippi, and the southeastern region; and

4. To advance the aims and objectives of the Jackson-Kush Plan, which are to attain self-determination for people of African descent and the radical, democratic transformation of the state of Mississippi (which we see as a prelude to the radical decolonization and transformation of the United States itself).

Controlling the means of production

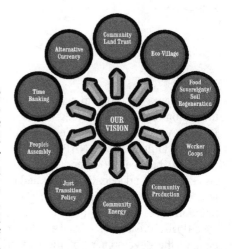

We define the means of production as labor power as well as the physical, non-human inputs that enable humans to transform the natural world to provide sustenance for themselves. The inputs in question are arable land, access to water, natural resources (wood, metals, minerals, etc.), and the tools and facilities that enable the cultivation of food and the transformation of raw materials into consumable goods and services, and the production or capturing of energy to power the tools and facilities. We also add control over processes of material exchange and energy transfer to our definition to give it greater clarity and force of meaning in line with our commitment to sustainability and environmental justice. The processes we feel are therefore necessary to control are the processes of distribution, consumption, and recycling and/or reuse. Without assuming some responsibility for these processes, we merely perpetuate the dynamics of externalization, particularly the production of pollution and the stimulation of waste from overproduction, that are inherent in the capitalist mode of production.

A population or people that does not have access to and control over these means and processes cannot be said to possess or exercise self-determination. The Black working class majority in Jackson does not have control or unquestionable ownership over any of these means or processes. Our mission is to aid the Black working class in Jackson, and the working class overall, to attain them.

Building the productive forces

On the question of building the productive forces in Jackson, it should be noted that while Jackson is the largest city in the state of Mississippi, and arguably the most industrialized city in the state, it is not and never has been a major center or hub of industrial production. Like most of the Deep South, Mississippi's development as a settler-colonial state has fundamentally been contingent upon the extraction of natural resources, such as timber for colonial and antebellum era ship building, and cash crop agriculture, such as cotton, tobacco, sugarcane, and rice, which were primarily sold as international commodities (see *"Exploiting Contradictions"* section below). Mississippi, like most of the South (North Carolina, Florida, and Texas being unique exceptions each in their own right), has not been able to break out of its historic position within the U.S. and world capitalist system of being a site of resource extraction and the super-exploitation of labor.[2] One of our primary tasks is to break this structural relationship by playing a leading role in industrializing Jackson, first and foremost, then the Kush district, and eventually the whole of Mississippi.

In many respects, we are positioning ourselves to act as a *"developer"*, which is normally a role that is exclusively played by the bourgeoisie, i.e. the capitalist class, or the state. We are aiming to upend this paradigm on many levels and in several strategic ways. One, we are seeking to negate the role of capital being the primary determinant of the social development of Jackson (see point below about exploiting the dynamic of uneven development within the capitalist system below), by situating this role in the hands of the working class through the agency of its own autonomous organizations and its control over the municipal state apparatus. But, we are not seeking to replicate the dynamics of *"development"* in the standard capitalist sense. The central dynamic in our quest is to upend the old aims, norms, processes and relationships of capitalist development, which have little to no regard for the preservation of the environment and ecology, and replace them with new norms that are fixed first and foremost on repairing the damage done to our environment and ecosystems, and creating new systems that will ultimately regenerate the bounty of life on our planet, in all its diversity. This will be possible by strategically incorporating, utilizing, and innovating upon the technologies of the third and (emerging) fourth waves of the industrial revolution, which will enable the elimination of scarcity, but within ecological limits (see more on this point below). What we aim to do is make Jackson a hub of community production, which is anchored by 3D-print manufacturing for community consumption, i.e. direct use-value consumption, and commodity production, to exchange value in consumer markets. How we plan to advance this initiative will be discussed in more detail below.

Democratically transforming the economy

In order to democratically transform the capitalist world-economy, we have to transform the agent central to this process, the working class, into a democratic subject. This transformation starts with the self-organization of the working class itself. Although not foreign to the working class historically by any means, particularly to the Black working class in the United States (which was often left solely to its own ends for self-defense and survival), worker self-organization is not a common feature of the class at present. This is a dynamic that we must change in Jackson (and beyond).

Now, to be clear on terms, self-organization means first and foremost workers directly organizing themselves through various participatory means (unions, assemblies, etc.) primarily at their places of work or points of production, but also where they live, play, pray, and study. The point of this self-organization is for workers to make collective, democratic decisions about how, when, and to what ends their labor serves, and about how to take action collectively to determine the course of their own lives and the animus of their own actions.

We will not and cannot accomplish any of the core ends described above without stimulating the self-organization of the Black working class in Jackson on a mass scale. While Cooperation Jackson, the Malcolm X Grassroots Movement and the broad forces aligned with the Jackson-Kush Plan have made some significant social and political advances and demonstrated our capacity to reach the masses, particularly in the electoral arena, we still haven't stimulated the self-organization of the Black working class on a mass scale. More work, profoundly more, must be done to accomplish the main tasks in this regard, which are to elevate and strengthen the class-consciousness of the community, foster and cultivate new relationships of social solidarity amongst the working class, and co-construct and advance new social norms and values rooted in radical ecological and humanitarian principles. In effect, what we are aiming to do is develop a new transformative culture.

In order to reinforce the development of this new culture within the present confines of Mississippi and the overall capitalist world-system, we have to harness the power of the Black working class and utilize it politically to eliminate the structural barriers blocking the "legal" development of the solidarity economy within the state. One of the main things we have to eliminate are the Mississippi legal statutes that presently restrict cooperatives to farming businesses, utilities, and credit unions. We have to create a new legal framework and paradigm that will enable any form of productive endeavor to become a cooperative or solidarity enterprise.

In the Jackson context, it is only through the mass self-organization of the working class, the construction of a new democratic culture, and the development of a movement from below to transform the social structures that shape and define our relations, particularly the state (i.e. government), that we can conceive of serving as a counter-hegemonic force with the capacity to democratically transform the economy. Again, we have taken some baby steps in this direction with the Mayoral election of Chokwe Lumumba in 2013 and the founding of Cooperation Jackson in 2014. But, we have a long way to get where we desire and need to be.

Advancing the Jackson-Kush Plan

"Politics without economics is symbol without substance". This old Black Nationalist adage summarizes and defines Cooperation Jackson's relationship to the Jackson-Kush Plan and the political aims and objectives of the New Afrikan People's Organization and the Malcolm X Grassroots Movement in putting it forward. Without a sound economic program and foundation the Jackson-Kush Plan is nothing more than a decent exposition of revolutionary nationalist politics. Cooperation Jackson is the vehicle we have collectively created to insure that we do more than just espouse good rhetoric, but engage in a concrete struggle to create a democratic economy that will enable Black and other colonized, oppressed and exploited people to exercise self-determination in Mississippi (and beyond).

We have to be clear, crystal clear, that self-determination is unattainable without an economic base. And not just your standard economic base, meaning a capitalist oriented one, but a democratic one. Self-determination is not possible within the capitalist social framework, because the endless pursuit of profits that drives this system only empowers private ownership and the individual appropriation of wealth by design. The end result of this system is massive inequality and inequity. We know this from the brutality of our present experience and the nightmares of history demonstrated to us time and time again over the course of the last 500 years.

We strive to build a democratic economy because it is the surest route to equity, equality, and ecological balance. Reproducing capitalism, either in its market oriented or state-dictated forms, will only replicate the inequities and inequalities that have plagued humanity since the dawn of the agricultural revolution. We believe that the participatory, bottom-up democratic route to economic democracy and eco-socialist transformation will be best secured through the anchor of worker self-organization, the guiding structures of cooperatives and systems of mutual aid and communal solidarity, and the democratic ownership, control, and deployment of the ecologically friendly and labor liberating technologies of the forth industrial revolution.

As students of history, we have done our best to try and assimilate the hard lessons from the 19th and 20th century national liberation and socialist movements. We are clear that self-determination expressed as national sovereignty is a trap if the nation-state does not dislodge itself from the dictates of the capitalist system. Remaining within the capitalist world-system means that you have to submit to the domination and rule of capital, which will only empower the national bourgeoisie against the rest of the population contained within the nation-state edifice. However, we are just as clear that trying to impose economic democracy or socialism from above is not only very problematic as an anti-democratic endeavor, but it doesn't dislodge capitalist social relations, it only shifts the issues of labor control and capital accumulation away from the bourgeoisie and places it in the hands of the state or party bureaucrats. We are clear that economic democracy and the transition to eco-socialism have to come from below, not from above. That workers and communities have to drive the social transformation process through their self-organization and self-management, not be subjected to it. This does not mean that individuals, organizations, and political forces shouldn't try to intervene or influence the development of the working class and our communities. We believe that we should openly and aggressively present our best ideas, programs, strategies, tactics and plans to the working class and to our communities in open forums, discussions, town halls, assemblies and other deliberative spaces, and debate them out in a principled democratic fashion to allow the working class and our communities to decide for themselves whether they make sense and are worth pursuing and implementing.

Confronting and defeating Black disposability

Above and beyond all of the lofty goals and ambitions mentioned above, there is one aim that we have above all others, and that is to counter the escalating threat of disposability confronting the Black working class.[3] The U.S. economy no longer needs the labor power of the Black working class, and as a result the Black working class constitutes a growing problem for the economic and social order of the empire, a problem in need of a solution.

Once the driving force behind the U.S. economy, constituting (as chattel) and producing over half of the country's wealth during the antebellum period, the Black working class is now a surplus population, one confronting ever greater levels of exploitation, precariousness, and material desperation as a direct result of the processes and forces of globalization and automation.[4] At the same time the agricultural sectors where the Black working class were concentrated until the early 20th century, have been largely mechanized or require even cheaper sources of super-exploited labor from migrant workers in order to ensure profits.[5]

To deal with the crisis of Black labor redundancy the U.S. ruling class has responded by creating a multipronged strategy of limited incorporation, counterinsurgency, and mass containment. The stratagem of limited incorporation sought to and has partially succeeded in dividing the Black community by class, as corporations and the state have been able to take in and utilize the skills of sectors of the Black petit bourgeoisie and working class for their own benefit. The stratagem of counterinsurgency crushed, divided and severely weakened Black organizations, particularly Black revolutionary organizations. And the stratagem of containment resulted in millions of Black people effectively being re-enslaved and warehoused in prisons throughout the US empire.[6]

This three-pronged strategy exhausted itself by the mid-2000 as core dynamics of it (particularly the costs associated with mass incarceration and warehousing) became increasingly unprofitable and therefore unsustainable. Experiments with alternative forms of incarceration (like digitally monitored home detainment) and the spatial isolation and externalization of the Black surplus population to the suburbs and exurbs currently abound, but no new comprehensive strategy has yet been devised by the ruling class to solve the problem of what to do and what politically can be done to address the Black surplus population problem. All that is clear from events like the catastrophe following Hurricane Katrina and the hundreds of Black people being daily, monthly, and yearly extra-judicially killed by various law enforcement agencies is that Black life is becoming increasingly more disposable. And it is becoming more disposable because in the context of the American capitalist socio-economic system, Black life is a commodity rapidly depreciating in value, but still must be corralled and controlled.

The capitalist system is demonstrating, day by day, that it no longer possesses the capacity to absorb dislocated and displaced populations into productive endeavors, and it is becoming harder and harder for the international ruling class to sustain the provision of material benefits that have traditionally been awarded to the most loyal subjects of capitalism's global empire, namely the "native" white working classes of Western Europe and the "whites" of the settler-colonial projects of the United States, Canada, and Australia.

When the capitalist system can't expand and absorb it must preserve itself by shifting towards "correction and contraction"—excluding and if necessary disposing of all the surpluses that cannot be absorbed or consumed at a profit.[7] We are now clearly in an era of correction and contraction that will have genocidal consequences for the surplus populations of the world if left unaddressed. The Black working class is now confronting this genocidal threat.

So, at its heart, this program and strategy, by attaining the four ends stated above, will create a model that provides a means to counter the escalating threat of disposability confronting the Black working class and provides some practical know-how pertaining to how to build a solid base of anti-capitalist transformation.

Exploiting contradictions

In order to concretely attain our four stated ends, we are seeking to exploit *three critical contradictions* within the capitalist world-system as a whole and the political economy of Mississippi and the United States in particular.

One of the primary contradictions we are trying to exploit is the *dynamic of uneven development*. Uneven development speaks to the fact that capitalism as a global system transforms the world through the concentration of human labor and human ingenuity (i.e. the production tools, industrial manufacturing, carbon based energy manipulation, advanced communications) to alter the physical environment for the pursuit of profit. Capitalism tends to concentrate the development of the productive and social forces in limited areas, while simultaneously restricting and distorting development and growth in other areas as part of the same process. Like the various modes of production that have preceded it, capitalism does not, and cannot, develop or transform the physical environments that humanity operates within and depends upon, uniformly. Meaning, in simple terms, that you can't build factories, power plants, freeways, strip malls, and grocery stores everywhere. Any serious attempt to do so would eliminate the limited concentration of surpluses the system extracts from workers and the earth itself.[8]

How Cooperation Jackson plans on exploiting this particular contradiction is by capitalizing on Mississippi's position as a weak link in the chain of capitalist production within the United States. Mississippi, like most of the southeastern portion of the United States, is grossly underdeveloped in comparison to the northeastern seaboard, the mid-western region, and the west coast. Since its colonial occupation by European settlers, the southeastern region, and Mississippi in particular, have primarily functioned as a site of resource extraction (like timber for ship building during the antebellum period) on the one hand or cash crop production (like "king" cotton) for international manufacturing and consumer markets on the other. Since the dominance of hydrocarbon (oil) dependent industrial production within the capitalist system from the early 19th century onwards, regions that concentrated on resource extraction and mono-cash crop production got locked into a position of relative dependency within the system that restricted their development.[9] As a site of dependent development, Mississippi has not been infused and developed by capital to possess advanced infrastructure outlays and networks (i.e. railways, highways, ports) or production clusters (factories, warehouses, logistic networks). As we note in "Casting Shadows",[10] the weak and relatively sparse concentration of capital in Mississippi creates a degree of "breathing room" on the margins and within the cracks of the capitalist system that a project like ours can maneuver and experiment within in the quest to build a viable anti-capitalist alternative.

We harness this breathing room by exploiting the fact that there is minimal competition in the area to serve as a distraction or dilution of our focus, a tremendous degree of pent up social demand waiting to be fulfilled and a deep reservoir of unrealized human potential waiting to be tapped.

The second critical contradiction we are trying to exploit is the *ecological limits of the capitalist system*. The capitalist system is a system bent on self-destruction. You cannot have limitless growth on a planet with finite resources. Something has to give. As it now stands, the capitalist system is rapidly destroying all of the vital, life giving and sustaining systems on our planet. Hydrocarbon dependent industrial production has forever altered our atmosphere. There is now more carbon in our atmosphere than at any time over the last 3 million years![11] CO_2, methane, and other climate altering gases induced by human production are beginning to cook the climate, with each year being progressively hotter than the previous one. The polar ice caps are disappearing right before our very eyes. The oceans are becoming more and more acidic, harboring ever-greater dead zones each year. And just as importantly, ocean currents, which regulate the flow of heat energy and weather patterns on the planet, are collapsing. And the constant resource extraction and drive to urbanize at the heart of the capitalist system are eliminating essential ecosystems and habitats that other complex life on this planet depend upon, resulting in the quickening of the 6th great extinction event, which might result in the loss of over 90% of the species currently living on the planet—including us.

As awkward and problematic as it may sound, we plan on exploiting this contradiction by getting out in front of the issue of climate change as much as we can politically and turning the economic strategies being proposed herein to address the climate crisis on their head. Our aim, as you will read in greater detail later, is NOT to foster and reinforce so-called "green capitalism".[12] Our aim is to help fashion and create a *regenerative economy*, one that not only restores and replenishes the resources its extracts from the earth, but aids in the actual restoration of our earth's ecosystems. We aim to do this by building a set of reinforcing institutions—such as green worker cooperatives, community land trusts, eco-villages, and centers of community production—that generate and redistribute both use values via mutual aid practices, and exchange values via the production of commodities, from the effort to recycle, reclaim, and reuse between 80 to 90% of essential resources and materials currently consumed and to introduce new zero-emission and zero-waste production methods on a large scale, starting with our municipality. We believe this regenerative orientation, coupled with sound solidarity economy practices, can and will be the basis for the development of economic democracy as an alternative to capitalism, and a prelude towards the democratic transition to eco-socialism.[13]

The third and final contradiction we are trying to exploit pivots on transcending the *productive limits of the capitalist system* that center on the conflict between the industrial, hydrocarbon dependent version of capitalist accumulation versus the emerging productive methods and technologies of the third and fourth industrial revolutions. These new methods and technologies potentially enable the development of a new mode of production and a radically different society and defining set of social relationships than those we have known over the past five hundred years. These emerging technologies and new social relationships lean towards the development of what some are calling a "post-capitalist" society, which is or could be a potential equivalent of what we call economic democracy. One of the chief proponents of this view, Paul Mason, holds that "postcapitalism is possible because of three major changes information technology has brought about".[14] Mason outlines three key components central to this contradiction, which enable a tremendous amount of maneuverability. He summarizes them thus:

> First, it has reduced the need for work, blurred the edges between work and free time and loosened the relationship between work and wages. The coming wave of automation, currently stalled because our social infrastructure cannot bear the consequences, will hugely diminish the amount of work needed—not just to subsist but to provide a decent life for all.

> Second, information is corroding the market's ability to form prices correctly. That is because markets are based on scarcity while information is abundant. The system's defense mechanism is to form monopolies—the giant tech companies—on a scale not seen in the past 200 years, yet they cannot last. By building business models and share valuations based on the capture and privatization of all socially produced information, such firms are constructing a fragile corporate edifice at odds with the most basic need of humanity, which is to use ideas freely.

> Third, we're seeing the spontaneous rise of collaborative production: goods, services and organizations are appearing that no longer respond to the dictates of the market and the managerial hierarchy. The biggest information product in the world—Wikipedia—is made by volunteers for free, abolishing the encyclopedia business and depriving the advertising industry of an estimated $3bn a year in revenue.

> Almost unnoticed, in the niches and hollows of the market system, whole swaths of economic life are beginning to move to a different rhythm. Parallel currencies, time banks, cooperatives and self-managed spaces have proliferated, barely noticed by the economics profession, and often as a direct result of the shattering of the old structures in the post-2008 crisis.[15]

These remarkable technological and productive advances are the product of the Third and Fourth industrial revolutions.[16] As noted, they are rapidly changing civilization, for better or worse depending on one's position, and making a dramatic new orientation to work and labor possible.

The Third Industrial Revolution (3IR), also known as the Digital Revolution, started in the 1960s, but exploded in the late 1980s and 1990s, and is still expanding today. This revolution refers to the advancement of technology from analog electronic and mechanical devices to the digital technologies we have now. The main technologies of this revolution include the personal computer, the internet, and advanced information and communications technologies, like our cell phones.

The Fourth Industrial Revolution (41R), also known as the Cyber-Physical Revolution, is marked by technological and knowledge breakthroughs that build on the Digital Revolution that are now fusing the physical, digital and biological worlds (including the human body). The main technologies of this revolution include advanced robotics, CNC (computer numeric control), automation, 3D printing, biotechnology, nanotechnology, big data processing, artificial intelligence, and autonomous vehicles.

These new technologies are not only changing everything in the world around us, they are also changing our social relationships and culture(s). In and of themselves, these technologies are somewhat value neutral—meaning neither good or bad. Their value and intent will be determined by humanity. They will either aid humanity in our collective quest for liberation, or they will help further our species inhumanity towards itself and mother earth. One thing is painfully clear, and that is if these technologies remain the exclusive property of the capitalist class and the trans-national corporations they control, these technologies will not be used for the benefit of the majority of humanity, but to expand the methods of capital accumulation and further consolidate the power of the 1% that rule the world. Under their control, these technologies will lead to a crisis of global unemployment on a scale unseen in human history. The end result will be global dystopia, that is a social nightmare predicated on massive poverty, lawlessness, and state repression, rather than the potential utopia these technologies have always foreshadowed.[17]

The only way we are going to come anywhere close to attaining anything like the utopia these technologies promise is to democratize and subject them to social production for the benefit of all, rather than continuing to allow them to be controlled and appropriated by the few. The democratization of the technologies of the Third and Fourth Industrial Revolutions, which we denote as #TechDemocracy, is one of the primary demands and areas of focus of Cooperation Jackson. We struggle for #TechDemocracy first and foremost by educating our members and the general public about the promises and perils of the technology so that people can make informed decisions. Our next course of action is self-organization to acquire as much of this technology as we can, with the explicit purpose of controlling these means of production and utilizing them for the direct benefit of our organization and our community. We call this self-organization "Community Production", and to this end, we are currently building our own Center for Community Production.[18]

Our third course of action is organizing our community for political and economic power to expand and reinforce our self-organization or Community Production efforts to gradually make them ubiquitous or ever present in our community, with the explicit intent of gradually replacing the exploitative and environmentally destructive forms of old production. Our fourth general course of action is to utilize our self-organization and political power to make demands on the government, the capitalist class, and the transnational corporations to remove the controls they have on the technology, like exclusive patents, to free it, and for government to make massive investments in technology to make them public utilities and to ensure that the capitalists and corporations make restorative investments in these utilities for the public good.

These are the core elements of our transformative program to utilize and participate in the development of the Fourth Industrial Revolution for the benefit of our community, the liberation of the working class and all of humanity.

This is the basic outline of our Transition City Vision. These are the components we are organizing to get the City of Jackson to adopt.

Our Concrete Program

Despite the limited capacity, experience, and resources of our organization, we dream big and plan big. There are some, friend and foe alike, who maintain that our program and strategy constitute an extreme case of overreach. There is undoubtedly some truth in this statement. But, we make no apologies for our approach. We firmly believe that we must demand the impossible, both of the world and of ourselves, in order to change both subjects. With effective organizing and sound strategy that capitalizes on exploiting the contradictions cited above, we believe our program will enable us to transform Jackson, Mississippi, the Deep South, and beyond.

To reiterate the general public framing of our mission and program, we state that:

>"*Cooperation Jackson is an emerging network of cooperative enterprises and supporting social solidarity institutions based in Jackson, MS. Our aim is to transform Jackson's economy and social order by building a vibrant local social and solidarity economy anchored by worker and community owned enterprises that are grounded in sustainable practices of production, distribution, consumption and recycling/*

The concrete programmatic activities Cooperation Jackson is currently working on to advance the Transition City vision.

reuse. Through these enterprises and institutions we aim to produce quality living wage jobs for our community; create sustainable and regenerative productive systems that affirm the life of our community; protect our community from the ravages of climate change; and to respect, protect and fulfill the human rights and human potential of all the residents in our community."[19]

To fully grasp our program and strategy, it is critical to understand what Cooperation Jackson is, on a structural basis. Cooperation Jackson is the sum-total of four interconnected and interdependent institutions.

1. **A Federation of emerging local cooperatives and mutual aid networks**. The Federation is and will be composed of a number of interconnected and interdependent worker, consumer, and community cooperatives cooperating as one overall, coherent, but democratic body. This body is and will be supported by various mutual aid institutions and practices that reinforce the solidarity of the Federation and provide various means to exchange value, labor, and time to improve the quality of life of all of the members of the Federation and the community in general.

2. **A Cooperative Incubator**. The incubator is the start-up training and development center of Cooperation Jackson. The Incubator aids new cooperators with basic training, feasibility studies, business plan development, financing, training in democratic management, etc.

3. **A Cooperative School and Training Center**. The primary purpose of

our Economic Democracy School is to ensure that Cooperation Jackson serves as an instrument of social transformation by constantly broadening the social consciousness of all its cooperators and continually enhancing their skills, abilities, and overall capacities to act as conscious actors in improving their social context and environment.

4. A Cooperative Credit Union and Bank. The credit union and bank, and other financial institutions will be used to start and strengthen all of the operations of Cooperation Jackson and serve as a means of self-capitalization and democratic investment to expand the initiative. At present, our efforts in this arena are being conducted through the Southern Reparations Loan Fund (SRLF), which was formally established by the Southern Grassroots Economies Project (SGEP) in in 2016. Cooperation Jackson is a founding member of SRLF and a board member of SGEP.[20]

All of Cooperation Jackson's programs and strategies are dependent upon and conducted through the aforementioned structures. However, our practical program and strategy is presently oriented around five intentionally, interlocked, interconnected, and interdependent focal points of execution. These focal points of execution include various campaign initiatives, projects and programs that you will read about in greater detail below. The five focal points are:

1. The development of green worker, self-managed cooperatives and an extensive network of mutual aid and social solidarity programs, organizations and institutions. This programmatic approach is translated into transformative policy as our effort to make Jackson a *Solidarity City*.

2. The development of an Eco-Village, community energy production, and sustainable methodologies and technologies of production and ecologically regenerative processes and institutions. This programmatic approach is translated into transformative policy as our effort to make Jackson a *Sustainable City*.

3. The development of a network of 3D print factories that anchor community production cooperatives and institutions. This programmatic approach is translated into transformative policy as our effort to make Jackson a *Fab City* (meaning Digital Fabrication Laboratory City).

4. The development of an all-embracing, class oriented Union-Cooperative to build genuine worker power from the ground up in Jackson. This programmatic approach is translated into transformative policy as our effort to make Jackson a *Workers City*.

5. The development of a Human Rights Institute to craft a human rights charter and commission for Jackson. This programmatic approach is translated into transformative policy as our effort to make Jackson a *Human Rights City*.

The transformative policy components attached to each of the focal points is a critical component, because none of the system(s) change processes we aim to make can or will be sustained in a non-revolutionary context without structural support and reinforcement from the state. The structural support and reinforcement in question entails legal justification, incentives, resource allocation, and monitoring and enforcement from operatives of the state and civil society, meaning civilian institutions that monitor the conduct and performance of government. These transformative policy components are fundamentally articulations of *"non-reformist reforms"*. The notion of non-reformist reforms, although conceptually far older than its articulation, was first concretely formulated by Andre Gorz, a French socialist, who posed the formulation as a means to bridge our short-term engagements for social justice in everyday life to our longer terms vision for an anti-capitalist world.[21] The formulation centers on waging struggle for demands and reforms that improve conditions in people's immediate lives, but which don't strengthen the capitalist system, but instead subvert its logic, up end its social relations, and dilutes its strength. These reforms seek to create new logics, new relations, and new imperatives that create a new equilibrium and balance of forces to weaken capitalism and enable the development of an anti-capitalist alternative. This is exactly what our transformative policy components seek to accomplish.

Green Worker Cooperatives, Mutual Aid Network, and Solidarity Economy Institutions

No one practice or form associated with the solidarity economy in and of itself is sufficient to transform the capitalist economy and build economic democracy as a transitional alternative. We subscribe to the theory that we have to develop and employ several complementary and reinforcing practices and forms of solidarity economics at once in mutual relationship with each other to subvert dynamics of the capitalist system, logic and imperative.[22]

The complement of solidarity institutions and practices that we are either currently building, with varying degrees of present implementation, or aiming to build are as follows.

1. *Community Land Trust (CLT)*. A CLT is a democratic, non-profit corporation that stewards and develops land and other community assets on behalf of a community. Our primary objective in developing this institution is to acquire and decommodify as much land as possible in Jackson to take it off the capitalist market (learn more about our CLT below in the *Sustainable Communities Initiative* section).

2. *Community Saving, Lending and Investing*. This practice includes a range of community-controlled financial institutions ranging from lending circles to credit unions. We are working to create and/or support existing

community financial institutions (as there are several grassroots funds in our community with which we are linked and related to) to create our own financing capacity, given that most of the "traditional" financial institutions will not lend to poor Black people with little, no, or bad credit. We have borrowed heavily from Mondragon[23] in this regard in prioritizing the work of creating a self-reinforcing financial institution to give us maximum control over capital and how we deploy it for our collective benefit.

3. *Price-based Mutual Credit*. Mutual Credit is a form of barter, where creditors and debtors constitute a network of people lending to each other through various forms of direct exchange and accounting for the goods and services exchanged. In the development of our model we are drawing heavily from the experiences of the Mutual Aid Network (MAN) in Madison, Wisconsin[24] in working to create a system that employs credit denominated by either the national currency (US dollar) or our local alternative currency (see below for more details). This will enable our Mutual Credit system to be transferable and practical to working class people in the community within standard capitalist oriented firms that willingly participate in the practice.

4. *Time Banking*. Time banking is a method for people to exchange services using time as currency instead of money. This practice allows everyone to contribute to the production of value in the community, enables skills and services that are not valued or are undervalued in the capitalist economy to be valued equally by valuing everyone's time equally, no matter the task. We are working on building this practice primarily to revalue women's work and to allow those presently excluded from the monetary economy to engage in the emerging solidarity economy on an equal footing in order to access the goods and services they need to improve their overall quality of life.

5. *Poshterity Budgeting*. Poshterity is individual and community budgeting that explores how to design and utilize the varieties of value exchange options available to replace monetary need. This practice helps people to improve their standard of living and quality of life by demonstrating where, when and how to utilize their limited resources to maximum effect. We are exploring the broad utilization of this practice to end the strangulation of impoverishment that afflicts the vast majority of city's residents.

6. *Alternative Currency*. An alternative currency is any form of currency used as a substitute to the national currency, in our case the US dollar. In the United States private individuals, corporations, or non-profit community institutions create these types of currencies to serve as a counterbalance to the standard currency. Alternative currencies enable

greater market mobility and connection to those with limited access to standard currency for lack of jobs and other forms of income. We are pursuing this practice to buttress our cooperatives and various financial institutions and to aid our city with its critical budgetary crisis as a means to support the struggle to retain the Black majority and Black political power against the pressing threats of gentrification, displacement, and privatization (see Sustainable Communities Initiative section for more details on our fight against gentrification and displacement).

7. *Tool Lending and Resource Libraries.* Tool libraries allow community members to check out or borrow tools, equipment and "how-to" instructional materials, either free of charge (with community norms and conditions) or for a rental fee (also with norms and conditions). We are pursuing this practice to eliminate aspects of over consumption in our community and to enable more people to have access to critical tools to engage in critical work projects and improve their quality of life.

8. *Participatory Budgeting.* According to Mike Menser and Juscha Robinson: "Participatory budgeting consists of a process of democratic deliberation and decision-making in which ordinary city residents decide how to allocate part of a public budget through a series of local assemblies and meetings. It is characterized by several basic features: community members determine spending priorities and elect budget delegates to represent their neighborhoods, budget delegates transform community priorities into concrete project proposals, public employees facilitate and provide technical assistance, community members vote on which projects to fund, and the public authority implements the projects. Various studies have suggested that participatory budgeting can lead to more equitable public spending, higher quality of life, increased satisfaction of basic needs, greater government transparency and accountability, increased levels of public participation (especially by marginalized residents), and democratic and citizenship learning. Most of the well-known examples of participatory budgeting involve city administrations that have turned over decisions over municipal budgets, such as its overall priorities and choice of new investments, to citizen assemblies. Other examples involve school budgets, housing project budgets, and the budgets of cooperatives and non-profit organizations".[25] We are developing this practice to humanize governance in Jackson and to institutionalize equity processes through governance.

9. *Community Energy Production.* Community Energy is the production and distribution of energy from renewable sources, i.e. solar, wind, geo-thermal and biophotovoltaics[26] (producing energy directly from plants) that is cooperatively owned and democratically managed. This energy can be utilized for direct consumption and production, or can be exchanged on the public energy utility grid for wider distribution for some form of

compensation or return to the community. We are developing this practice to reduce our community's carbon footprint, to make a concrete contribution towards the development of sustainable energy systems, and to create energy self-reliance and self-determination in our community.

All of the above mentioned solidarity institutions and practices are still emerging and in very rudimentary stages of development. As of this writing (April 2017), we are currently prioritizing the building of three interrelated and interconnected green cooperatives. These are: 1) Freedom Farms, an urban farming cooperative, 2) Nubia's Place Cafe and Catering Cooperative, and 3) the Green Team, a landscaping, organic waste gathering and composting cooperative.

Freedom Farms is an urban farming worker-owned cooperative, based in West Jackson. Freedom Farms currently produces on 2 acres of land in the emerging Fannie Lou Hamer Community Land Trust, held by Cooperation Jackson. Freedom Farms specializes in organic vegetables, and is in the process of expanding production into fruits and fish. Freedom Farm's produce is primarily being sold and consumed at Nubia's Place Café and Catering Cooperative.

Nubia's Place Café and Catering Cooperative is a healthy oriented café and catering worker-owned cooperative that operates out of the Lumumba Center. It is designed to fight the chronic obesity and diabetes related afflictions that threaten the lives of many of our community's residents. Organic waste from Nubia's Place is handled and processed by The Green Team.

The Green Team is a yard care and composting worker-owned cooperative. It focuses on gathering and processing organic yard waste into compost to keep it from the landfill and water drainage systems. It also gathers organic materials from grocery stores and restaurants and turns this organic waste into compost that is sold to gardeners, farmers and hardware and home supply stores.

We are very intentional about creating a cooperative eco-system that reinforces and builds upon itself. With these three cooperatives, we have created a reinforcing value chain wherein Freedom Farms produces food that is sold and consumed at Nubia's Place Café, the waste from which is utilized by The Green Team to create organic compost that nourishes the crops produced by Freedom Farms. This is an example of the types of sustainable and regenerative enterprises and productive systems that we are intentionally constructing. Some of the additional green cooperatives that we are working to develop are:

- A Housing Cooperative
- A Recycling Cooperative
- A Construction Cooperative
- A Childcare Cooperative
- A Solar Installation and Green Retrofitting Cooperative

However, these three green cooperatives are not enough to create a truly reinforcing and self-sustaining economy of scale that can transform our local economy. Given both the existing political economy in our region and the new economy we are trying to develop, we have to build our own supply and value chains.[27]

Value chains are the decision making processes by which cooperatives, or any form of business, receive and process raw materials, add value to the raw materials through various labor and technical processes to create a finished product, and then sell and/or exchange the end product to customers and communities through effective distribution and marketing.

A supply chain is the entire network of entities (directly or indirectly) interlinked and interdependent in serving the same customer base or market. It comprises vendors who supply raw materials and natural resources, producers who convert these materials and resources into finished products, warehouses that store the products, distribution centers and networks that deliver the products to retailers, and retailers who present the products to communities and sell them to consumers. Supply chains underlie value chains because without them no producer has the ability to give customers what they want, when and where they want it, at prices that they want and/or can afford. In standard capitalist market dynamics, producers compete with each other only through their supply chains, reducing the degree of value increase from improvements on the producers end, which cannot make up for deficiencies in the supply chain that reduce the producer's ability to compete.[28]

To foster the development of a non-capitalist alternative, we have to socialize every step of the productive process required to create, distribute, and recycle a product to collective ownership and democratic management to increase the effective scale and scope of the solidarity economy. It is only by creating solidarity oriented value chains and supply chains that we can and will effectively displace and replace the capitalist economy. Our emphasis on intentionally creating mutually interconnected and interdependent cooperatives and solidarity networks is fundamental to how we will ensure the attainment of our end pursuits locally, regionally and beyond.

Sustainable Communities Initiative

To improve the quality of life in our City and for the sake of our children, grandchildren, and great-grandchildren we can and must end the overlapping environmental, climatic and human rights crises confronting us. Cooperation Jackson believes that we can solve these crises by organizing our communities to execute a comprehensive program that will protect our environment, curb our carbon emissions, stimulate employment, and democratically transfer wealth and equity.

We call this comprehensive program a *Just Transition Program*[29] which is premised on ending our systemic dependence on the hydro-carbon industry and the capitalist driven need for endless growth on a planet with limited resources, while creating a new, democratic economy that is centered around sustainable methods of production, distribution, consumption and recycling that are more localized and cooperatively owned and controlled. Cooperation Jackson's specific contribution to a Just Transition program is our *Sustainable Communities Initiative (SCI)*. The Sustainable Communities Initiative has four primary components:

1. Green Worker Cooperatives (*see above*)

2. Building an Eco-Village

3. Developing Food Sovereignty

4. Just Transition Policy Reform

The *Sustainable Communities Initiative* (SCI) was the first major initiative launched by Cooperation Jackson. At this stage in the organization's development and the execution of this initiative, our Sustainable Communities Initiative is primarily a neighborhood-based strategy that centers on transforming a key neighborhood in West Jackson by creating a live work *"Eco-Village"*. The Eco-Village will be anchored by a *Community Land Trust* (CLT) and a network of interlocking and interdependent institutions that will help stabilize rents, provide affordable "green" housing, create quality high paying jobs, and lay a foundation for the sustainable transformation of Jackson's economy through cooperative enterprise and solidarity economics.

We are targeting West Jackson because it is the working class gateway to Downtown Jackson, which is the heart of the State Government of Mississippi and the economic engine of Jackson. And because it is critical to stopping the advance of gentrification and maintaining Jackson's Black working class majority, which is quintessential to the Jackson-Kush Plan as a comprehensive political project. Over the past 30 plus years, West Jackson has suffered from rapid capital flight and divestment, driven in large part by white flight. Since the late 1970s West Jackson has become a Black working class community, with high concentrations of poverty. Since the late 1980s, large parts of West Jackson have become dilapidated and abandoned. It is now estimated that there are over 1,832 vacant lots and 832 abandoned structures out of a total of 6,748 lots in the community (it is estimated that 41% of the parcels in the community are unused). The community has an estimated 13,890 people, the vast majority of whom are Black (an estimated 92%).[30]

Four major real estate and so-called economic development initiatives adjacent to West Jackson are driving speculative pressures on the community, which is confronting it with the threat of gentrification and race and class based displacement. The four development initiatives are the mid-town based Medical Corridor initiative (being driven by the University of Mississippi and funded by the State government), the Downtown-One Lake Redevelopment initiative (being driven by Greater Jackson Chamber of Commerce and proposed and planned out in "Plan 2022"), the development of a sports and entertainment complex in Downtown Jackson (being driven by the destruction of the old stadium in the Medical Corridor development area and Jackson State University's desire for a larger stadium), and the Capitol Complex Bill or Downtown Annexation Bill (being driven by some neo-colonial forces which aim to create an exclusive zone of political control and economic development controlled by the Governor and big developers within the very heart of the capitol city).[31] Each initiative is at a different stage of development, but all have committed financial streams and widespread support amongst local and state elites.

The primary force driving the encroaching gentrification is the Medical Corridor. The Medical Corridor was approved after Hurricane Katrina, and capitalized primarily by the federal relief funds secured for the state of Mississippi by former Governor Haley Barbour, who was and is a very adept politician and a close friend of then President George H. W. Bush. The Corridor's secure capitalization provides the economic conditions that enable and drive the other developments. Over the course of the next decade, the Corridor's expansion will provide hundreds of short-term construction jobs, and thousands of long-term term medical and medical support jobs. All of these new doctors, nurses, technicians, pharmacists and other support and spin off workers will need places to live, shop, dine, play, and worship. Many will want to avoid long suburban commutes and have easy access to various living amenities and various types of entertainment. Knowing these needs and anticipating the long-term profits that can be drawn from them, speculators and developers have literally consumed most of Fondren, Midtown, and Central City and are rapidly encroaching on the northern borders of West Jackson due to its strategic location, accessibility and cheap real estate values to fulfill these needs.

None of the aforementioned development initiatives are designed to incorporate the existing population living in West Jackson in their long-term plans. This is where Cooperation Jackson and the Sustainable Communities Initiative come into the picture. Our first task is to stop gentrification and displacement, which we are trying to contain at what we call the "Fortification Line". The Fortification Line is our line in the sand. It is the point we are declaring to the forces of gentrification "you cannot pass". Fortification Street defines the Line, which is one of the main horizontal east-west thoroughfares in West Jackson that separates the northern section of the community from the central heart of the community. As noted before, there are parts of the northern section of West Jackson, those directly adjacent to Mid-Town and Central City, that are already being bought up by real estate speculators. And there are parts of the community below the Fortification Line that are already in contest between our forces and the forces of gentrification.

One of the stated gentrification projects below the Fortification Line is the "Capitol Street Corridor" project. This project is being defined and pushed by the Greater Jackson Chamber of Commerce and is aimed at developing West Capitol Street.[32] Their aim is to acquire as much of the depressed value real estate on and around West Capitol Street to turn into market rate "middle income" housing, that will be catered to by a new commercial district that will be directly linked to the Jackson Zoo and retrofitting of the Golf Course adjacent to Hawkins Field airport.[33] We are working diligently to counter this gentrification move by purchasing as much of the available real estate as we can afford and holding it in our Community Land Trust. This blocks the capital forces pushing gentrification from getting a consolidated hold on the street, as we will never sell our property, nor will we consent to their plans, which will inevitably lead to the displacement of the Black working class community, either through higher real estate values, higher taxes, or higher rents for renters.

Holding the forces of gentrification and displacement at the Fortification Line is central to maintaining a Black working class majority in Jackson. As the Medical Corridor develops and expands, Mid-town, Central City and Fondren and adjacent neighborhoods are going to become majority non-Black areas. The forces behind the gentrification of Jackson are deliberately trying to dilute the numerical strength of the Black working class in Jackson in order to change the political character of the city. The Black working class is the social base for the radical politics that has been expressed in the city. Without this base, Chokwe Lumumba, a revolutionary New Afrikan nationalist, would never have been elected to office. Jackson is presently over 80% Black.[34] The political calculation of the reactionary forces pushing for displacement and seeking to profit from gentrification, is that in order break the bloc of radical political forces in Jackson, they have to reduce the Black population considerably. Based on deductions from the last two municipal elections, they have to get the Black numbers below 60% of the overall population.[35] If they can accomplish this, they will ensure that no one politically comparable to Chokwe Lumumba will get elected again. This is why we are trying to hold the Fortification Line, as we need to ensure that the city retains at least 70% of its present Black working class population in order to sustain the radical political orientation of the city.

That said, Cooperation Jackson is not adverse to *"economic development"*, which West Jackson, and many other Black working class communities throughout the city are in desperate need. However, we are for *sustainable, community driven and controlled development without displacement.* We firmly believe that the existing community must equitably benefit from the new developments that are being planned, and that the community must self-determine and execute its own community revitalization and wealth building initiatives. The Sustainable Communities Initiative is one of the few bottom-up development initiatives in Jackson. The project is being driven by the membership of Cooperation Jackson through extensive community outreach, but its foundations were laid by the long-standing organizing efforts of the Malcolm X Grassroots Movement and the Jackson People's Assembly. The Sustainable Communities Initiative's success will neutralize the attempt to displace the Black working class community of West Jackson and create an array of eco-friendly and worker- and community-owned cooperative businesses and institutions that will be accessible to the long standing and potentially new residents of West Jackson.

The anchor of our grand vision for a Sustainable City is the West Jackson Eco-Village. The Eco-village is being organized in the heart of the "Downtown Gateway" section of West Jackson. This community is situated in municipal Wards 3 and 5, and is primarily populated by Black working class residents.

The community is almost exclusively a bedroom community with few employment opportunities at present. The largest employers in the community are Jackson State University (JSU) and Jackson Public Schools (JPS). Vast tracts of this community, as previously noted, are either vacant or dilapidated and abandoned. The community is also in an extensive food desert. Residents of the community typically have to travel two to three miles to access quality produce, fruits, and meats.

The Eco-village seeks to radically alter the quality of life in West Jackson over the next several years by increasing and improving the housing stock, creating quality living wage jobs, and servicing essential energy, food, and entertainment needs. The base of the Eco-village is quality cooperative housing that is green, off the utility grids, and deeply affordable. In its broad dimensions, the Eco-village will contain a significant portion of the Freedom Farms Urban Farming Cooperative, which will provide a significant number of quality jobs through the green worker cooperatives listed earlier, in addition to a multi-stakeholder grocery cooperative and a comprehensive arts and culture entertainment complex owned and managed by our emerging Revolutionary Resonance Arts and Culture Cooperative.

The ecological component of the community is centered on creating a "living-systems" integrated community anchored by a solar-thermal, recycling, and composting network that will provide deeply affordable and sustainable energy and green jobs that will help fight ecological degradation and climate change. Per the terms of "cooperative living" that we are adopting, adapting and developing, all of the residents of the housing cooperative will participate in the village's recycling and composting programs that will create a protected market for our Urban Farming Cooperative as well as our emerging Composting and Recycling Cooperatives. In addition, all of our houses will primarily operate off of solar energy and be connected to an internal community energy production grid that will foster energy efficiency and sustainability throughout the village. The exercise of collective land, home, and energy ownership and the provision of permanent affordability will enable us to fight the encroachment of gentrification and displacement threatening the predominantly Black working class community of West Jackson.

We are currently pursuing several strategies to acquire a significant number of vacant lots and abandoned homes in West Jackson. We currently possess over 40 properties in our target community, including the Lumumba Center for Economic Democracy and Development, and have applied for several properties currently owned by the State of Mississippi, the City of Jackson and the Jackson Redevelopment Authority. We are also seeking to acquire several vacant lots and abandoned homes that are privately owned.

Following our land acquisition drive, the second major step in developing the Eco-Village is the Ewing Street Initiative. We currently own 90% of Ewing Street between Robinson and Central Streets, and are actively in the process of acquiring the remaining 10%. We are targeting this property because it is the most contiguous property we presently have, and it is zoned in a manner that will give us the greatest organizing and operational flexibility. The first step of the Ewing Street Initiative is cleaning and clearing the lots. Remediating the soils on the lot, which will lead the expansipm of our agricultural production and provide a higher level of food security to our members and the West Jackson community. The next step is creating our first community energy production unit on the block, which will then be followed by the introduction of off the grid, digitally fabricated houses. We plan on this phase of the development coming into fruition over the course of the next 3 years. The successful implementation will provide us with a model to replicate on a broader scale throughout Jackson that will demonstrate the benefits of a new way of living to our community and effectively combat the gentrification and displacement threatening it.

The broader Just Transition component of our overall initiative focuses on instituting policies that curb ecological destruction and climate change and incentivize the creation of sustainable jobs and cooperative enterprises in our city. We are committed to helping the city realize the vision of the Lumumba administration of making Jackson the most "sustainable city" in the South (if not the country), by committing the city government to institute policies that will enable Jackson to become a *Zero-Emissions* and *Zero-Waste* city by 2025.[36]

Our *Zero-Emissions* program calls for the following:

1. *Weatherization and Energy Efficiency Retrofitting.* We want to push the City of Jackson to retrofit and weatherize all of the buildings that it owns and operates, so that they conserve heat in the winter and naturally cool the facility in the summer. We also want the City to incentivize this type of retrofitting in the private and non-profit sectors of the economy with grants, low-interest loans, tax-credits, etc.

2. *Solar-Thermal Energy Production.* We want to encourage the City of Jackson to place solar panels on all of the buildings and facilities it possesses that have the capacity to host the equipment. We also want to encourage the City to install solar-thermal converters in all of the facilities it controls that have the capacity to regulate their energy use via this technology. We also want to encourage the City to incentivize private solar-thermal energy conversion and production and enable residents and businesses to supply excess energy to the main power grid to aid the energy company in eliminating its dependence on fossil fuels.

3. *Zero-Emissions Fleet.* We want to push the City of Jackson to gradually replace its entire operating fleet, including all police vehicles, with electric vehicles. We also want to encourage the City to incentivize the purchasing of electric cars and to create publicly owned and operated electric fueling stations throughout the city to accommodate this transition.

4. *Expanded and Sustainable Public Transportation.* We want to push the City of Jackson to gradually acquire a fully electric public transportation fleet and to expand its public transportation vehicles, routes and hours to accommodate more efficient and accessible transportation throughout the city and metro-region.

Our *Zero-Waste* program calls for the following:

1. *Comprehensive Recycling.* We want to encourage the City of Jackson to create a comprehensive recycling program, that includes mass public education, and a system of inducements and rewards for residents, businesses and civil institutions in the city to recycle all that can be recycled to reduce the burden on the city's landfill and to create more private and public sectors jobs in waste management and recycling.

2. *Comprehensive Composting.* We want to encourage the City of Jackson to create a comprehensive composting program that gathers all of the organic refuse produced by households, businesses and civil institutions and include the requisite public education necessary to encourage individuals, families, businesses and institutions to participate and to adhere to all of the necessary sanitary standards.

3. *Comprehensive Oil Reuse.* We want to encourage the City of Jackson to create a comprehensive cooking oil gathering program that calls for all restaurants and food service businesses and institutions producing mass amounts of used cooking oils for their food production such as schools, colleges, universities, and hospitals to recycle these materials so they can be reused for other energy and production needs and help eliminate the need for their extended production and disposal at public expense.

4. *Local Food Production.* We want to encourage the City of Jackson to create a Local Food and Production Charter, to encourage and incentivize local food production and distribution, to create more jobs and reduce carbon emissions by eliminating the need for extended transportation systems and refrigeration. The incentive program should focus exclusively on supporting producers who reside in Jackson and are drawn from historically discriminated and capital deprived communities.

A critical component of our Just Transition work is *Food Sovereignty*. Food Sovereignty is critical to our mission and the realization of our end goals.

Food sovereignty is defined as, "the right of peoples to healthy and culturally appropriate food produced through ecologically sound and sustainable methods, and their right to define their own food and agricultural systems. It puts the aspirations and needs of those who produce, distribute and consume food at the heart of food systems and policies rather than the demands of markets and corporations."[37]

Despite the overabundance of food in the United States, which is largely produced by heavily subsidized transnational corporations utilizing the most extreme and unsustainable industrial agricultural methods, most Black working class communities are confronted with various types of food access deprivations, what many are calling food apartheid.[38] These deprivations range from food deserts, to little to no access to fresh and healthy foods, to super exploitative overpricing. All of these deprivations are the direct result of white supremacy and the exploitative efficiencies inherent to capitalism. In order to become self-determining subjects, we have to be able to securely provide our communities with the food and nutrients needed to sustain healthy and productive lives.

And we have to do it sustainably, because industrial agriculture is one of the leading contributors to climate change and a driving force of the sixthth great extinction event through which we are living. Industrial agriculture is eviscerating our ecosystems and destroying our soils and the ability for humanity to provide sustenance sustainability. According to the United Nations Food and Agriculture Organization (UN FAO), humanity only has 60 years of top soil remaining (as of 2014). The Food and Agriculture Organization further states that, "unless new approaches are adopted, the global amount of arable and productive land per person in 2050 will be only a quarter of the level in 1960, ...due to growing populations and soil degradation".[39]

In order to attain a modicum of Food Sovereignty in Jackson over the course of the next five to ten years, we have to create our own comprehensive, interconnected and interdependent supply and value chains—that is, our own network of cooperative farms, processing centers, food hubs, compost and soil generators, food processors, canneries, shipping and trucking cooperatives, grocery stores, etc. Our first major initiative to actually realize food sovereignty in Jackson starts with our People's Grocery Initiative. The People's Grocery Initiative[40] is the effort to transform a previously owned Black grocery store in West Jackson into a multi-stakeholder community cooperative that will serve, in part, as a food bank, a farmers market, a community supported agricultural provider, a market aggregator, and an anchor of our first Eco-Village.

The proposed site of the People's Grocery is within our Eco-Village zone, situated at the intersection of W. Capitol and Rose Streets, and is central to our effort to hold the Fortification Line discussed above. This initiative is being launched with the support of the Mississippi Association of Cooperatives (MAC) and a network of Black farmers throughout Mississippi. The first step is to work with this initial network to build a level of food security as a first step towards attaining food sovereignty. We aim to create an interconnected and interdependent network of urban farms, with Freedom Farms being the anchor, that links with rural Black and organic farmers throughout the state and region, that are willing to strategically coordinate and practice sustainable zero-waste methods of production, distribution, pricing, and aggregate consumption and gathering for composting. Starting from here and collectively making a plan of gradual expansion based on statewide and regional integration of producers, workers, and consumers (see *Regional Considerations, Plans and Aspirations* below for more details) dedicated to the solidarity economy and the struggle for economic democracy, we can create value chain with enough significant scale and scope to attain food sovereignty for our community that will help us realize our Just Transition and self-determining goals.

As these points illustrate, there are viable and attainable solutions that we can implement now that will help our city work its way out of its health, human rights, environmental, and climate change contributing crisis. We want to encourage everyone in Jackson to support us in advancing this cause by becoming a member or supporter of Cooperation Jackson. This course of actoion would help us build and execute the Sustainable Communities Initiative to engender our collective power and advance a just transition to a new economy and social horizon.

Community Production Initiative

As noted earlier in this essay, Cooperation Jackson has launched a critical initiative to own and control the means of industrial production called the Community Production Initiative. Community Production is industrial manufacturing based on a combination of 3rd and 4th generation industrial technologies, namely the combination of digital technology and automated production with 3-D printing and quantum computing, that is collectively owned and democratically operated by members of geographically and/or intentionally defined communities. The Community Production Initiative is centered on building the Community Production Cooperative (CPC), and the Center for Community Production (CCP).

The Community Production Cooperative is an emerging multi-stakeholder cooperative specializing in 3D print/digital fabrication manufacturing. The stakeholders involved include Cooperation Jackson, our tech operators who operate as worker-owners and a class of community owners and investors.

The Center for Community Production will serve as a Fab Academy training center, a coding and digital programming innovation hub, a community maker space[41], and a workforce development entry point. A Fab Lab is defined by "a technical prototyping platform for innovation and invention, providing stimulus for local entrepreneurship."[42]

Combined the Community Production Cooperative and the Center for Community Production have three fundamental divisions of production:

1. The Education Division

2. The Commercial Manufacturing Division, and

3. The Community Production Division.

The *Education Division* will primarily, but not exclusively, focus on training members and the community on how to use the 3D printing machines and other 4th Industrial Revolution technologies, in part through the Fab Lab network. It will also teach members, students, and the community how to code. And finally, this division will partner with various workforce development programs throughout Jackson and the region to aid workers create their own jobs or secure high paying jobs in the dog-eat-dog capitalist system.

The *Commercial Manufacturing Division* will primarily focus on providing build to order, high quality, high volume 3D printed products. It will also aid businesses with designing and prototyping new products. The commercial division will also produce its own specialty products, ranging from toys to medical aids and tools. In addition, the commercial division will also provide precision laser and water jet cutting services.

The *Community Production Division* will focus on providing a range of maker space services to the community, where members and customers can work individually or collaboratively to produce products for their own use or for the market. However, the primary aim of our community production division is to produce directly for community need. Utilizing this technology as a democratically governed "public good" or "public utility" will help us address several essential production needs in our community, like the need to create "sustainable" or "green" manufacturing businesses, and our need for quality, affordable "off the grid" green housing, which digital fabrication makes possible. But, that's not all. 3D printing will also enable us to produce everything from recyclable consumer goods and services, advanced medical aids and tools, and the next generation(s) of 3D printing machines on the road to advancing the means of production to non-commodified forms as witnessed in futuristic sagas like Star Trek.

The Community Production Initiative is a critical investment in the liberation of our community, and its emancipation from the terrors of scarcity and the agonies of hard labor that Black people have been subjected to in the US empire. Democratizing the fourth generation of industrial innovation and technology from the bottom up is central to humanizing the new social relationships that will be fostered by the new "robot era" and defeating the rapid genocidal advance of capitalism's disposable age.

The Jackson Union-Cooperative Initiative

The Union-Cooperative Initiative is a long-term initiative to organize the working class in its totality—meaning unionized and non-unionized workers, cooperators, and the under and unemployed – throughout Jackson to address their common needs and interests, build genuine worker power from the ground up, and serve as the core transformative force to democratize the local economy and society. The objective is to create a class and community oriented syndicate,[43] one big union, with multiple autonomous divisions that would democratically introduce and enforce economic, social and cultural rights (ESCR)[44] norms and standards in Jackson via workers and people's assemblies, and other democratic institutions and processes (see the connection to the Jackson Human Rights Institute below).

The primary objectives of this Initiative are to:

1. Train the future generation of working class militants in Jackson and throughout Mississippi.

2. Create a dynamic, new model of community unionism in Mississippi.

3. Build militant class-consciousness in Jackson and throughout Mississippi.

4. Change social relations between class forces in Jackson and throughout Mississippi.

5. Win collective bargaining rights and overturn the Taft-Hartley "right-to-work [for less] regime" in Mississippi.

The 5 aforementioned objectives will be accomplished by building the following institutions:

1. The Mississippi Organizing Institute

    1.1. Will train workers in participating unions in the arts of union and community organizing.

    1.2. Will train various sectors of the community in the arts of union and community organizing.

2. Mississippi Workers Union

    2.1. Will serve as a class-based community union that will embrace all workers, regardless of trade and/or occupation.

    2.2. Will engage in campaigns to protect workers in all trades and occupations.

    2.3. Will engage in campaigns that challenge the various laws that exploit and/or limit the rights of workers and organized labor.

3. Union Cooperatives

3.1. Work to build democratic unions in the cooperatives that develop in Jackson and throughout Mississippi and help the worker-owners fortify their democratic practice and sustain ongoing relations with workers in non-cooperative enterprises.

3.2. Work to convert existing businesses into union-shop cooperatives.

3.3. Work at creating union initiated and supported worker cooperatives.

To help build its base and its transformative potential, the Jackson Union-Coop Initiative will support and advance the following initiatives which are aimed at building working class power and transforming social relationships in Mississippi to create economic democracy, a generative economy and the fulfillment of human rights. These core initiatives include:

1. The *Jackson Just Transition Plan*. The Just Transition Plan puts workers in the lead of a municipal process to create a regenerative local economy grounded in sustainable development and provides real, worker-owned green jobs. (For more details see the *Green Worker Cooperatives, Mutual Aid Network, and Solidarity Economy Institutions* section above)

2. The *Human Rights Charter Initiative*. The Charter Initiative aims to radically transform municipal governance by having Jackson adopt human rights norms, standards and procedures and adhere to them in its governing and administrative processes and activities. This initiative will enable many progressive things, but key amongst them are enabling policies that will protect workers, guarantee collective bargaining rights, support worker ownership and workplace democracy. (For more details see the section on the *Jackson Human Rights Institute* below).

The Jackson Human Rights Institute

The Jackson Human Rights Institute (JHRI) is a project of Cooperation Jackson. The Human Rights Institute is a human rights training and organizing institute that is focused on fulfilling one of the key policy planks of the Jackson-Kush Plan, which was and is making Jackson a "Human Rights City". In December 2014, Cooperation Jackson and the Malcolm X Grassroots Movement initiated and led a progressive coalition that pressured the City Council to pass a resolution committing it to make Jackson a Human Rights City.[45]

Making Jackson a Human Rights City entails creating a Human Rights Charter for the City of Jackson that is enforceable by law and based on the major covenants, conventions, and treaties of the United Nations (UN) that define international law. It also entails creating a Human Rights Commission, which will be governed by specially elected officials who will enforce the charter and its statutes, and work to ensure that our municipal government respects, protects and fulfills the entire complement of our human rights, particularly the complement of positive rights so vehemently denied in the United States, like the right to water, food, housing, education, and health care, enshrined in Economic, Social, and Cultural Rights (ESCR).[46]

The Commission will have several divisions that address areas of social concern beyond the standard measures of remediation addressed through the limited scope of law enshrined in the United States' constitution or the constitution of the state of Mississippi, which are predominantly oriented around the protection of "negative rights". Negative rights are fundamentally what we call "civil and political rights", that require that the state or private entities abstain from coercing or interfering with an individuals activities. These types of rights constitute things such as "freedom of speech", "freedom of religion", the "right to a fair trial", habeas corpus, etc.[47]

One of the primary divisions of the Commission will center on protecting and enforcing the Economic, Social, and Cultural Rights (ESCR) of the people of Jackson. This division is necessary to help aid the people of Jackson relieve the grinding impoverishment they are subjected to by the capitalist system and the forces that control and wield it to serve their own narrow interests of capital accumulation. By enforcing and protecting economic, social, and cultural rights, we are helping the workers of Jackson overcome the racist limitations of the Taft-Hartley regime and the right to work laws, that is the "right to work for less", which give licence to define the relations between capital and labor in Mississippi.[48] In striving to protect these rights, we are also reinforcing the imperatives of democracy, solidarity, equity and justice that underlie our work to build economic democracy in Jackson.

Regional Considerations, Plans and Aspirations

The vast majority of what you have read so far primarily focuses on our operations within Jackson and our aims to transform it. Jackson isn't our only focus. We have a vision, program and strategy to transform Mississippi and our greater region. Our drive in this regard is driven by necessity. The supply chains and value chains that we need to create cannot be created exclusively in Jackson. While we have learned a lot from studying numerous efforts around the world that focus on the importance of going local and building "municipal socialism".[49] We do not believe that socialism, or economic democracy, can be built in isolation on a local level, as it is neither economically viable or ecologically sustainable. You have to have wider relationships and links to other areas to access or acquire the resources you need to survive, and ultimately, thrive.

What is presented below is an outline of our Southern regional organizing vision, program, and strategy. Our mission is to create a more democratic and equitable economy in the South through the fostering of sustainable solidarity economics and the development of a network of interconnected cooperative enterprises throughout the region.

Although the economy of the southeastern region is diversifying—including more manufacturing, technological research and development, biomedical expansion, and tourism—it is still largely dependent on agricultural production and the extraction of natural resources. The existing cooperative infrastructure in the region reflects this reality, as the vast majority of cooperatives are either agricultural or service the needs of agriculture or agricultural (rural) areas, such as the rural utility cooperatives or credit unions.

In order to build a more dynamic, democratic, sustainable, and transformative economy in the region, we will have to simultaneously build upon, strengthen, and expand the existing cooperative enterprises and infrastructure AND diversity and expand into new areas, economic niches, and markets. The new areas we will focus on are the expanding metropolitan areas in the region. The new niches will primarily be in the manufacturing, recycling, new energy, distribution, and service industries. And the new markets will of necessity be emerging markets, expanded local and regional markets, and greater entrée into national and international markets.

In order to execute this strategy, we will have to create a broad multiracial and multiclass alliance. This alliance will be rooted in cooperative principles, promote the self-determination of historically oppressed peoples and communities, and promote sustainability and a just transition to a new economy and society. This alliance will prioritize organizing working class communities in the south, in both urban and rural areas, to accomplish its mission. Organizing youth and students, particularly high school and college students, will also be a priority. In addition to organizing workers, youth and students to build cooperative enterprises, this alliance will also campaign to create a comprehensive policy regime that will support cooperative development and sustainable methods of production, distribution, and consumption throughout the south. It will also campaign for divestment from extractive industries, particularly hydrocarbon based industries, and for community reinvestments that will help democratize public and private finance on a regional, global, and international scale.

To reach our constituents and move the mission and agenda, these are some of the concrete steps and means we will undertake to accomplish our goals.

Core Cities

In order to diversify and transform the regional economy on a whole, the Southern cooperative movement will have to make some critical inroads in creating dynamic cooperative ecosystems in key metropolitan areas. These metropolitan based ecosystems should include a mix of worker, producer, and consumer cooperatives that mutually reinforce and support each other by dedicating themselves to engaging in cooperative business planning, production, and purchasing to create our own protected markets, security and operating leverage in our local markets.

We also should seek to create 1 or 2 cooperatives of scale in each core city over the course of the next 10 years. We should use a number of strategies to get us to scale up in each locale, based on the opportunities present. One strategy is to engage in extensive community and worker led campaigns to move Anchor Institutions (i.e., placed based major institutions with considerable purchasing power) to "localize" their supply chains and procurement by serving the wealth building needs of oppressed and marginalized communities by partnering with cooperatives built by and based in these communities. This strategy may enable us to create a number of relatively large-scale cooperatives that employ 50 or more people, whom all receive living wage incomes. Large scale cooperatives that could potentially emerge via this strategy include health care workers (nurses and other direct health service providers), laundries, food management and distribution, transportation, alternative energy installation and servicers, urban farming, and waste management to name a few. Another likely strategy entails creating innovative cooperatives to address new market needs, particularly those pertaining to climate change and environmental sustainability. This strategy might entail creating comprehensive recycling cooperatives that not only gather and sort through recyclable materials, but also create new products out of recycled materials or reuses or repurposes recyclable items for other uses.

Rural/Urban Production Networks

The existing infrastructure that connects agricultural cooperatives with credit unions not only needs to be maintained, but expanded. We can effectively expand upon it by creating a series of interconnected Rural/Urban Production Networks that link our Core Cities with agricultural cooperatives that are adjacent (or relatively near) to these metropolitan areas. The production networks will be based on creating protected markets for the agricultural cooperatives through the collective purchasing of the urban cooperatives and by creating cooperative restaurants, food hubs, food processing centers, food manufacturing enterprises (producing canned goods, dried goods, fish and poultry cuts, etc.), and food distribution and transportation companies. We will work with the various credit unions that service these urban areas and the agricultural enterprises that are a part of this network, to create special investment funds and portfolios that support and reinforce these productive networks and link these directly to the regional and climate reinvestment funds.

New Energy Production and Transition

Per our commitment towards ending the extractive economy and creating sustainable methods of production, we have to strategically invest in the infrastructure that will enable this transition. We have to get the Rural Energy Utilities to transition to solar and wind energies and divest from coal, natural gas, and oil. We also have to encourage the urban utilities to make this transition, and in many states to allow for solar producers to resale back to the power grid. Both orientations will require popular campaigns to create the policy shifts needed.

While we are pushing for new policy regimes, we should start by developing incipient, small-scale infrastructure to lay the groundwork for the transition by creating new energy installation and production cooperatives that will create low-scale solar energy markets in our Rural/Urban Productive Networks. Converting all of our cooperative enterprises into solar power users and distributors, and by recruiting businesses, public and private institutions, and homeowners to also convert to being solar power users and distributors will create this new energy market. The objective is to slowly create and grow the new energy market infrastructure that over time, ideally a period of 5 to 10 years, will compel the utilities and the legislatures to make the necessary policy changes that will support a just transition.

By Way of Conclusion

So, here dear readers are snapshots of the comprehensive programmatic and strategic vision of Cooperation Jackson. Please note that we have taken great risk in presenting this information. Parts of what have been laid out in this essay will give fodder to our many enemies and detractors in the state of Mississippi and beyond. We know it can and will be used against us, and may in fact be a factor in aiding our enemies to get a few steps ahead of us. However, we are taking this risk because we think it is essential that other progressive forces understand what we are doing, why, and how we are thinking and planning on achieving it. We think this is critical because, even if we should fall short or utterly fail in our efforts, we hope that there is enough laid out here for others to be inspired by and learn from to be able to pick up the mantle and continue to run forward with it in the pursuit of liberation.

We also put this out to elicit the solidarity and mutual aid of you the reader. We can't accomplish all of this on our own. We need your help. We need non-extractive, patient capital to move on many fronts, like Community Production and the Community Land Trust initiatives and to defeat gentrification and displacement. We need cooperation and mutual aid between cooperatives and social enterprises to build the necessary value and supply chains needed to create and sustain a viable alternative. We need technical assistance in numerous areas, particularly in how to develop anti-capitalist business plans and models. And we are going to need political support. We need forces throughout the US empire and the world to provide us with various forms of political support to keep the reactionary state and federal governments off our backs, and to help advance our efforts to enact the non-reformist reforms we are campaigning to enact.

As our actions in Jackson, Mississippi, over the past decade demonstrate, we can change the world for the better by working together in solidarity. We ask that you join us in this effort by offering whatever mutual aid and support you can provide and by organizing a Cooperation _____ wherever you live that is directly linked with grassroots efforts to build democratic people's power from the bottom-up and forming mutual bonds with us and formations like us throughout the US and the world. This is how we will give birth to the new world waiting to be born.

Notes

1. For more information see "The Jackson-Kush Plan and the Struggle for Black Self-Determination and Economic Democracy" by Kali Akuno at http://navigatingthestorm.blogspot.com/2012/05/the-jackson-kush-plan-and-struggle-for.html.

2. For more information see "Cotton in a Global Economy: Mississippi, 1800—1860", by Eugene R. Dattel at http://www.mshistorynow.mdah.ms.gov/articles/161/cotton-in-a-global-economy-mississippi-1800-1860, and "Antebellum Mississippi", by Max Grivno at http://www.mshistorynow.mdah.ms.gov/articles/395/antebellum-mississippi.

3. For more information on our "Disposability Thesis", see "Until We Win: Black Labor and Liberation in the Disposable Era", by Kali Akuno http://www.counterpunch.org/2015/09/04/until-we-win-black-labor-and-liberation-in-the-disposable-era/.

4. For more information see *The Half Has Never Been Told: Slavery and the Making of American Capitalism*, by Edward E. Baptist, New York: Basic Books, 2014, and *Empire of Cotton: A Global History*, by Sven Beckert, New York, Vintage; reprint edition 2015.

5. For more information see Slavery by Another Name: The *Re-Enslavement* of *Black Americans: From the Civil War* to *World War II*: Douglas A. Blackmon, New York: Anchor, 2009 and *Empire of Cotton: A Global History*, by Sven Beckert, New York, Vintage; reprint edition 2015.

6. For more information see *Lockdown America: Police and Prisons in the Age of Crisis*, by Christian Parenti, *Golden Gulag: Prisons, Surplus, Crisis and Opposition in Globalizing California*, by Ruth Wilson Gilmore, *Racialized Mass Imprisonment: Counterinsurgency and Genocide*, by Kevin "Rashid" Johnson, and *Incarcerating the*

Crisis: Freedom Struggles and the Rise of the Neo-Liberal State, by Jordan T. Camp.

7. For more information see *Global Capitalism and the Crisis of Humanity*, by William I. Robinson, *A Theory of Global Capitalism: Production, Class and State in the Transnational World*, by William I. Robinson, and *The Implosion of Contemporary Capitalism*, by Samir Amin.

8. For more information see *Uneven Development*, by Neil Smith.

9. For more information see *Uneven Development: An Essay on the Social Formations of Peripheral Capitalism*, by Samir Amin, and *Uneven Development and Local Inequality in the U.S. South: The Role of Outside Investment, Landed Elites, and Racial Dynamics*, by Donald Tomaskovi-Devey and Vincent J. Roscigno.

10. For more information see "Casting Shadows: Chokwe Lumumba and the Struggle for Racial Justice and Economic Democracy in Jackson, MS", Kali Akuno http://www.rosalux-nyc.org/casting-shadows/.

11. For more information see "There's more Carbon Dioxide in the air now than any time in 3 million years", by Phillip Bump https://www.theatlantic.com/international/archive/2013/05/weve-got-new-carbon-dioxide-record-well-soon-rocket-past/315305/.

12. For more information see *Green Capitalism: Why it Can't Work*, by Daniel Tanuro.

13. For more information see *The Ecological Rift: Capitalism's War on the Earth*, by John Bellamy Foster, Brett Clark, and Richard York, *Ecosocialism: A Radical Alternative to Capitalist Catastrophe*, by Michael Lowy, and *The Enemy of Nature: The End of Capitalism or the End of the World*, by Joel Kovel.

14. For more information see "The End of Capitalism has begun", by Paul Mason https://www.theguardian.com/books/2015/jul/17/postcapitalism-end-of-capitalism-begun.

15. For more information see, "The End of Capitalism has begun", by Paul Mason https://www.theguardian.com/books/2015/jul/17/postcapitalism-end-of-capitalism-begun.

16. For more information see, *The Fourth Industrial Revolution*, by Klaus Schwab.

17. For more information see, *Four Futures: Life After Capitalism*, by Peter Frase, and *Technology vs. Humanity: The Coming Clash between Man and Machine*, by Gerd Leonhard.

18. We are establishing the Center of Community Production on W. Capitol Street, which is across the street from our Chokwe Lumumba Center for Economic Democracy and Regenerative Development. The official name of our Center for Community Production is the Imari Abubakari Obadele Center for Community Production, in honor of the late Imari A. Obadele, who was contemporary and partner of Malcolm X and a founder of several major Black Liberation organizations and institutions including the Group On Advanced Leadership (GOAL), the Republic of New Afrika (RNA), and the National Coalition of Blacks for Reparations in America (NCOBRA).

19. For more information see www.cooperationjackson.org.

20. For more information see http://sgeproject.org/about/southern-reparations-loan-fund/.

21. For more information see, *Strategy for Labor: A Radical Proposal*, by Andre Gorz, and *Activism and Social Change: Lessons for Community Organizing*, by Eric Shragge.

22. For more information see, *Envisioning Real Utopias*, by Erik Ollin Wright, and *Alternatives to Capitalism: Proposals for Democratic Economy*, by Robin Hanhnel and Erik Olin Wright.

23. For more information see, Mondragon at http://www.mondragon-corporation.com/eng/, and *New Paths to Socialism: Essays on the Mondragon Cooperatives and Workplace Democracy, Green Manufacturing, Structural Reform and the Politics of Transition*, by Carl Davidson.

24. For more information about the Mutual Aid Network see http://www.mutualaidnetwork.org/gears/.

25. This definition was taken from, *Participatory Budgeting: from Puerto Alegre, Brazil to the US*, by Mike Menser and Juscha Robinson. The document can be found at https://www.scribd.com/document/16362300/Participatory-Budgeting-and-the-Solidarity-Economy.

26. For more information on Biophotovoltaics see https://biophotovoltaics.wordpress.com/ or https://iteamsonline.org/bio-photovoltaics/.

27. For more information on value and supply chains see, "What is the difference between a value and a supply chain" at http://www.investopedia.com/ask/answers/043015/what-difference-between-value-chain-and-supply-chain.asp.

28. This definition of supply chain was adapted from the definition provided at http://www.businessdictionary.com/definition/supply-chain.html.

29. For more information the definition of Just Transition closest to ours see Movement Generations Just Transition Zine at http://movementgen.electricembers.net/justtransition/.

30. For more information about West Jackson see "West Jackson Master Plan" at https://www.duvalldecker.com/west-jackson-master-plan/ and http://www.city-data.com/city/Jackson-Mississippi.html.

31. For more information see, "Jackson Pushes Health Care Corridor" at http://www.clarionledger.com/story/news/2015/09/28/jackson-pushes-health-care-corridor/73012020/, "One Lake bill moves forward: fed money, approval pending" at http://www.clarionledger.com/story/news/politics/2017/02/21/one-lake-bill/98214952/, "Gov. Bryant unexpectedly revives talk of new Jackson State stadium" at https://mississippitoday.org/2016/03/30/gov-bryant-unexpectedly-revives-talk-of-new-jackson-state-stadium-2/, and "Capitol Complex would fund (parts of) Jackson" at http://www.jacksonfreepress.com/news/2016/mar/09/capitol-complex-district-would-fund-parts-jackson/.

32. For more information see, "Hinds County helping to pave West Capitol Street", by Jimmie E. Gates at http://www.clarionledger.com/story/news/2015/11/29/hinds-county-help-pave-west-capitol-st/76451412/.

33. For more information see, "Could Capitol Street Corridor transformation stabilize Zoo?" at http://www.msnewsnow.com/story/29948444/could-capital-street-corridor-transformation-stabilize-zoo.

34. For more information see https://suburbanstats.org/population/mississippi/how-many-people-live-in-jackson.

35. For more information see, "Jackson mayor election results by precinct" see http://www.clarionledger.com/story/news/local/2014/04/23/jackson-mayor-election-results-by-precinct/8062809/.

36. For more information see "Jackson Rising Statement" written by Kali Akuno at https://www.scribd.com/document/226528780/Jackson-Rising-Policy-Statement-Mayor-Chokwe-Lumumba.

37. Definition originally crafted from the "Declaration of Nyeleni, Mali", which was the first global forum on food sovereignty in 2007. For more information on the concept see http://usfoodsovereigntyalliance.org/what-is-food-sovereignty/.

38. For more information see, "Food Apartheid: The Silent Killer in the Black Community", by Tracy at http://atlantablackstar.com/2015/06/16/food-apartheid-the-silent-killer-in-the-black-community/, and "Covering Food Deserts: Tips to bringing context to a complex story", by Christopher Cook at https://www.centerforhealthjournalism.org/resources/lessons/covering-food-deserts.

39. For more information see "Only 60 years of farming left if soil degradation continues" at https://www.scientificamerican.com/article/only-60-years-of-farming-left-if-soil-degradation-continues/.

40. The People's Grocery name is intentional. There is the obvious association of the people's with the working masses of Jackson, but the deeper meaning is historical. The deeper meaning is drawn from the People's Grocery Cooperative operated and managed by Thomas Moss in 1888 in Memphis, Tennessee that was burned to the ground and Thomas Moss, along with two others, were lynched in 1892. The lynching was documented and presented to the world by Ida B. Wells, who was a friend of Thomas Moss. Ms. Well's reporting on this case was the start of our critical anti-Lynching campaign and career. See http://historic-memphis.com/biographies/peoples-grocery/peoples-grocery.htmland http://www.commercialappeal.com/story/news/local/2017/03/09/125th-anniversary-peoples-grocery-lynching-remembered/98607052/ for more background and details.

41. A "maker space" is a physical location where people gather to share resources and knowledge, work on projects, network and build. Definition provided by ELI 7 things you should know about Makerspace's at https://net.educause.edu/ir/library/pdf/eli7095.pdf.

42. For more information see, "What is a Fab Lab", from the Fab Foundation at http://www.fablabconnect.com/fab-lab/.

43. For more information on Syndicalism see, "Syndicalism", by Daniel De Leon at https://chomsky.info/19760725/, "Anarchosyndicalism: Theory and Practice", by Rudolf Rocker at https://theanarchistlibrary.org/library/rudolf-rocker-anarchosyndicalism, "The Relevance of Anarcho-Syndicalism: Noam Chomsky interviewed by Peter Jay" at https://chomsky.info/19760725/.

44. For more information on the International Covenant on Economic, Social and Cultural Rights see http://www.ohchr.org/EN/ProfessionalInterest/Pages/CESCR.aspx.

45. For more information see, "Historic Human Rights City Resolution passed in

Jackson, MS to create 1st Human Rights Charter and Commission in the South" at http://www.cooperationjackson.org/announcementsblog/2015/1/10/historic-human-rights-city-resolution-passed-in-jackson-ms-to-create-1st-human-rights-charter-and-commission-in-the-south.

46. For more information see, "Introduction to Economic, Social and Cultural Rights", by ESCR-Net at https://www.escr-net.org/rights.

47. For more information on the concept of "Negative Rights" see http://www.globalization101.org/negative-vs-positive-rights/.

48. For more information see, "Labor Unions and Taft-Hartley", by David Macaray at http://www.counterpunch.org/2008/01/02/labor-unions-and-taft-hartley/, and "Taft-Hartley: A Slave-Labor Law?", Nelson Lichtenstein at http://scholarship.law.edu/cgi/viewcontent.cgi?article=1478&context=lawreview.

49. For more information on the notion of "Municipal Socialism" see, *Social Ecology and Communalism*, by Murray Bookchin, and *Municipal Socialism Then and Now: Some lessons for the Global South*, by Ellen Leopold and David A. MacDonald at http://www.municipalservicesproject.org/sites/municipalservicesproject.org/files/publications/Leopold-McDonald_Municipal_Socialism_Lessons_Global_South_2012.pdf.

2.

Toward Economic Democracy, Labor Self-management and Self-determination

Kali Akuno & Ajamu Nangwaya

To recapitulate: we cannot follow the class structure of America; we do not have the economic or political power, the ownership of machines and materials, the power to direct the processes of industry, the monopoly of capital and credit. On the other hand, even if we cannot follow this method of structure, nevertheless we must do something. We cannot stand still; we cannot permit ourselves simply to be the victims of exploitation and social exclusion. —William Edward Burghardt Du Bois.[1]

"The new militancy on the part of blacks and many young whites have caused, not only in the Deep South but the North as well, to realize that racism is an unnecessary evil which must be dealt with by "men and governments" or by "men and guns." If survival is to be the name of the game, then men and governments must not move just to postpone violent confrontations, but seek ways and means of channeling legitimate discontentment into creative and progressive action for change.

Politics will occupy the attention of the nation in the '70s as the Black man makes his reentry into the political arena. Step by step he will achieve many victories as we have seen in our northern big cities. While this is important, I believe that the key to real progress and the survival of all men, not just the Black man, must begin at the local, county, and state levels of governments. While politics will not cure all of our ills, it is the first step toward erecting a representative and a responsive government that will deal with the basic needs.

"Land, too, is important in the '70s and beyond, as we move toward our ultimate goal of total freedom. Because of my belief in land reform, I have taken steps of acquiring land through cooperative ownership. In this manner, no individual has title to, or complete use of, the land. The concept of total individual ownership of huge acreages of land, by individuals, is at the base of our struggle for survival. In order for any people or nation to survive, land is necessary. However, individual ownership of land should not exceed the amount necessary to make a living. Cooperative ownership of land opens the door to many opportunities for group development of economic enterprises, which develop the total community, rather than create monopolies that monopolize the resources of a community.

—Fannie Lou Hamer[2]

The revolution can only achieve the emancipation of labor only by gradual decentralization, by developing the individual worker into a more conscious and determining factor in the processes of industry by making him [or her] the impulse whence proceeds all industrial and social activity. The deep significance of the social revolution lies in the abolition of the mastery of [humans over humans], putting in its place the management of things. Only thus can be achieved industrial and social freedom. —Alexander Berkman[3]

Part 1: Introduction and Reasoning: Short Narrative of an Experiment

For many people in Jackson, Mississippi, Tuesday, February 25th, 2014 will forever be remembered as a day of infamy. On this day, Jackson Mayor Chokwe Lumumba died without warning or clear explanation. And with Chokwe's untimely death, the hope and promise he embodied for Jackson was nearly extinguished, for when he died the vision of liberation he projected and the transformative plan he offered to attain it was almost buried with him.

Some of what was concretely lost is best illustrated by outlining what Mayor Lumumba was intending on doing on this fateful day to help advance some of the objectives of the Jackson-Kush Plan. February 25, 2014 was a regularly scheduled City Council meeting and at this particular meeting the Lumumba administration was set to launch three critical items. The first was to secure the formal approval of the council for the administration's choice of director for the department of public works. The second was to secure the council's approval of the *"Jackson Rising: New Economies Conference"*. And the third was to layout his administration's plans to facilitate the building of a vibrant, social and solidarity economy in Jackson to improve the overall quality of life and transform the social relationships in the community.

Unfortunately, none of these items were ever presented to or considered by the council. When Chokwe died, the council delayed engaging or initiating any critical action for months to concentrate on the special election that was called to determine who his successor would be. This was further complicated by the fact that two members of council ran in the special election for Mayor.[4] Chokwe Antar Lumumba, the youngest son of Chokwe Lumumba, also ran for Mayor during the special election. However, he finished second in the race, losing the Mayoral seat to former councilman Tony T. Yarber. It should be noted that Chokwe Antar won the majority of the Black vote during the special election, but lost the election on account of two interrelated factors: a historically high white voter turnout in support of councilman Yarber and a relatively low Black voter turnout.

In many people's minds, this electoral defeat was interpreted as the death of the Jackson-Kush Plan. Many equated the plan with Chokwe Lumumba and electoral politics, and did not think there was more to the work in Jackson other than Chokwe's notoriety and popularity. As time has demonstrated, nothing could be further from the truth.

There should be no doubt about it, Chokwe's death was a hard blow to the New Afrikan People's Organization, the Malcolm X Grassroots Movement, the People's Assembly, and progressive forces in Jackson overall, as the accumulated experience, knowledge, skill, and leadership capacities developed by Chokwe were fundamentally irreplaceable. But, what turned out to be the fundamental saving grace for the revolutionary forces in Jackson was the Jackson-Kush Plan. The Plan has served as our guiding light, our North Star.

The Jackson-Kush Plan is grounded in over forty years of community organizing and base building by the likes of forces such as the Provisional Government of the Republic of New Afrika (PG-RNA), the New Afrikan People's Organization (NAPO), and the Malcolm X Grassroots Movement (MXGM). It is not a fly by night idea. It is a vision and plan with an organic base that has long been committed to the politics of revolutionary transformation and far beyond being dependent upon one man or one organization.

After Chokwe's death, the forces guided by the Jackson-Kush Plan rallied to fulfill many of the uncompleted or half completed tasks central to the plan. The New Afrikan People's Organization and the Malcolm X Grassroots Movement rallied to get Chokwe Antar Lumumba elected in the immediate months following Chokwe's death. The People's Assembly successfully held a session just days after Chokwe's passing, and played a key role in launching the Coalition for Economic Justice in January 2016 to fight a series of policy threats that were hostile to Jackson's municipal sovereignty and Black political control.[5] The motion to advance the Jackson-Kush Plan was certainly stunted by Chokwe's death, but it was not halted.

The first clear indication that the Plan did not die with Chokwe was the hosting of the Jackson Rising Conference and the launch of Cooperation Jackson. Cooperation Jackson was launched on Thursday, May 1st, 2014 and the Jackson Rising Conference was held Friday, May 2nd through Sunday, May 4th, 2014. Both events indicated that the forces associated with the Jackson-Kush Plan still possessed the will, fortitude, and capacity to move forward with the expansion of the Plan as designed.

The Jackson Rising Conference was originally planned and conceived as a joint initiative of the Lumumba administration and the Malcolm X Grassroots Movement. It was supported by the Southern Grassroots Economies Project (SGEP), which included Cooperation Texas, the Federation of Southern Cooperatives (FSC), the Fund for Democratic Communities (F4DC), and the Highlander Research and Education Center. However, upon Chokwe's death, the conference lost support from the City, and became the exclusive province of the Malcolm X Grassroots Movement and the conference planning committee. The conference was originally planned and designed to rollout the Lumumba administration's plans to foster the growth of a vibrant, locally grounded solidarity economy.

Some of the things that the administration was planning on rolling out were: a) the creation of a unit within the city's economic development department that would focus on promoting cooperative development and supporting new cooperative enterprises with technical assistance; b) the creation of a loan fund that would be jointly capitalized by the city and several local, regional, and national credit unions; and c) the introduction of new municipal policies and procedures that would incentivize the development of cooperatives and allow the city to serve as an anchor institution in advancing their development.

However, given the absence of governmental support, the Jackson Rising Conference was utilized to launch the next phase of the Jackson-Kush Plan's execution: the development of a strong, autonomously oriented social and solidarity economy. Cooperation Jackson was created to execute this pillar of the Jackson-Kush Plan and in the three intervening years since Chokwe's passing it has worked diligently to build a dynamic and integrated solidarity economy in Jackson anchored by a growing network of worker cooperatives, a community land trust, a growing network of urban farms, along with the steady incorporation of a number of mutual aid practices. In order for Cooperation Jackson to reach the scale and scope of the development of the solidarity economy envisioned in the Jackson-Kush Plan it has a long, long way to go before it attains some of its mid-term goals, such as making cooperatives responsible for over 10% of Jackson's Gross Domestic Product (GDP). However, the initiative has been launched and we are indeed "making the road while walking it", as is demonstrated in the "Build and Fight" chapter in this volume written by Kali Akuno.

Cooperation Jackson it trying to make cooperative economics, labor self-management, ecological sustainability, and the democratization of new technologies central to the project of revitalizing the Black liberation movement, to establishing the collective ownership of the means of production and the emancipation of the working class. White supremacy, settler colonialism, capitalist exploitation and patriarchal domination have prevented the Black working class from exercising substantive control over their lives for centuries. To counter these systems of oppression, Cooperation Jackson maintains that its preferred path of "build and fight" development is a necessity to transform the oppressive social relations conditioned by the advance of late-capitalism in its neoliberal form. This orientation draws on a long tradition of self-help, mutual aid, collective entrepreneurship and group economics practiced by Black people in the United States. A snapshot into the depth of this history is captured in the book *Entrepreneurship and Self-Help Among Black Americans: A Reconsideration of Race and Economics.*[6] The harsh reality of American apartheid in the South and de facto segregation in the North forced Blacks to depend on their collective resources in the pursuit of self-determination and collective liberation.

Cooperation Jackson is promoting cooperative economics as an alternative to capitalism and not just as a way to pragmatically get by in an anti-Black economic, social and political environment. Cooperation Jackson embraces cooperative economics because it is primarily centered on putting people before profits and the promotion of democracy at work. These are necessary practices to facilitate worker control, ownership and management of the economic enterprise and supports the practice of self-reliance amongst workers that underscores the quest for self-determination long pursued by the forces of the Black liberation movement.

From its inception as an idea in a Malcolm X Grassroots Movement study group, the organizers of Cooperation Jackson have identified labor self-management, that is workers exercising the intellectual, strategic and operational control of the workplace, as central to the project of building economic democracy through the social and solidarity economy. Under labor self-management, the workers own, manage and control their place of work and make all of the decisions around matters such as the level of employment, introduction of technology, the level of profit to set aside for distribution, making hiring decisions and determining the level of investment. Essentially, the workers make all the decisions in a worker cooperative or labor self-managed firm. We must never forget, that it was capitalism's need for a servile, available and dependable source of plantation labor that was the driving force behind the importation and enslavement of millions of Afrikans in the Americas. Cooperation Jackson's commitment to cooperative economics and labor self-management is an effort to eliminate the dynamic of labor exploitation that is at the heart of capitalism. It is also addressing the need to create workplaces that give workers control over how their labor is used and how the value created from this labor is disbursed or shared.

The Focus of this Work

The purpose of *Jackson Rising: the Struggle for Economic Democracy and Black Self-determination in Jackson, Mississippi*, is to share some of the collective experience that has been accumulated by the forces advancing the Jackson-Kush Plan over the last decade. The collection of essays assembled in this work represent the best summations of the struggle in Jackson in the humble opinion of the editors. The book covers a broad range of subjects and experiences, including reflections of the Jackson-Kush Plan itself, the organizing work leading to the election of Chokwe Lumumba as councilman of Ward 2 in 2008 and 2009, the campaign to elect Chokwe Lumumba mayor in 2012 and 2013, experiences from the mayoral administration of Chokwe Lumumba from July 2013 through February 2014, and numerous reflections on the social and political impact of Chokwe's death and what organizers in Jackson did in response to sustain and advance the Jackson-Kush Plan.

However, we have placed a particular focus on the effort to advance cooperative economics and build economic democracy. Why this emphasis? As the old saying goes, "politics without economics is symbol without substance". We think that economic transformation is central to the project of dismantling the capitalist and imperialist systems and creating new transformative relationships that heal society and foster harmony with the life generating and sustaining systems of our planet. Unfortunately, in our view, too much emphasis has been placed on electoral politics in reference to the Jackson-Kush Plan, both by the mainstream capitalist press and in left and progressive media circles. This emphasis reflects a deep, manufactured bias in bourgeois societies that orients the public towards paying more attention and giving more credence to the illusions of alleged "democratic governance", rather than the real contests for political and social power reflected in the motion of capital and the perpetuation of capitalist social relationships which the sham of democratic governance enables in these societies (even with reforms or moderations in the case of left or social democratic governments in bourgeois states). We aim to re-center every reader's gaze towards the challenges to the "free" motion of capital (meaning the domination of capital over labor and the natural world) and the rejection of capitalist social relationships represented by the thought, strategy, and work of Cooperation Jackson.

Part 2: The Necessity of Cooperative Economics, Labor Self-Management and the Struggle for Economic Democracy

Compelling Reasons for Cooperative Economics and Labor Self-management

A compelling reason for us to embrace cooperative economics and labor self-management is tied to the simple fact that capitalism is not working for hundreds of millions of people across the globe. It is creating chronic joblessness, underemployment, poverty, homelessness, limited access to educational opportunities, exploitative and insecure work-life that is closely mimicking the nasty and brutish experience of nineteenth century capitalism and concentrating income, power and wealth in the hands of the ruling class and their enablers (the bourgeoisie). On the latter issue of wealth and concentration of income in the hands of the economic elite, the United States leads the pack with the top twenty per cent of income earners capturing over fifty per cent of its national income on an annual basis.[7] In 2012, the top ten per cent of the households in the United States commandeered seventy-seven per cent of its net worth, while the bottom forty per cent of households had a negative or zero net worth.[8] In countries such as Austria, The Netherlands, Germany, the top ten per cent of households grabbed over sixty per cent of the net worth in 2012, while in Portugal, Luxembourg Norway and France over fifty per cent of the net worth is controlled by the top ten per cent of households.[9] Even Sweden, which is often seen as a socialist paradise by some political liberals in North America, had the second highest Gini coefficient[10] score for wealth inequality in 2014, which stood at 79.90, while that of the United States came in at 80.56.[11] Since capitalist societies encourage selfish, individualistic and self-regarding values and behaviors, this level of wealth hoarding in the hands of a class that is hostile and antagonistic to the interest and wellbeing of the laboring class cannot be a positive development.

In capitalist societies across the globe, the operational logic and practice of the old adage: "He [or she] who pays the piper calls the tune" is in effect. Given the fact that getting elected is a very expensive affair and deep-pocketed donors are essential to campaign financing, this state of affairs has enabled the bourgeoisie to get its preferred laws and policies in the realm of liberal capitalist democracy. In the article, "Why 21st Century Capitalism Can't Last," the editor and publisher of the socialist magazine *Jacobin* Bhaskar Sunkara shares his perspective on the corrosive mixture and unholy alliance of money and power in society:

> It isn't that the rich are getting richer; it's that they're also getting more powerful. Across the world, inroads against economic democracy — collective bargaining rights and robust social welfare programs — since the 1970s have undermined political democracy, and that's going to make mere policy shifts even more difficult to achieve. Workers aren't pushing for wealth redistribution anymore; in fact, they're actually losing battles to preserve gains won in past generations. No longer threatened at the grassroots, the ability of the world's wealthiest citizens to shape politics is nearly absolute.
>
> Developments in the United States, such as the Citizens United and McCutcheon rulings eliminating limits on campaign fundraising restrictions, have made the connection between financial wealth and political influence even more apparent. But despite public outrage — almost 90 percent of Americans think there's too much money in politics — reform appears to be a faint hope.[12]

Cooperative economics and labor self-management provide the members of the laboring classes who experience class exploitation and domination and non-class forms of oppression with practical economic tools to challenge the economic and political power of the economic and political elite. The oppressed are in a position to build a counterhegemonic practice that mirrors the embryonic values and institutions of the future socialist society, while living within the existing capitalist, patriarchal and racist social order.

It was not an accidental occurrence or for flippant reasons that Karl Marx and Mikhail Bakunin saw cooperative economics and labor self-management as useful tools in the struggle for socialism and the undermining of capitalism. In 1864, Marx made the comment below on cooperative economics and labor self-management over production:

> But there was in store a still greater victory of the political economy of labor over the political economy of property. We speak of the cooperative movement, especially of the cooperative factories raised by the unassisted efforts of a few bold

'hands'. The value of these great social experiments cannot be over-rated. By deed, instead of by argument, they have shown that production on a large scale, and in accord with the behest of modern science, may be carried on without the existence of a class of masters employing a class of hands; that to bear fruit, the means of labor need not be monopolised as a means of dominion over, and of extortion against, the laboring man himself; and that, like slave labor, like serf labor, hired labor is but a transitory and inferior form, destined to disappear before associated labor plying its toil with a willing hand, a ready mind, and a joyous heart.[13]

Marx saw the labor self-managed factories as spaces that prepared the workers for life in the communist society. Further, the practice of labor self-management provides proof of the capabilities of the workers to self-organize without the oppressive overlordship of capital or its representatives.[14]

Bakunin viewed the cooperatives as preparatory arenas of struggle for the stateless, self-managed and classless (anarchist communist) society:

Let us, whenever possible, establish producer-consumer cooperatives and mutual credit societies [credit unions] which, though under the present economic conditions they cannot in any real or adequate way free us, are nevertheless important inasmuch as they train workers in the practice of managing the economy and plant the precious seeds for the organization of the future.[15]

Bakunin was quite perceptive in his understanding that the institutional environment of capitalism, which would be the operational context of the producer, consumer and financial cooperatives would not by themselves emancipate the laboring classes and other oppressed groups. There must be a political struggle to wrest power from the ruling class and start the process of creating the classless, stateless and self-managed society of socialism. The initiative to create a solidarity economy in Jackson cannot divorce itself from social movement activism and the class struggle. To do so would be tantamount to conceding that capitalism is the only game in town.

The collapse of the former Soviet Union and, with it, its version of socialism has led many members of society to believe that there is no viable alternative to capitalism. The proponents of capitalism have used all available means to reinforce the preceding perception, even while conceding that there are problematic behaviour among certain agents of this economic system:

The revival of anti-capitalist rhetoric owes much to the financial crisis of 2008 and its aftermath. The crisis was merely the latest example of the inherent stability of capitalism, a process that, while allowing the economy to benefit from "creative destruction", causes a lot of collateral damage along the way. The real problem is that capitalism has become associated with high finance, rather than the heroic entrepreneurship of Thomas Edison, whose inventions still surround us. It is not just that few people can see the benefits of complex financial products like credit default swaps. He adds that "bankers have undoubtedly done their best to give capitalism a bad name. The extraordinary scale on which big banks have been rigging interest rates and foreign-exchange markets and ripping off their customers is almost beyond comprehension."[16]

Contrary to the propagandistic claim about capitalism being the only game in town, there are alternatives to this system. One example that demonstrates in practice elements of a post-capitalist practice is the Mondragon cooperative experiment in the Basque region of Spain. Some key lessons from this experiment are documented in *Making Mondragon: The Growth and Dynamics of the Worker Cooperatives Complex* and *Values at Work: Employee Participation Meets Market Pressure at Mondragon.*[17] The Mondragon Corporation is a network of cooperatives and other organizations with worker cooperatives at its centre. In 2015, the Mondragon Corporation generated €12.11 billion in income, provided 74,335 jobs, invested €317 million in its operation, achieved the figure of 43 per cent of the worker members being women and had workers owners constituting 81 per cent of the cooperatives' workforce.[18] The Jackson–Kush Plan and the emerging cooperative experiment in Jackson are heavily influenced by the Mondragon experiment and its interrelationship with the Basque movement for self-determination and sovereignty. In these movements, we have found many parallels with our struggle for self-determination and economic democracy in Mississippi and throughout the Black Belt region of the US South.

The Basque history of organizing their people for self-reliance, as reflected in the Mondragon experiment, is a compelling reason to embrace cooperative economics in general and labor self-management in particular. Cooperative economics is based on organizing and meeting the needs of your members or community and doing so with the strategic objectives of satisfying self-determined human needs and social bonding, not the generation or pursuit of profits. In the process of the people reflecting on why the institutional context in which they are located has prevented them from being able to adequately meet their need for high quality and affordable goods and services, the revolutionary or progressive organizers have the opportunity to pose questions that encourage the people to think critically and interrogate the structural shortcomings of capitalism. In other words, as a result of posing questions about the basic features of capitalism and the predictable anti-people or anti-working class economic, social and political outcomes that it produces, a critical mass of people might come to the conclusion that capitalism must become history in order for them to lead decent, just and ecologically sustainable lives.

The revolutionary organizers ought to predicate their organizing intervention among the oppressed around their self-defined needs. By utilizing the critical problem-posing methodology of the late Brazilian educator Paulo Freire, on the basis that the exploited are and can act as the architects of their own emancipation, we increase the likelihood of turning the people on to a radically transformative approach to relating to the world:

Critical and liberating dialogue, which presupposes action, must be carried on with the oppressed at whatever stage of their struggle for liberation. The content of that dialogue can and should vary in accordance with historical conditions and at the level at which the oppressed perceive reality. But to substitute monologue, slogans, and communiqués for dialogue is to attempt to liberate the oppressed without their reflective participation in the act of liberation is to treat them as objects which must be saved from a burning building: it is to lead them into the populist pitfall and transform them into masses which can be manipulated.

At all stage of their liberation, the oppressed must see themselves as women and men engaged in the ontological and historical vocation of becoming more fully human. Reflection and action become imperative when one does not erroneously attempt to dichotomize the content of humanity from its historical forms.

The insistence that the oppressed engage in reflection on their concrete situation is not a call to armchair revolution. On the contrary, reflection — true reflection — leads to action. On the other hand, when the situation calls for action, the action will continue an authentic praxis only if its consequences become the object of critical reflection. In this sense, the praxis is the new raison d'etre of the oppressed; and the revolution, which inaugurates the historical moment of this raison d'etre, is not viable apart from their concomitant conscious involvement.[19]

When cooperatives employ a genuine participatory and democratic framework of labor self-management to address the needs of the people for food, housing, employment, childcare services and other basic necessities, it helps enable people to better compare and contrast the difference between the capitalist system and the emerging post-capitalist systems that are emerging. The first contrast typically emerges in the arena of decision-making and operational control. Democratic, self-managed cooperatives enable workers to have greater control over the decisions that impact their lives as opposed to the authoritarian and alienating organizational structures and processes that are associated with capitalism.

Organizing people around their needs, which includes their social and cultural needs for human contact and connection, enables our social movements to make quantum leaps towards the development of a protagonistic consciousness that calls on people to utilize and/or create opportunities to engage in transformative practice. As Amilcar Cabral, the revolutionary, educator, organizer and military strategist from Cape Verde and Guinea-Bissau makes it clear, our organizing strategy must center experiences of the people and address their concrete material needs:

Always remember that the people do not fight for ideas, for the things that exist only in the heads of individuals. The people fight and accept the necessary sacrifices. But they do it in order to gain material advantages, to live in peace and to improve their lives, to experience progress, and to be able to guarantee a future for their children. National liberation, the struggle against colonialism, working for peace and progress, independence – all of these will be empty words without significance for the people unless they are translated into real improvements in the conditions of life.[20]

The people are likely to make greater sacrifices and commitments to social change projects that respond to their here-and-now daily needs, but which also offer a vision of how to solve the major issues confronting society that limit their freedom and constrain their aspirations. Cooperatives and the practices of democratic self-management, mutual aid and solidarity, we believe, present the Black working class in Jackson (and well beyond) with an organizational form and philosophical outlook that literally allows them to put their future in their hands.

Another compelling reason for cooperative economics and labor self-management is the emphasis that it places on developing the capacities of the members or cooperators to shape the world in their image and interest. When we refer to capacity building, we are highlighting the necessity of equipping the cooperators with the requisite knowledge, skills and attitude to collectively build the economic and social infrastructure of a humanistic, caring and participatory democratic present and future. A key principle of the international cooperative movement affirms the need to educate and train cooperative stakeholders and the sharing of information with the public:

> Co-operatives provide education and training for their members, elected representatives, managers, and employees so they can contribute effectively to the development of their cooperatives. They inform the general public – particularly young people and opinion leaders – about the nature and benefits of cooperation.[21]

We believe the commitment to 'developing the individual worker into a more conscious and determining factor in the processes of industry'" will only emerge from the systematic and purposive educational program that must be carried out among the cooperators, or targets of liberation, as noted by Berkman.[22] Our character and psychological predisposition have been shaped under undemocratic, authoritarian relations and processes and our possession of the requisite knowledge, skills and attitude of self-management and participatory democracy is uneven. As a result, we tend to demonstrate behaviours that are not unlike those of our oppressors and exploiters. Critical education is essential to the process of exorcising the ghosts of conformity within the status quo from the psyche and behaviour of the oppressed to enable the development of a cultural revolution. Cultural revolutions typically precede political revolutions, as the former creates the social conditions for a critical mass of the people to embrace new social values that orient them toward the possibility of another world. Therefore, training and development programs, the constant dissemination of critical information, and mass educational initiatives are central to the goal of preparing the people for self-management and self-determination.

The abilities and knowledges that worker collectives need to manage their own affairs, or oppressed people need to exercise self-determination are unevenly distributed and developed. And without education initiatives to intervene, the better skilled and more formally educated members in our collectives and organizations often dominate decision-making and organizational processes. The preceding condition often unintentionally recreate relations of domination within our cooperative or labor self-managed structures. But, to be truly effective our education initiatives have to be fortified by clear accountability and harm reduction practices that reinforce our democratic practices and strivings for human development.

Another compelling reason to embrace and promote cooperative economics and labor self-management in this period of triumphant neoliberal capitalism is their capacity to serve as antidotes to liberal individualism, selfishness and rampant competition. On the collectivism/individualism continuum, the United States and its inhabitants are classified as being highly individualist. Sadly, Black people tend to score high on individualism in these studies and the article "Cultural Orientations in the United States: (Re)Examining Differences Among Ethnic Groups," provides contextual factors that explain this behavioural phenomenon among Blacks.[23] Economic and social cooperation will encourage and cultivate values such as unity, self-determination, collective work and responsibility, collective purpose, solidarity, in-group trust and faith. It would certainly help in reversing the unacceptably high level of individualism in the Afrikan community and the general society inside the United States. The ideological realm is a site of struggle in winning the people over to socialism and away from their commitment to philosophical liberalism, which is the dominant ideology in the United States and other societies in the global North. The possibility of revolution in capitalist society, in particular this capitalist society with its settler-colonial foundations and imperialist imperatives, becomes stronger when a critical mass of people embrace the antidote of cooperation, collectivism, solidarity, mutual aid, and sharing in thought and action. This is what we are trying to cultivate and build in Jackson.

Enabling Structures and Supportive Organizations for Cooperative Economics

The act of thinking about the possibility of another world outside of capitalism, white supremacy and patriarchy meets an untimely demise when it rams into the iceberg of a non-enabling social and economic environment. In other words, the ideas of emancipation that are grounded in the construction of alternative institutions are thrown into the barren soil of an institutional environment that only nurtures and supports structures, which facilitate exploitation and top-down or authoritarian relations with the people. Cooperative economics and labor self-management can only thrive and expand, if they have the necessary enabling structures and organizations that will allow them to successfully compete and challenge capitalist firms for the hearts and souls of the people in their capacity as the purchasers of goods and services. We are not looking to establish an alternative economic practice that is a quaint little infrastructure that exists on the margins of the mainstream economy. Our aim ought to be the development of a counterhegemonic, liberating economic and social infrastructure whose aim is the liquidation of the predatory, exploitative and alienating economic system that is making the lives of the dispossessed a living hell. Capitalism cannot exist in the absence of the support that it gets from varied institutions and programmes abroad in society.

What exactly are we alluding to when we make reference to 'enabling structures and supportive organizations' for cooperative economics and labor self-management? We are going to attempt an answer to the preceding question by illustrating how essential they are to the survival of capitalist firms. The companies that follow the capitalist ownership patterns, method of handling workers, and approach to operating and managing a business benefit from the business education and conventional economic programmes that are taught in primary or elementary, secondary and tertiary levels of the education system. The taxes from the laboring classes are used to finance the business regime that exploit the workers and make capitalist business ideas and practices second nature in our consciousness. It ought to be clear to the reader that the public education system is an enabling structure that provides the existing economic system with ideologically prepared and technically trained or educated personnel to function in capitalist firms. Most of the students who take high school economics and business management courses are not normally expose to consumer, financial and worker cooperatives as viable business forms that promote economic democracy and privilege the needs of their members—not the making of profits for their stakeholders.

Even at the college and university level of the education system, only a few students are trained to work in cooperatives and worker self-managed firms. The educational programmes that address the need of the cooperatives for cooperators and staff with the knowledge, skills and attitude to effectively and efficiently function in these democratic, member owned and controlled economic enterprises were specifically designed for this purpose. Cooperative economics and labor self-management projects do not have an available pool of prospective cooperators who are trained at taxpayers' expense or trained at all as is the case with economic initiatives that are following the orthodox path of capitalist economic development. The Mondragon cooperatives have created their own educational structures over the years to meet their need for trained cooperators at the shop-floor, technical and administrative levels of the cooperative workforce.[24]

The Mondragon University was created in 1997 and it offers undergraduate and graduate degree programs. The "university is in effect the training and research-and-development arm of a wider network of interlocking cooperatives" and it is governed by the students, members and the stakeholders in the other cooperatives. Mondragon has other training and development entities within its Knowledge Group such as the Politeknika Ikastegia Txorierri, the Lea

Artibailkastetxea, and the Otalora as well as research and development organizations. We cannot exaggerate the importance of educating the members in Cooperation Jackson and the community at large for this developing economic democracy and self-determination project.

The conservative path to creating or running businesses finds a much more enabling environment in the area of access to start-up and working capital than cooperatives. Conventional businesses, especially large corporations, have supportive financial structures such as the stock exchange and venture capital funds and institutions such as commercial and investment banks to finance their projects. The Rochdalian cooperatives have been around (in one form or another) since the 1840's, but are still viewed in both mainstream and alternative economic circles as strange organizational creatures with their collectivistic pattern of ownership and control, especially worker cooperative and labor self-managed firms. In the modern era, almost all businesses need loans in order to survive and grow. Consumer and worker cooperatives are at a distinct disadvantage in this respect. Small businesses, which constitute the vast majority of cooperatives worldwide, are usually undercapitalized. But, the problem is quite severe for cooperatives because of the orientation of most banks and financial institutions, which were constructed to fortify capitalism, capitalist social relations, and firms that adhere to capitalist logic. Most banks and other financial institutions are not comfortable or willing to support social enterprises structured around collective ownership. They view them as extremely risky investments. Throughout its history, the cooperative movement has created its own financial institutions to address this problem. However, most have been grossly inadequate to address the comprehensive needs of the movement. But, there are several successful models that are worth noting, studying and emulating based on critical assessments of one's space, time and conditions.

Mondragon's Caja Laboral Popular is perhaps the most instructive. The Caja Laboral Popular (CL), is the provider of financial services and technical assistance, advice and promotion to the Mondragon cooperatives. The Caja Laboral was instrumental in establishing the insurance and social security infrastructure of the Mondragon cooperative confederation, the Seguros Lagun Aro. With respect to the supportive financial structures of the Mondragon cooperatives, Ramon Flecha and Ignacio Santa Cruz illuminate the indispensable role these financial and technical assistance institutions play in the success of the Mondragon cooperatives:

The creation of the Mondragon Corporation and its financial group, organized through Caja Laboral and Lagun Aro, allowed the cooperatives to develop a wide range of reciprocal and mutually supportive mechanisms. These included knowledge transfer, the reallocation of capital and workers (when required) between cooperatives, shared support services, the creation of common funds, a shared strategy for new entrepreneurial projects, and a specific strategy to cover basic needs, such as social security.[25]

The Caja Laboral Popular is a major mobilizer of capital for the cooperatives by way of the savings of the people in the Basque Country and the rest of Spain. It is one of the largest financial institutions in the country. In addition to the Mondragon experience, there are two additional large-scale experiences that are worth citing. These include the Desjardins Group of financial institutions, mainly credit unions, in Quebec (and beyond), and the cooperative Populari banks in Emilia Romagna and throughout Italy (although these have come under serve political attack over the last decade or more by neoliberal political forces).[26] These examples have much to offer, both positive and negative, to Cooperation Jackson and those of us seeking to make another world possible under the constraints of living under the oppressive conditions of the current world-system.

As these examples illustrate, credit unions, as financial cooperatives, will have an important part to play in the development of Cooperation Jackson and the solidarity economy movement in Jackson. Following the example of Caja Laboral Popular, people of a progressive persuasion in Jackson and beyond could start shifting their savings and financial transactions from banks to credit unions or other forms of mutual financial aid to help capitalize cooperatives in the city. They would have to complement this action with being active in the running of the credit unions, and charting a new direction for them as instruments of the class struggle.

As you will read throughout this work, Cooperation Jackson is developing a mutually integrated systems approach to the organizing of the cooperatives it is building and will rely on a high degree of coordination and mutual aid among the cooperatives and supporting organizations to be successful. The cooperatives will have to balance their desire for autonomy with the objective need for integration. A principle of the cooperative movement in general is cooperation amongst cooperatives and cooperatives have to develop the structures and organizations that will transform them into a cohesive and integrated system. This type of cooperative development on a large scale would enable democratic enterprises to both defend themselves from capitalist organizations and compete for the hearts and minds of the people in the struggle over how best to balance the delivery of essential goods and services with social justice and ecological balance. As these cooperating cooperatives with their supportive structures bulk up in size, they would be better able to withstand the competitive onslaught of conventional capitalist firms. They would also be able to strategically extract some level of support from the state for various reasons that are relevant to the particular contexts of struggle.

Role of the State in Cooperative Economics and Labor Self-management

At present, the state is a fact of life that the agents of anti-capitalist and post-capitalist struggle are compelled to contend with and address in their strategic pursuit of liberation. In spite of the state being an agent and enabler of the wealthy and other socially dominant groups, the state controls economic resources that are the product of the labor of the working class. The working class must struggle to control these resources, and not just surrender them to the capitalists and the dominant operative forces that manage the state to reinforce and reproduce capitalist social relations. These captured and appropriated resources can and should be used to advance the development of the social and solidarity economy. Through working class struggle on a mass scale, the possibility exists to recapture and redirect the resources controlled by the state in the form of social and income-security programs, like universal basic income (UBI), or the provisioning of cooperatives and other social economy projects that may undermine and gradually transform the operative social relationships that presently exist to reinforce capitalism in the long-term.

One of the functions of the state in advanced capitalist countries like the United States, Canada, Germany, Sweden and others with liberal bourgeois democratic political systems is the legitimizing of the social order in the eyes and worldviews of the masses. This function is critical to the construction of hegemony in capitalist societies, which is primarily executed through social institutions such as schools, the media, the police, and health and welfare agencies. This legitimation function compels the liberal capitalist state to carry out minimally necessary initiatives that alleviate the lot of the oppressed, often through welfare programs. This action on the part of the state also assists in staving off the masses' receptivity to radical and revolutionary ideas of social movements. This legitimation function often compels the masses to project the fulfillment of their hopes and aspirations onto the same system that is crushing their dreams and systematically exploiting and oppressing them. When the bourgeois state regulates certain outrageous actions of capitalist firms or other power brokers in society, it is done to prevent the system from falling into disrepute and inspiring revulsion against it. The preceding act is an expression of the liberal bourgeois state fulfilling its legitimation function to ensure the reproduction of systems of extraction and the private appropriation of socially produced value that define the capitalist system.

History has demonstrated that strong working class and people's movements can create tremendous tensions within liberal bourgeois states that challenge their legitimation function and apparatus. They do this by creating tension between the function of the state as a facilitator of capital accumulation and a guarantor of "basic" democratic rights. It is by exploiting the structural tensions within the bourgeois state, particularly the legitimation function of its hegemonic apparatus, that interventions can be made by radical activists to compel the state to utilize some of the resources it has extracted from the people to support cooperative economic development. Ajamu Nangwaya's article in this volume speaks to the ways that the state is able to provide cooperatives with valuable support, such as financing, education, technical assistance and other services.

In order for cooperatives to be utilized as a tool of revolutionary social transformation their members must constantly struggle against being coopted by the institutions and other instruments of the bourgeois state. To sustain a revolutionary orientation and practice, our cooperatives cannot become dependent upon the concessions or largess of the bourgeois state, nor the protected markets the state confers in limited cases. Sadly, however, there is a long history of cooperatives pursuing this route and succumbing to the logic of capitalism and the perpetuation of the system. As a result, many cooperatives simply come to see themselves as one sector in the capitalist political economy alongside the private and public sectors. This political orientation has enabled many cooperatives to be viewed as non-threatening to the system, and relatively safe to the operatives of the state.

However, in most cases where progressive political parties or social forces have employed cooperatives and other types of mutual aid institutions and practices to help advance a socialist or non-capitalist path of development, they were viewed as a dire threat to the established social order by the dominant forces of capital and the state, and were often the target of destabilization or repression. This was definitely the case in Jackson when the administration of Chokwe Lumumba promoted cooperatives as an essential plank in its platform for the transformation of the municipality, which is duly noted by Nathan Schneider in "the Revolutionary Life and Strange Death of a Radical Black Mayor".[27]

Outline of the Book

The focus of this book is the sharing of the story of how the Jackson-Kush Plan emerged, how the forces that are committed to it have planned and worked to bring it to fruition, and what lessons we have learned from our collective successes and failures. As previously noted, the book gives particular focus to the effort to develop the social and solidarity economy pillar of the Jackson-Kush Plan through the work of Cooperation Jackson.

Jackson Rising includes nine new works, never published on any website, newspaper, or book. These include a Forward by Rukia Lumumba that speaks to the contributions of her late father, Mayor Chokwe Lumumba. It also includes Afterwords by internationally organizers, Ajamu Baraka and Hakima Abbas, encouraging people to critically examine the struggle in Jackson, Mississippi and to apply its lessons wherever Afrikan people are struggling.

The first section of the book, "*Groundings*", lays the critical foundation to understand how Cooperation Jackson is expanding the vision of the Jackson-Kush Plan towards fulfilling its mission to build a dynamic, social and solidarity economy in Jackson to provide a solid material foundation for the transformation that is being envisioned and struggled for. "Build and Fight", written by Kali Akuno on behalf of Cooperation Jackson, is the most comprehensive statement written to date on the theory and programmatic outline of the work that Cooperation Jackson is pursuing. We think it can and will be instructive to practitioners everywhere.

The second section of the book, *"Emergence"*, provides us with the public write up of the now famous Jackson-Kush Plan, written by Kali Akuno. It also provides us with several other works that address dimensions of how the Jackson –Kush Plan emerged and was unveiled to the world. The first chapter in this section, is written by human rights activist and attorney Kamau Franklin, and outlines the early electoral work conducted under the auspices of the Jackson-Kush Plan, which focused on getting Chokwe Lumumba elected to the city council, and how this was buttressed by decades of base building work in the community. Kali Akuno wrote the next two works in this section, the *"People's Assembly Overview"* and the *"Jackson Rising Policy Statement"*. The People's Assembly Overview was written to demonstrate to a broad public audience how the Assembly emerged in Jackson and what its basic historic characteristics have been. The Jackson Rising Statement was written on behalf of the Mayoral administration of the late Chokwe Lumumba. This statement outlined the core elements of the transformative vision and programs that the Lumumba administration was working towards to make Jackson a Transition City. The last chapter in this section, *"Seek ye first the worker self-management kingdom"*, was written by one of the co-editors, Ajamu Nangwaya, to highlight the transformative potential of the Jackson-Kush Plan, and how the municipalist orientation of the plan could enable the transformation of Jackson's economy through cooperative development and worker self-management.

The third section of the book, *"Building Substance"*, focuses on the process of organizing the Jackson Rising conference and some of the immediate outcomes that emerged from it. The first essay in this section, *"Free the Land"*, is a narration from one of the last interviews given by Mayor Chokwe Lumumba to Bhaskar Sunkara, the founder and editor of Jacobin magazine. In this interview, Bhaskar outlines some of ways Chokwe was envisioning taking on the question of democratically transforming the economy, including engaging in ongoing initiatives like the Jackson Rising conference. The second essay in this section comes from veteran radical organizer and intellectual, Carl Davidson, who wrote one of the first insightful articles to correctly grasp the link between our efforts to use electoral politics to build power and transform the local economy. The final article in this section, written by militant journalist and former Black Panther Party member, Bruce Dixon, focuses on the centrality of Black working class organizing to the effort to democratically transform the economy through cooperative economics. It also addresses, how this type of self-organization is a necessary heightening of the class struggle within the Black community.

The fourth section of the book, *"Critical Examinations"*, addresses a number of key issues and challenges confronting Cooperation Jackson and the execution of the Jackson-Kush Plan. The first essay, *"Why the Left should look to Jackson, Mississippi*", by human rights lawyer and activist Michael Siegel, takes a short look at how left forces in Jackson are seeking to address many of the structural and political challenges that have been haunting the left for decades. The second essay, *"The Centrality of Land and the Jackson-Kush Plan"*, by renowned housing and human rights activist Max Rameau, addresses the question of land ownership and property relations, and how these systems and how they are controlled are central to any people's struggle for liberation. The third essay, *"The City as Liberated Zone"*, by movement strategist and theoretician Makani Themba, addresses the critical role of people's assemblies in the struggle to build municipal democracy and socialism. The fourth essay, "A Long and Strong History with Southern Roots", by Jessica Gordon-Nembhard, the chief intellectual on Black cooperative history and development in our age, attempts to situate the birth and development of Cooperation Jackson in the long thread of Black cooperative development in the South. The fifth essay of this section, *"The Challenge of Building Urban Cooperatives in the South"*, by Elandria Williams and Jazmine Walker, addresses the challenges confronting Cooperation Jackson in its effort to build viable, self-sustaining worker cooperatives in Jackson. The final work of this section, "Coming Full Circle: the Intersection of Gender Justice and the Solidarity Economy", is an interview by renowned journalist Thandisizwe Chimurenga with Cooperation Jackson co-founder and executive committee member, Sacajawea "Saki" Hall. The interview addresses how Cooperation Jackson is struggling to eliminate the systemic dynamics of sexism, patriarchy and heterosexism and incorporate a dynamic analysis and practice of inter-sectionality into its work and worldview.

The fifth and final section of this book, *"Going Forward"*, provides us with a series of reflections on the overall work to implement the Jackson-Kush Plan, and what lessons can and should be drawn from these experiences. The first essay, "After the death of a Radical Mayor", by award winning progressive journalist Laura Flanders, is the last interview given by Chokwe Lumumba. This is a critical essay, as it presents the most in-depth illustration of what Chokwe was thinking shortly before his death, and where he was planning on heading, as he was reflecting on his first seven months in office. The second essay in this section, *"The Jackson Just Transition Plan"*, written by Kali Akuno, outlines Cooperation Jackson's basic vision for how it is going to aid the city of Jackson fulfill the pledge made by the Lumumba administration to become the greenest, most sustainable city in the United States empire. The third essay in this section, *"A green utopia in Mississippi"*, by progressive journalist Sara Bernard, highlights how Cooperation Jackson links the local with the global in the struggle institute systems change to halt climate change and eliminate the extractive and exploitative logic of the capitalist system. The forth essay in this section, *"Casting Shadows"*, was written by Kali Akuno nearly a year after the death of Chokwe Lumumba to provide a public assessment of the experiences of the first Lumumba administration. After more than two years since its publication, the work remains as critical and insightful as ever, which is why we are including it in this critical work. The fifth and final essay in this section is, *"The Socialist Experiment: a new-society vision for Jackson Mississippi"*, by Katie Gilbert. This essay is the newest work in this entire volume. It was published by the Oxford American, with the support Economic Hardship Reporting Project in September 2017, after more than 2 years of in-depth interviews with Chokwe Antar Lumumba, Sacajawea "Saki' Hall, Kali Akuno, brandon king and several other members of Cooperation Jackson, the Malcolm X Grassroots Movement, the Coalition for Economic Justice, and the People's Task Force. The essay is one of the most comprehensive works written about the ongoing effort to implement the Jackson-Kush Plan, and the various internal and external struggles that have arisen in the course of this work, and some lessons that can be learned from it.

Work, Reflect, Study, Improve! And Repeat.

Notes

1. W.E.B. DuBois, *Dusk of Dawn: An Essay Toward an Autobiography of a Race Concept.* Oxford University Press, 2007.

2. *The Speeches of Fannie Lou Hamer: To Tell It Like It Is.* Maegan Parker Brooks, 2001.

3. Alexander Berkman, 'The Pattern of Life Under Decentralized Communism,' In *Patterns of Anarchy: A Collection of writings on the Anarchist Tradition,* ed., Leonard I. Krimerman and Lewis Perry, New York: Anchor Books, 1966, 344.

4. The two council member's that ran for Mayor during the special election of 2014 were Tony Yarber and Melvin Priester, Jr.

5. For more background on the Coalition for Economic Justice (CEJ) see, "Countering the Confederate Spring: the Assault on Black Political Power in Jackson, MS", by Kali Akuno at http://navigatingthestorm.blogspot.com/2016/03/countering-confederate-spring-assault.html.

6. John Sibley Butler, *Entrepreneurship and Self-Help Among Black Americans: A Reconsideration of Race and Economics*, Albany, New York: State University of New York Press, 1991, 79-142.

7. Christopher Ingraham, "If you thought income inequality was bad, get a load of wealth inequality," *The Washington Post*, May 21, 2015. Accessed from https://www.washingtonpost.com/news/wonk/wp/2015/05/21/the-top-10-of-americans-own-76-of-the-stuff-and-its-dragging-our-economy-down/?utm_term=.e7e7031bad7f.

8. Ibid.

9. Ibid.

10. For more information on the Gini coefficient see, "Who, What, Why: What is the Gini coefficient", at http://www.bbc.com/news/blogs-magazine-monitor-31847943.

11. Erik Sherman, "America is the richest, and most unequal, country," *Fortune*, September 20, 2015. Accessed from http://fortune.com/2015/09/30/america-wealth-inequality/.

12. Bhaskar Sunkara, "Why 21st Century Capitalism Can't Last," Al Jazeera America, April 26, 2014. Accessed from http://america.aljazeera.com/opinions/2014/4/thomas-piketty-capitalism21stcentury.html.

13. Bruno Jossa, "Marx, Marxism and the Cooperative Movement," *Cambridge Journal of Economics*, 29 (2005): 4.

14. Ibid., 6.

15. Sam Dolgoff, ed., *Bakunin on Anarchism*, Montreal: Black Rose Books, 1980, 173.

16. *The Economist*, "What's the alternative?," *The Economist*, August 15, 2015. Accessed from http://www.economist.com/news/books-and-arts/21660952-capitalism-not-perfect-its-better-other-systems-whats-alternative. The quote in the excerpt is from John Plender's book *Capitalism: Money, Morals and Markets*.

17. George Cheney, *Values at Work: Employee Participation Meets Market Pressure at Mondragon*, Ithaca: Cornell University Press, 1999; William Foote Whyte and Kathleen King Whyte, *Making Mondragon: The Growth and Dynamics of the Worker Cooperatives Complex*, Ithaca: Cornell University Press, 1988.

18. Mondragon Corporation, "Highlights," Accessed on February 18, 2017, http://www.mondragon-corporation.com/eng/about-us/economic-and-financial-indicators/highlights/.

19. Paulo Freire, *Pedagogy of the Oppressed*, 30th Anniversary Edition, New York: Continuum, 2000, 65-66.

20. Lar Rudebeck, *Guinea-Bissau: A Study of Political Mobilization*, Uppsala, The Scandinavian Institute of African Studies, 1974, 91.

21. International Co-operative Alliance, *Co-operative identity, values & principles*.

22. See Note 1

23. Heather M. Coon and Markus Kemmelmeier, "Cultural Orientations in the United States: (Re)Examining Differences Among Ethnic Groups," Journal of Cross-cultural Psychology, 32, No. 3, (2001).

24. Sharryn Kasmir, *The Myth of Mondragon: Cooperatives, Politics, and Working-class Life in a Basque Town*, Albany: State University of New York Press, 1996, 153-154.

25. Ramon Flecha and Ignacio Santa Cruz, "Cooperation for Economic Success: The Mondragon Case," *Analyse & Kritik*, 33, 1 (2011): 163. Accessed from http://burawoy.berkeley.edu/Public Sociology, Live/Flecha&Santacruz.Mondragon.pdf.

26. For the attacks on the Popolari see "Not so Popolari: Reform of Italy's biggest cooperative banks will help the sector to consolidate" at http://www.economist.com/news/business-and-finance/21640571-reform-italys-biggest-cooperative-banks-will-help-sector-consolidate-not-so-popolari.

27. To read this article view https://www.vice.com/en_us/article/5gj7da/free-the-land-v23n2.

II

EMERGENCE

3.

The New Southern Strategy: The Politics of Self-determination in the South

Kamau Franklin

A view from 2009

In October 2008, the Malcolm X Grassroots Movement (MXGM) made a strategic decision to run one of its founders, Chokwe Lumumba, for the Ward 2 City Council seat in Jackson, Mississippi. We took on this strategy in part because over 10 months ago[1] the US electorate, partly due to an economic meltdown, open-ended wars abroad and the changing demographics of the U.S. population, voted in a moderate Black Democrat as its President. That President has gone through great pains to appear as race neutral as possible in both content and rhetoric. Which means that although there has been a substantial amount of hope and resources invested in him the possible returns on such an investment remains unclear for the Black community. With many constituents to please, the new president was guessing that he could not afford to look as if he was overly responsive to the needs of the Black community.

Moderate Black elected officials who are beholden to the Democratic Party similarly dominate the southern Black population. These politicians filled a void vacated by the veterans of the Civil Rights and Black Power movements of the 60's and 70's, who were forced to abandon the development of a coherent political strategy due to the severe attacks the movements were subjected to by the US government, big corporations and white reaction. These careerist forces filled the void by becoming beholden to the Democratic Party. The needs of the community took a back seat to their own individual career paths. It is in this context that MXGM saw an opening to support the candidacy of Chokwe in Jackson, Mississippi. Jackson is an overwhelmingly Black city, where Black elected officials, or as they may prefer, elected officials who just happen to be Black, dominate city politics.

This domination has not led however, to the Jackson populace's participation in true city decision making, to better governmental services, more job's, better health care or a safer and cleaner environment. With no commitment to anything, beyond getting elected these officials don't bring any overarching principles to city-government beyond the principle of careerism. This gave us the opportunity to respond with a candidate who could highlight real choices to areas that we have a majority Black population. In no other place other than the South, where over 50% of the U.S. Black population still lives could we highlight the politics of self-determination versus the politics of careerism and moderation.

If there is any place where a strategy of self-determination should be implemented it's a place where our people are the clear majority and where issues of race can actually be succumbed to ideas on how to improve the lives of people. The south allows us to argue in an unapologetic way, our case that the way out of this economic, social and cultural mess of our community, in terms of electoral work, is to support candidates that are connected to the concept of self-determination, the use of the government apparatus to serve the needs of the local community and direct resources to those communities. Candidates with the politics of self-determination look to support the creation of institutions and control of institutions through the community. Candidates steeped in the tradition of self-determination come from an established base that can hold them accountable to their politics.

There is a practice that is beginning to catch fire amongst left organizers in the states that are involved in electoral politics, that we have borrowed from our comrades in Latin America, that is Peoples' Assembly's. Gathering the community into an organized bloc that begins to set the agenda for what candidates that are elected should be fighting for as opposed to just hearing what candidates are saying they are going to do, we only support people who run on what the community has determined is in their self interest. Making candidates responsive to our community needs must be done in an intentional way, one that involves planning for what the city/community should look like and how should it be governed.

Jackson seems to be an ideal place to start such a campaign. To see if the Black public when given the option of politicians who are moderate democrats versus a candidate who believes in Black self determination, who would they choose. In a national election the Black majority was well rehearsed to say that race did not matter as 95% voted for the Black candidate. In this local election where all the candidates were Black, what separated the candidates was their politics and their plans for the future of Jackson. The other seven candidates sounded the same. They were for winning the City Council seat but had no ideas about what to do with it. Only one candidate based on his history in the movement for self-determination was prepared with ideas on what needs to be done in his district and the rest of the city, based on conversations with his soon to be constituents.

On May 19, 2009 the anniversary of the birth of Malcolm X, the politics of self-determination was the clear winner in Jackson, with little resources but lots of support the electorate in Ward 2 voted in overwhelming numbers for a out-spoken revolutionary nationalist to represent the interest of the community, they voted for beginning the process to transform the local government apparatus into a vehicle for economic and political change, guided by the principle of self-determination.

§

A view from 2013

Many people I know expressed surprise at me moving to Jackson, MS, being from Brooklyn (back when it was the BK- but that is another story).[2] The surprise is even more startling for Jackson folks under 30 who with amazement in their eyes ask WHY WOULD YOU LEAVE NEW YORK? Part of the answer is that I have committed myself to the fulfillment of certain ideas. So my career is the politics of Black self-determination. It does not pay well by any means; you can't always get the most qualified people to fulfill certain positions and the hours suck; but over 20 years ago I was bitten by the bug of revolutionary Black politics. Those politics have cost me financially and sanity wise, but at the same time they have led me on a life mission, some great comrades and the love of my life. So on balance I still feel as if I am coming out ahead, however back to Jackson, MS.

I would like to believe that as a committed organizer that the work I do has a larger purpose. That it is coordinated in such a way to gain results that are tangible and that build towards greater community control over social, economic and political institutions. I came to Jackson, MS with such ideas in mind. The thinking is that the city of Jackson due to its size, demographic makeup and history could be a great place to re-test ideas both historic and current in the struggle for Black self-determination.

It is way too early to suggest success; however my first twelve weeks in Jackson is a good guide to early satisfaction with the actual move. I have done more multilayered organizing here than I have in the last 5 years in either New York or Atlanta. I have met and worked with various groups and individuals from people in community civic leagues, church groups, home associations, electoral candidates, cops, preachers, politicians, farmer groups, civil rights workers, and international allies, but relatively few of the pro-Black militants or overt left radicals that I have worked with most of my organizing life. Obviously most of these folks don't necessarily share the full range of my politics but we have enough in common to work on various initiatives that can lead to progressive/radical changes in Jackson. My debates have been substantive and have led to action as opposed to conversations that only ignite plans without success because of follow thru abilities, desire, finances, scale, or scope. I have worked on achieving economic development, international solidarity, electoral strategies, and food justice issues.

More specifically we have already established the largest community garden/farm in Jackson (over 5 acres). A campaign for policy changes on healthy food is in the works. We have supported the successful election of the first Black Sheriff in Hinds County Mississippi (Hinds was incorporated in 1820), which encompasses Jackson and is over 70% Black. This is a victory coming on the heels of electing Chokwe Lumumba to the city council two years ago. We are now beginning work on a second city-council race and looking into buying property for a center and we have purchased our fist property for economic development purposes.

The overt work of struggling for self-determination in the south predates me by a few hundred years; however 40 years ago the groundwork was laid for a modern struggle that recognized the south as a battleground in an ideological and at times physical battle for self-determination. In 1968 the Provisional Government of the Republic of New Afrika (RNA) was formed and later in the 1980s the New Afrikan Peoples Organization (NAPO) provided a revolutionary nationalist position for organizing in the South where the majority of Black people still live today. People have changed their lives, uprooted their families and died for attempting to convince Black people that the south could be more than just a place of oppression but it could also be a place of rejuvenation and control.

Two years ago a new phase of this struggle began. Momentum has been built over that time when we got directly involved in the previously mentioned electoral candidacy of Chokwe Lumumba for City Council. We made several other attempts in nearby cities to do similar work but the time seemed overtly right this time to focus on Jackson, MS.

As noted previously, the majority Black centers in the south are dominated by moderate Black Democratic Party careerists. The political void left by the retreat of the Black social movements of the 1950's, 1960's and 1970's was filled by "safe" politicians who did not do much to upset the economic balance of power that favored white power brokers and embraced moderate Democratic Party rhetoric and positioning on governing. As a result, Jackson is in many respects like post apartheid South Africa, where Black electoral power never translated into actual political power, and in the main only supported the Black petty-bourgeois class happy to live off the scraps of the minority white capitalist class that really calls the shots.

It is in this context that MXGM saw an opening to support the candidacy of Chokwe Lumumba. For the Black political class the needs of the community take a back seat to their own individual career paths. With no commitment to anything, beyond getting elected these officials don't bring any overarching principles to city-government beyond the principle of careerism. This gave us the opportunity to respond with a candidate who could highlight real choices. In no other place except the South could we play on a city wide basis, where over 50% of the U.S. Black population still lives and where in major cities in the South blacks still represent over 50% of the electorate. It is here where we can highlight the politics of self-determination versus the politics of careerism and moderation.

We have also borrowed from our friends in places like Venezuela with the concept of Peoples' Assemblies. Organizing the community into specific blocs for a more direct democracy that begins to set the agenda for what candidates that are elected should be fighting for as opposed to just hearing what candidates say they are going to do. This work must be done in an intentional way, one that involves planning for what the city/community should look like and how it should be governed. Even if candidates don't overtly share our politics they are responsive to them for the first time. In addition the Peoples' Assembly is a larger base where policy through community organizing can be achieved. We are developing Assemblies for each of the seven wards in Jackson and by the beginning of 2012 we should be supporting the start of two additional Assemblies in Jackson.

On the challenging side the politicizing of young people will take a while. The idea of politics being outside of mainstream discussions is now a foreign concept to many young people. The idea that life chances are all about personal responsibility now once again dominate discourse and that will change only through more victories. In addition despite my needed respite from only working with "professional" organizers the need to expand what we have is great if we are to keep the momentum going. As Lenin and others have pointed out the vanguard party cannot easily be discarded when thinking through strategy and planning.

We hope to facilitate several mechanisms for people close to us to move to Jackson through some of our economic development plans, but that is a few years away. Unlike the past where activists would move based on what were the strategic needs of a movement they were a part of, today's organizer is less likely to make such a move unless it's tied to the adventure of an international struggle or a semi-natural disaster. We don't want to overwhelm Jackson with transplants but I believe with ten more trained organizers steeped in the politics and practice of self-determination we could test our theories that much faster. My goal and hope is that within two years this work will produce real results in making Jackson a capital of Black progressive change and positioning the Malcolm X Grassroots Movement to serve as a leading community force, that even if not liked by all, will certainly be recognized as one to reckon with.

Notes

1. An earlier version of this article was originally written and published in September 2009 on Kamau Franklin's blog, Grassroots Thinking https://grassrootsthinking.com/2009/09/29/the-new-southern-strategy-the-politics-of-self-determination-in-the-south/.

2. As part and parcel of his political commitment, Kamau Franklin moved to Jackson, MS in 2011 to help advance the work of the Jackson-Kush Plan, which he played a central role in constructing as a core member of the strategic think tank within the Malcolm X Grassroots Movement that devised the plan between 2001-2012. An earlier version of this article first appeared in Organizing Upgrade http://www.organizingupgrade.com/index.php/modules-menu/community-organizing/item/46-kamau-franklin-the-new-southern-strategy.

4.

The Jackson-Kush Plan: The Struggle for Black Self-determination and Economic Democracy

Kali Akuno

A major progressive initiative is underway in Jackson, Mississippi. This initiative demonstrates tremendous promise and potential in making a major contribution towards improving the overall quality of life of the people of Jackson, Mississippi, particularly people of African descent. This strategy is the *Jackson Plan* and it is being spearheaded by the Malcolm X Grassroots Movement (MXGM) and the Jackson People's Assembly.

The Jackson Plan is an initiative to apply many of the best practices in the promotion of participatory democracy, solidarity economy, and sustainable development and combine them with progressive community organizing and electoral politics. The objectives of the Jackson Plan are to deepen democracy in Mississippi and to build a vibrant, people centered solidarity economy in Jackson and throughout the state of Mississippi that empowers Black and other oppressed peoples in the state.

The Jackson Plan has many local, national and international antecedents, but it is fundamentally the brain child of the Jackson People's Assembly. The Jackson People's Assembly is the product of the Mississippi Disaster Relief Coalition (MSDRC) that was spearheaded by MXGM in 2005 in the wake of Hurricane Katrina's devastation of Gulf Coast communities in Mississippi, Louisiana, Alabama and Texas. Between 2006 and 2008, this coalition expanded and transformed itself into the Jackson People's Assembly. In 2009, MXGM and the People's Assembly were able to elect human rights lawyer and MXGM co-founder Chokwe Lumumba to the Jackson City Council representing Ward 2.

What follows is a brief presentation of the Jackson Plan as an initiative to build a base of autonomous power in Jackson that can serve as a catalyst for the attainment of Black self-determination and the democratic transformation of the economy.

Program or pillars

The J-K Plan has three fundamental programmatic components that are designed to build a mass base with the political clarity, organizational capacity, and material self-sufficiency to advance core objectives of the plan. The three fundamental programmatic components are:

- Building People's Assemblies
- Building a Network of Progressive Political Candidates
- Building a broad-based Solidarity Economy

People's assemblies

The People's Assemblies that MXGM are working to build in Jackson and throughout the state of Mississippi are designed to be vehicles of Black self-determination and autonomous political authority of the oppressed peoples' and communities in Jackson. The Assemblies are organized as expressions of participatory or direct democracy, wherein there is guided facilitation and agenda setting provided by the committees that compose the People's Task Force, but no preordained hierarchy. The People's Task Force is the working or executing body of the Assembly. The Task Force is composed of committees that are organized around proposals emerging from the Assembly to carry out various tasks and initiatives, such as organizing campaigns and long-term institution building and development work.

Rooted in a history of resistance

The People's Assemblies model advanced by MXGM has a long, rich history in Mississippi and in the Black Liberation Movement in general. The roots of our Assembly model are drawn from the spiritual or prayer circles that were organized, often clandestinely, by enslaved Africans—to express their humanity, build and sustain community, fortify their spirits and organize resistance. The vehicle gained public expression in Mississippi with the organization of "Negro Peoples Conventions" at the start of Reconstruction to develop autonomous programs of action to realize freedom as – Blacks themselves desired it and to determine their relationship to the Union.

This expression of people's power remerged time and again in Black communities in Mississippi as a means to resist the systemic exploitation and terror of white supremacy and to exercise and exert some degree of self-determination. The last great expression of this vehicle's power in Mississippi occurred in the early 1960s. It was stimulated by a campaign of coordinated resistance organized by militant local leaders like Medgar Evers that drew on the national capacity and courage of organizations like the Student Non-Violent Coordinating Committee (SNCC) and the Congress of Racial Equality (CORE). This campaign created the democratic space necessary for Black communities in Mississippi to organize themselves to resist oppression more effectively. Broad, participatory based People's Assemblies were the most common form of this self-organization.[1] One of the most memorable outgrowths of this wave of Peoples Assemblies in Mississippi was the creation of the Mississippi Freedom Democratic Party (MSFDP), which tested the concrete limits of the Voting Rights Act and challenged white hegemonic control over the Democratic Party in the state of Mississippi and throughout the south.

It is this legacy of People's Assemblies that MXGM is grounding itself in, and one we encourage others, particularly those in the Occupy movement, to study to help guide our collective practice in the present to build a better future.

A comprehensive electoral strategy: Mounting an effective defense and offense

MXGM firmly believes that at this stage in the struggle for Black Liberation that the movement must be firmly committed to building and exercising what we have come to regard as "dual power"—building autonomous power outside of the realm of the state (i.e. the government) in the form of People's Assemblies and engaging electoral politics on a limited scale with the expressed intent of building radical voting blocs and electing candidates drawn from the ranks of the Assemblies themselves. As we have learned through our own experiences and our extensive study of the experiences of others that we cannot afford to ignore the power of the state.

First and foremost our engagement with electoral politics is to try to negate the repressive powers of the state and contain the growing influence of transnational corporations in our communities. From police violence to the divestment of jobs and public resources, there are many challenges facing our communities that require us to leverage every available means of power to save lives and improve conditions. We also engage electoral politics as a means to create political openings that provide a broader platform for a restoration of the "commons",[2] create more public goods utilities (for example, universal health care, public pension scheme, government financed childcare and comprehensive public transportation), and the democratic transformation of the economy. One strategy without the other is like mounting a defense without an offense or vice versa. Both are critical to advancing authentic, transformative change.

Fundamental to our engagement with electoral politics is the principle that we must build and employ independent political vehicles that are not bound to or controlled by either of the two monopoly parties in the United

States. We are particularly focused on building an independent political force that challenges the two-party monopoly and empowers oppressed people and communities throughout the state of Mississippi. In the effort to build on the legacy of independent electoral engagement by Blacks in Mississippi, MXGM's members are all registered members of the Mississippi Freedom Democratic Party (MSFDP) and are starting to work as activists within the party to extend its reach and impact.

It is this combination of building and exercising dual power—building autonomous People's Assemblies and critical engagement with the state via independent party politics—that are the two fundamental political pillars of the Jackson Plan.

To date, some of the accomplishments of this model beyond the 2009 election of Chokwe Lumumba include:

- Leading the campaign to elect the first ever Black Sheriff of Hinds County, Tyron Lewis, in August 2011;[3]

- Leading the campaign to Free the Scott Sisters, which won their release in January 2011;[4]

- Successfully campaigned to save the J-Tran city public transportation in Jackson from devastating austerity cuts planned by current Mayor Harvey Johnson;

- and united with the Mississippi Immigrant Rights Alliance (MIRA) and other progressive forces to pass an anti-racial profiling ordinance in Jackson and to defeat Arizona styled anti-immigrant legislation in Mississippi in 2011 and 2012 respectively.[5]

Building a local solidarity economy

The critical third pillar of the Jackson Plan is the long-term commitment to build a local Solidarity Economy that links with regional and national Solidarity Economy networks to advance the struggle for economic democracy.

Solidarity Economy as a concept describes a process of promoting cooperative economics that promote social solidarity, mutual aid, reciprocity, and generosity.[6] It also describes the horizontal and autonomously driven networking of a range of cooperative institutions that support and promote the aforementioned values ranging from worker cooperatives to informal affinity based neighborhood bartering networks.

Our conception of Solidarity Economy is inspired by the *Mondragon Corporation*, a federation of mostly worker cooperatives and consumer cooperatives and, based in the Basque region of Spain[7] but also draws from the best practices and experiences of the Solidarity Economy and other alternative economic initiatives already in motion in Latin America and the United States.

We are working to make these practices and experiences relevant in Jackson and to facilitate greater links with existing cooperative institutions in the state and elsewhere that help broaden their reach and impact on the local and regional economy. The Solidarity Economy practices and institutions that MXGM is working to build in Jackson include:

- Building a network of cooperative and mutually reinforcing enterprises and institutions, specifically worker, consumer, and housing cooperatives, and community development credit unions as the foundation of our local Solidarity Economy

- Building sustainable, Green (re)development and Green economy networks and enterprises, starting with a Green housing initiative

- Building a network of local urban farms, regional agricultural cooperatives, and farmers markets. Drawing heavily from recent experiences in Detroit, we hope to achieve food sovereignty and combat obesity and chronic health issues in the state that are associated with limited access to healthy and affordable foods and unhealthy food environments

- Developing local community and conservation land trusts as a primary means to begin the process of reconstructing the "Commons" in the city and region by decommodifying[8] land and housing

- Organizing to reconstruct and extend the Public Sector, particularly public finance of community development, to be pursued as a means of rebuilding the Public Sector to ensure there is adequate infrastructure to provide quality health care, accessible mass transportation, and decent, affordable public housing, etc.

In building along these lines, we aim to transform the economy of Jackson and the region as a whole to generate the resources needed to advance this admittedly ambitious plan.

Turning theory into action: Organizing campaigns and alliance-building

These fundamental program components or pillars of the Jackson Plan will only be built through grassroots organizing and alliance building. The key to the organizing component of the overall plan is the launching and successful execution of several strategic and synergistic organizing campaigns. The most critical of these organizing campaigns are:

- The Amandla[9] Education Project

- Take Back the Land
- Operation Black Belt
- 2013 Electoral Campaigns

The Amandla Education Project

The Amandla Project is a youth and community education project specializing in skill building for civic engagement and participation. The Project provides training to youth and community members in the People's Assembly and the broader civil society in Jackson on community organizing, conflict resolution, critical literacy, media literacy, journalism and media advocacy, political theory, political economy, human rights advocacy, cooperative planning and management, participatory budgeting, the principles and practices of solidarity economy, sustainable economic development, and ecological sustainability. The Project also specializes in teaching the rich history of social struggle in Jackson and Mississippi in general, focusing on the legacy of struggle to deepening and expanding democracy in the state and the lessons from these struggles that can be employed today to enhance civic engagement and participation.

In its first year, the Amandla Project will recruit, train, and organize 100 youth and community organizers. These 100 individuals will serve as the core organizing cadre for the Jackson Plan. Our objective is to place 10 organizers in each of Jackson's 7 wards and to utilize the remaining 30 to enhance the overall organizing capacity of progressive forces in the state of Mississippi.

These organizers will be trained by a team of experienced organizers drawn from the ranks of MXGM, Mississippi Chapter of the National Association for the Advancement of Colored People, Mississippi Workers Center for Human Rights and other allied organizations that support the People's Assembly and the Jackson Plan.

Training 100 organizers is a critical start, but is in no way sufficient to meet the comprehensive needs of the Jackson Plan. To develop and train the cohorts and cadre of organizers needed to realize the objectives of this plan, MXGM, MS NAACP and the Praxis Project are working in alliance to build a training school by the start 2013 that will serve as the cornerstone of this long term educational initiative.

The Take Back the Land Campaign

The Take Back the Land campaign is an initiative to create a network of urban farms and farmers' markets to promote a healthy diet, affordable produce, and food sovereignty in the city. It also aims to create a land trust network, cooperative housing, and a workers' cooperative network to provide a base of employment for many of the unemployed and under-employed residents of Jackson.

The Take Back the Land campaign will focus on occupying vacant land, abandoned homes and industrial facilities and converting them into usable agricultural land for urban farming, refurbished green housing to establish a cooperative housing network, and community space to establish training facilities, business centers and recreational spaces.

Aspects of this campaign have already been launched by MXGM with the healthy foods initiative and Fannie Lou Hammer Gardens Project. This initiative is also conceptually linked with the National Take Back the Land Movement that was launched in 2009 by the Land and Housing Action Group (LHAG) of the US Human Rights Network (USHRN), which originally consisted of MXGM, Survivors Village, Chicago Anti-Eviction Campaign, and Take Back the Land Miami.[10]

Operation Black Belt

Operation Black Belt is a campaign to expand worker organizing in Jackson and Mississippi overall, concentrating particularly on Black and immigrant workers. The aim is to organize these workers into associations and unions to provide them with collective voice and power and improve their standards of living.

The long-term objective of this campaign is to challenge, and eventually overturn, the "right to work" laws and policies in Mississippi. These laws and polices play a major role in sustaining the extreme rates of poverty and health disparities in the state, and must be overturned to improve the living standards of the vast majority of its residents. MXGM and the People's Assembly aim to partner with the Mississippi Workers Center for Human Rights to build and expand this critical long-term campaign.

2013 electoral campaigns

For the 2013 City Elections in Jackson, the Jackson People's Assembly and MXGM are prepared to run two candidates. One candidate, Attorney Chokwe Lumumba, who currently serves as the City Councilman for Ward 2, will run for Mayor. The other candidate is June Hardwick, who is also an Attorney, will run for City Council in Ward 7.

The objective of running these candidates and winning these offices is to create political space and advance policies that will provide maneuverable space for the autonomous initiatives of the Jackson Plan to develop and grow. They are also intended to be used to build more Ward based People's Assemblies and Task Forces in Jackson, base build for the overall plan, and raise political consciousness about the need for self-determination and economic democracy to solve many of the longstanding issues effecting Black people.

- In order to create the democratic space desired, we aim to introduce several critical practices and tools into the governance processes of the Jackson city government that will help foster and facilitate the growth of participatory democracy. Some of these processes and tools include: *Participatory Budgeting* to allow the residents of Jackson direct access and decision making power over the budgeting process in the city

- *Gender-Sensitive Budgeting* to address the adverse impact of policy execution as reflected in budget priorities that negatively impact women and children

- *Human Rights Education and Promotion* will require all city employees to undergo human rights training to ensure that their policies and practices adhere to international standard of compliance with the various treaties ratified by the United States government and the results based norms established by the United Nations

We also aim to make several critical structural changes to the city of Jackson's governance structure. The most critical change we will propose and fight for is:

- Creating a Human Rights Charter to replace the existing city charter as the basis of sovereignty and governance for the city

And finally, we aim to advance several economic and social changes on a structural level in Jackson via the governance process. These include:

- Expanding Public Transportation, by increasing transport lines and launching a fleet of green vehicles that utilize natural gas, ethanol, and electric energy

- Creating a network of solar and wind powered generators throughout the city to expand and create a sustainable power grid

- Creating a South-South Trading Network and Fair Trade Zone, that will seek to create trading partnerships with international trading blocs such as CARICOM (the Caribbean Community and Common Market) and ALBA (the Bolivarian Alliance for the Americas)

Alliance-building

Following the example of Malcolm X and countless Black political strategists and organizers before and after him, MXGM is a major advocate for strategic alliance building and united front politics. We are clear that none of our strategic objectives and demands can be attained simply by the forces we can muster. And few of our transitional goals and objectives can be reached without creating substantive alliances with strategic partners and allies. The Jackson Plan, as a transitional plan, is no exception to the rule.

Alliance building has been central to the operations of MXGM in Jackson. In many fundamental respects, the roots of the Jackson People's Assembly rest with the principled alliance of Black progressive organizations like Southern Echo, MS NAACP, MS Workers Center, Nation of Islam, MS ACLU, N'COBRA, MIRA, MS Freedom Democratic Party, NCBL, etc., assembled in the early 1990's to combat environmental racism, labor exploitation, and various aspects of institutional racism in Mississippi. Some of the key alliances we have formed or helped support over the last 20 plus years include the Andre Jones Justice Committee, MS Justice Coalition, Concerned Citizens Alliance, Jackson Human Rights Coalition, Concerned Workers of Frito Lay, Johnnie Griffin Justice Committee, Anti-Klan Coalition, Kwanzaa Coalition, Chokwe Lumumba Legal Support and Defense Committees, Workers United for Self Determination, City Wide Coalition for Selective Buying Campaign, Grassroots Convention, Committee to Free the Scott Sisters and the Full Pardon Committee for the Scott Sisters.

In order for the Jackson Plan and its objectives to be realized, we are going to have to build a broad alliance in the city that is aligned with the principal aims of the Plan and the initiatives that emerge from the People's Assemblies. This alliance will intentionally be multi-national in its outlook and orientation, but be based in and led by Black working class communities and forces. We assess our strategic allies being the growing Latino/Latina community and various immigrant populations that are migrating to the state seeking employment in the agricultural, construction, and professional service sectors. The strategic nature of these forces rests with our common interest in eradicating white supremacy and institutional racism. This alliance will also give due focus to building principled relationships with white progressive forces throughout the city and state who are essential to the current and foreseeable balance of power in the state. Our immediate aim is to win enough of these forces over to our vision and program so as to weaken, if not altogether neutralize, aspects of white conservative power in the state.

The objectives of the Jackson Plan require the building of coalitions and alliances that far exceed the borders of Mississippi. We envision the coalitions and alliances we are seeking to build in Mississippi as being an essential cornerstone to the building of a strategic South by Southwest radical peoples' alliance, rooted in the rebuilding of principled alliances amongst the primary oppressed peoples' in the U.S., namely Blacks, Xicanos, and Indigenous Nations. When and if linked with the growing immigrant population, this grand alliance possesses within it the potential to transform the United States into an entirely new social project.

What you can do to help promote and advance the J-K Plan

MXGM believes that for organizing initiatives like the Jackson Plan to be successful, it will take a balance of self-reliant initiative, will and resourcing combined with genuine solidarity and joint struggle on the part of our allies. To help see this initiative to fruition, we are calling on our allies and supporters to build with us in the following concrete ways:

Promotion and education

The first critical task is to spread the word about the Jackson Plan. Promote it amongst your family, friends and comrades and wherever you live, work, play, rest or pray. Promote the democratic potential that the plan represents and educate people about the importance of this initiative, the lessons that can be learned from it, how it can be applied in their context, and how they can support it.

Resource generation

No major social initiative such as the Jackson Plan can succeed without resources. The Jackson Plan needs a broad array of resources, but the two most fundamental resources it needs are money and skilled volunteers.

We need money for a great number of things, but more specifically to help support and build our organizing drives and campaigns, which includes paying organizers, covering work expenses (transportation, operations, facilities, etc.), and producing and promoting educational and agitation materials. If all of our allies and supporters were to make small individual donations, we firmly believe we could raise millions to support this critical work. In this spirit, we are challenging everyone who supports the Jackson Plan and the work of MXGM to make a contribution of $5 or more to this work to ensure that it succeeds. You can make a tax deductible contribution by donating to Community Aid and Development, Inc., which is our 501c3 fiduciary agent, by visiting http://www.cadnational.org/.

The types of skills we need are in the areas of organizing, management, fundraising, entrepreneurship. Additionally in the technical fields of social networking, farming, construction, engineering, journalism and media, and health care, we are looking for volunteers to come to Jackson and make commitments to help at strategic times for short-term campaign initiatives, mainly for one or two weeks. And, when and where possible, to make more long term commitments for several months or years to work under the discipline of MXGM and the People's Assemblies.

Solidarity and joint campaigns

Political support for the Jackson Plan and the many initiatives within it is just as essential as resource support. We strongly encourage folks in the South to join us in building and extending Operation Black Belt, as this campaign ultimately needs to be a Southern wide initiative in order to be successful. The Amandla Project needs book and curriculum donations, pedagogical exchanges, and volunteer trainers to help it get started. We further call on our allies and supporters everywhere to support our 2013 electoral campaigns by joining one of our volunteer brigades that will start in the summer of 2012 to carry out the will of the People's Assembly. And of course make generous financial contributions to the campaign coffers of Chokwe Lumumba and June Hardwick.

More critically however, we would like to encourage our allies and supporters outside of Mississippi to form local and regional *Jackson Solidarity Circles* to support the Plan and relate directly with MXGM and the People's Assembly to support some or all of the aforementioned initiatives. We want to strongly encourage organizing and organizational development anywhere to enable social transformation to happen everywhere.

We are also looking to inspire, encourage, and support Jackson like plans in other Black Belt regions of the South. In particular, Black Belt regions with mid-sized cities like Jackson with similar race and class demographics, as these represent the greatest potential for success given the current balance of forces in the US, primarily because these cities don't possess the same degree of consolidated transnational capital to contend with as do larger cities. We would hope that over time Jackson Plan Solidarity Committees throughout the Black Belt South would take up this call to action and build their own local political bases of support to engage in dual power initiatives that can link with the forces advancing the Jackson Plan to empower Black and oppressed communities in the South.

If people would like to work more closely with MXGM to build the Jackson Plan we strongly encourage people of Afrikan descent to join MXGM. People interested in joining should contact our national organizer Kamau Franklin at kamauadeaabiodun@yahoo.com. We strongly encourage whites and other non-Afrikan peoples' who are committed to anti-racist, anti-imperialist, anti-sexist politics interested in working directly with us to join the Malcolm X Solidarity Committee (MXSC). People interested in joining the MXSC should contact malcolmxsolidaritycommittee@gmail.com.

Forward!

The Jackson Plan is a major initiative in the effort to deepen democracy and build a solidarity economy. To the extent that this plan calls for a critical engagement with electoral politics, we take heed of the lesson and warning issued by Guyanese Professor Walter Rodney, who stated:

> I say this very deliberately. Not even those of us who stand on this platform can tell you that the remedy in Guyana is **that a new set of people must take over from old set of people, and we will run the system better.** That is no solution to the problems of Guyana. **The problem is much more fundamental than that.** We are saying that **working class people will get justice only when they take the initiative. When they move themselves!** Nobody else can give (freedom) as gift. Someone who comes claiming to be a liberator is either deluding himself or he is trying to delude the people. He either doesn't understand the process of real life. Or he is trying to suggest that you do not understand it. And so long as we suffer of a warped concept of politics as being leadership, we're going to be in a lot of trouble.– Walter A. Rodney, *In the Sky's Wild Noise*

We draw two lessons from this statement and the history associated with it. One, that to engage is to not be deluded about the discriminatory and hierarchal nature of the system, nor deny its proven ability to contain and absorb resistance, or to reduce radicals to status quo managers. The lesson we draw from Rodney's statements are that we have to fight in every arena to create democratic space to allow oppressed and exploited people the freedom and autonomy to ultimately empower themselves. The second lesson regards leadership. MXGM believes that leadership is necessary to help stimulate, motivate, and educate struggling people, but that leaders and leadership are no substitutes for the people themselves and for autonomous mass movement with distributed or horizontal leadership. As the legendary Fannie Lou Hamer said, *"we have enough strong people to do this. For peoples to win this election, it would set a precedent for other counties in the state. People need a victory so bad. We've been working here since '62 and we haven't got nothing, excepting a helluva lot of heartaches."*[11]

The Jackson Plan ultimately aims to build a strong people, prepared to improve their future and seize their own destiny. We hope you will join us in its building and advancement.

Unity and Struggle!

For updates and more information about the Jackson Plan please visit the following websites and social media sources: Malcolm X Grassroots Movement www.mxgm.org or https://www.facebook.com/MXGMnational.

This paper was first published at https://mxgm.org/the-jackson-plan-a-struggle-for-self-determination-participatory-democracy-and-economic-justice/ on July 12, 2017

Notes

1. See *I've Got the Light of Freedom: the Organizing Tradition and the Mississippi Freedom Struggle*, by Charles M. Payne; *Local People: the Struggle for Civil Rights in Mississippi*, by Charles Dittmer; *The Origins of the Civil Rights Movement: Black Communities Organizing for Change*, by Aldon D. Morris; *A Little Taste of Freedom: the Black Freedom Struggle in Claiborne County, Mississippi*, by Emilye Crosby; and *Freedom is an Endless Meeting: Democracy in Action in Social Movements*, by Francesca Polletta.

2. The "Commons" refers to the resources of the earth that everyone is dependent upon and must utilize to survive and thrive. The essential "Common's" are land, water, and air.

3. See Black Agenda Morning Shot August 29, 2011 interview with Kamau Franklin by Kali Akuno at http://youtu.be/IIJcginZkpw. And "Lewis prepares for the Future", by Elizabeth Waibel at http://www.jacksonfreepress.com/index.php/print_view/47994.

4. See "Lumumba says Scott sisters released because of supporters" at http://youtu.be/oXBm_szT_5E. And "Scott Sisters Finally Set Free" at http://colorlines.com/archives/2011/01/scott_sisters_finally_set_free.html.

5. See "A New Kind of Southern Strategy", by Susan Eaton at http://www.thenation.com/article/162694/new-kind-southern-strategy.

6. For more information on Solidarity Economy see the works of Ethan Miller, particularly "Solidarity Economy: Key Concepts and Issues" at http://www.communityeconomies.org/site/assets/media/Ethan_Miller/Miller_Solidarity_Economy_Key_Issues_2010.pdf.

7. For more information on the Mondragon visit http://www.mondragon-corporation.com/ENG.aspx.

8. Decommodifying: rejecting as a commodity, that is something for sale, and strengthening the social elements, making citizens less dependent on the market.

9. *Amandla* is a Xhosa or Zulu word for "Power". It is used in a fashion like the slogan, "Black Power" by the BLM in the United States. It is used in call and response form, and the response is *Awethu*, which means "to us". Combined it means "Power to the People", as made popular in theUnited States by the Black Panther Party for Self-Defense. This slogan was and remains common in the Azanian (i.e. South African) Freedom Movement.

10. For more background on the National Take Back the Land Movement and its history visit http://navigatingthestorm.blogspot.com/ or http://www.takebacktheland.org/.

11. Quote taken from *This Little Light of Mine: The Life of Fannie Lou Hammer*, by Kay Miles, page 176.

5.

People's Assembly Overview: The Jackson People's Assembly Model

Kali Akuno for the New Afrikan People's Organization and the Malcolm X Grassroots Movement

"We must practice revolutionary democracy in every aspect of our Party life. Every responsible member must have the courage of his responsibilities, exacting from others a proper respect for his work and properly respecting the work of others. Hide nothing from the masses of our people. Tell no lies. Expose lies whenever they are told. Mask no difficulties, mistakes, failures. Claim no easy victories...."
— *Amilcar Cabral*

Brief Synopsis

People denied their agency and power and subjected to external authority need vehicles to exercise their self-determination and exert their power. A *People's Assembly* is a vehicle of democratic social organization that, when properly organized, allows people to exercise their agency, exert their power, and practice democracy—meaning "the rule of the people, for the people, by the people" – in its broadest terms, which entails making direct decisions about the economic, social and cultural operations of a community or society and not just the contractual ("civil") or electoral and legislative (the limited realm of what is generally deemed to be "political") aspects of the social order.

What the People's Assembly Is

A People's Assembly first and foremost is a mass gathering of people organized and assembled to address essential social issues and/or questions pertinent to a community.

"Mass" can be and is defined in numerous ways depending on one's views and position, but per the experience of the New Afrikan People's Organization (NAPO) and the Malcolm X Grassroots Movement (MXGM) in Jackson, Mississippi, we define it as a body that engages at least 1/5th of the total population in a defined geographic area (neighborhood, ward or district, city, state, etc.). We have arrived at this 1/5th formula based on our experience of what it takes to have sufficient numbers, social force, and capacity to effectively implement the decisions made by the assembly and ensure that these actions achieve their desired outcomes.

"Addressing essential social issues", means developing solutions, strategies, action plans, and timelines to change various socio-economic conditions in a desired manner, not just hearing and/or giving voice to the people assembled.

Secondly, another defining characteristic of a truly democratic Assembly is that it calls for and is based upon "one person, one vote". Agency is vested directly in individuals, regardless of whether the Assembly makes decisions by some type of majoritarian voting procedures or consensus. This aspect of direct engagement, direct democracy, and individual empowerment is what separates a People's Assembly from other types of mass gatherings and formations, such as Alliances or United Fronts, where are a multitude of social forces are engaged.

However, given these two basic defining characteristics, it should be noted that there are still different types of People's Assemblies. Within NAPO/ MXGM we break Assemblies down into 3 essential types.

1. *United Front or Alliance based Assembly*. This type of Assembly is typically a democratic forum that is populated and driven by formally organized entities (i.e. political parties, unions, churches, civic organizations, etc.) that mobilize their members to participate in broad open decision making sessions with members from other organizations and/or formations. What makes this different then from a typical alliance or coalition is that the organizations and their leaders do not make the decisions on behalf of their members in these spaces; members make decisions as individuals within the general body. The main limitation with this type of Assembly formation is that they tend to remain "top heavy". The various organizational leaders often to do not disseminate adequate information about meetings, or inform their members about decisions and activities of the Assembly. And there is the problem that many organizations do not have consolidated members or a base that they can turn out, instead they are legitimated by their history, social position, or the charisma of their leadership.

2. *Constituent Assembly*. This type of Assembly is a representative body, not a direct democratic body of the people in their totality. This type of Assembly is dependent on mass outreach, but is structured, intentionally or unintentionally, to accommodate the material (having to work, deal with childcare, etc.) and social limitations (interest, access to information, political and ideological differences, etc.) of the people. The challenge with this type of Assembly is that if it doesn't continue to work to bring in new people (particularly youth) and struggle and strive politically to be mass in its character, then it tends to become overly bureaucratic and

stagnant over time.

3. *Mass Assembly.* The Mass Assembly is the broadest example of people's democracy. It normally emerges during times of acute crisis, when there are profound ruptures in society. These types of Assemblies are typically all-consuming, short-lived entities. Their greatest weakness is that they typically demand those engaged to give all of their time and energy to the engagement of the crisis, which over time is not sustainable, as people eventually have to tend to their daily needs in order to sustain themselves, their families, and communities.

The Jackson Assembly Model

At present, the Jackson People's Assembly operates in a space in-between a Constituent and Mass Assembly. In the main, it operates as a Constituent Assembly, engaging in a number of strategic campaigns (such as defending the 1% Sales Tax which was voted in by the residents of Jackson in January 2014) and initiatives (such as support for *Cooperation Jackson,* see www.CooperationJackson.org for more details) to address the material needs of our social base and to extend its power. This is based primarily on the material limitations imposed on the base and the members of the People's Task Force (see below for more details on the Task Force) by the daily grinds of the capitalist social order (i.e. tending to work, child care, health, and transportation challenges, etc.). There have also been some political challenges it has confronted over the past year adjusting both to the Mayoral ship of Chokwe Lumumba and how to relate to it, and how to address the sudden loss of Mayor Lumumba and the counter-reaction to the people's movement that facilitated the election of Mayor Tony Yarber in April 2014. However, during times of crisis the Assembly tends to take on more of a mass character, such as during the immediate passing of Mayor Lumumba in late February 2014 to defend the People's Platform (devised by the Assembly) and many of the initiatives the Lumumba administration was pursuing to fulfill it. It should be noted however, that even though the current practice in Jackson tends towards the Constituent model, the aim is to grow into a permanent Mass Assembly.

The basic outlines of the Jackson People's Assembly model can be found in the Jackson-Kush Plan (see http://navigatingthestorm.blogspot.com/2012/05/the-jackson-kush-plan-and-struggle-for.html for the full document). A synopsis of the model, taken from the Plan, outlines it as:

The People's Assemblies that MXGM and NAPO are working to build in Jackson and throughout the state of Mississippi, particularly its eastern Black belt portions, are designed to be vehicles of Black self-determination and the autonomous political authority of the oppressed peoples' and exploited classes contained within the state. The Assemblies are organized as expressions of participatory or direct democracy, wherein there is guided facilitation and agenda setting provided by the committees that compose the People's Task Force, but no preordained hierarchy. The People's Task Force is the working or executing body of the Assembly. The Task Force is composed of committees that are organized around proposals emerging from the Assembly to carry out various tasks and initiatives, such as organizing campaigns (like Take Back the Land) and long-term institution building and development work (like land trusts and cooperative housing).

The People's Assemblies model advanced by MXGM and NAPO as a core component of the J—K Plan have a long, rich history in Mississippi and in the Black Liberation Movement in general. The roots of our Assembly model are drawn from the spiritual or prayer circles that were organized often clandestinely by enslaved Afrikans to express their humanity, build and sustain community, fortify their spirits and organize resistance. The vehicle gained public expression in Mississippi with the organization of "Negro Peoples Conventions" at the start of Reconstruction to develop autonomous programs of action to realize freedom, as Afrikans themselves desired it and to determine their relationship to the defeated governments of the Confederacy and the triumphant government of the Federal Republic.

This expression of people's power re-emerged time and again in the New Afrikan communities of Mississippi as a means to resist the systemic exploitation and terror of white supremacy and to exercise and exert some degree of self-determination. The last great expression of this vehicle of Black people's self-determined power in Mississippi occurred in the early 1960's. It was stimulated by a campaign of coordinated resistance organized by militant local leaders like Medgar Evers that drew on the national capacity and courage of organizations like the Student Non-Violent Coordinating Committee (SNCC) and the Congress of Racial Equality (CORE). This campaign created the democratic space necessary for New Afrikan communities in Mississippi to organize themselves to resist more effectively. Broad, participatory-based People's Assemblies were the most common form of this self-organization. One of the most memorable outgrowths of this wave of Peoples Assemblies in Mississippi was the creation of the Mississippi Freedom Democratic Party (MSFDP), which challenged the hegemonic control over the Black vote on a state and local level since the New Deal, and remains a vehicle that serves as a constant reminder of the need for genuine Black equality and self-determination to this day.

Basic Functions of a People's Assembly

Regardless of their type, People's Assemblies have two broad functions and means of exercising power:

1. *They organize "autonomous", self-organized and executed social projects.* Autonomous in this context means initiatives not supported or organized by the government (state) or some variant of monopoly capital (finance or corporate industrial or mercantile capital). These types of projects range from organizing community gardens to forming people's self-defense campaigns to housing occupations to forming workers unions to building workers cooperatives. On a basic scale these projects function typically as "serve the people" or "survival programs" that help the people to sustain themselves or acquire a degree of self-reliance. On a larger scale these projects provide enough resources and social leverage (such as flexible time to organize) to allow the people to engage in essential fight back or offensive (typically positional) initiatives.

2. *They apply various types of pressure on the government and the forces of economic exploitation in society.* Pressure is exerted by organizing various types of campaigns against these forces, including mass action (protest) campaigns, direct action campaigns, boycotts, non-compliance campaigns, policy shift campaigns (either advocating for or against existing laws or proposed or pending legislation), and even electoral campaigns (to put someone favorable in an office or to remove someone adversarial from office).

How to Carry Out the Functions of the Assembly

In order to carry out these critical functions, an Assembly must organize its proceedings to produce clear demands, a coherent strategy, realistic action plans, and concrete timelines. It must also organize itself into units of implementation, committee's or action groups, to carry out the various assignments dictated by the strategy and action plans.

When considering these functions and how they are executed In Jackson, it is critical to note that our model makes clear distinctions between the Assembly as an "event", the Assembly as a "process", and the Assembly as an "institution". In Jackson, the Assembly, as an event, is where we take up general questions and issues and deliberate and decide on what can, should, and will be done to address it. The process of the Assembly, where the more detailed questions of strategy, planning, and setting concrete timelines, measurable goals, and deliverables are refined is conducted through the People's Task Force and the various committees and working groups of the Assembly. The Assembly as an institution is a product of the combined social weight of the Assemblies events, processes, actions, and social outcomes.

Basic Organizing Assumptions

There are three basic assumptions that are being made in this paper that must be surfaced for anyone thinking of organizing a People's Assembly (following this model or any other model in our experience and study). In our experience, forces attempting to organize a People's Assembly that don't explicitly address these assumptions tend to struggle and/or outright fail. These assumptions are:

1. The social forces organizing the People's Assembly must have the ability to mobilize and assemble a significant amount of people to participate and engage in a democratic process (review our 1/5th formula above). This typically means that the social force or forces organizing the Assembly have already built a significant base and are able to or committed to scaling up.

2. The social forces organizing the People's Assembly have experience participating in, and ideally facilitating broad democratic processes (participating in democratic processes is more important than having experience facilitating a process, as facilitation is a skill we encourage all to learn and should not be a prerequisite of participation).

3. The social forces organizing the People's Assembly are willing or experienced in engaging in broad democratic processes guided by norms established, accepted, and self-enforced by the assembled body (see Key Components below).

Key Components of the Assembly "Event"

In order to make sure that the Assembly as an event is effective, we recommend that each of the following be clearly articulated and in place.

1. *Group Norms and Codes of Conduct.* These should be co-constructed by the participants of the Assembly, and should be crafted at the start of an Assembly formation. These Norms and Codes should cover everything from how to facilitate a meeting, how to raise a question, how to raise an objection, how to keep the Assembly from being dominated by a few individuals, how check with various forms of privilege and power, and how to arrive at decisions and conclusions. The Norms and Codes should be visited and/or referenced at each Assembly event to ensure that all

participants, old and new, know what they are and that they constitute the
guiding operating principles of the Assembly that ensure that it is
productive and truly democratic.

2. *Clear Agenda*. To the greatest extent possible, everyone who attends
the Assembly should know the Agenda before the meeting. Even when
this has been communicated, it is essential that the Agenda be reviewed at
the beginning of each and every Assembly meeting so that all participants
are clear on what it is and what the Assembly is seeking to accomplish.

3. *Clear Goals and Objectives*. Each Assembly event should be clear on
what it is focused on accomplishing. It is trying to investigate an issue, is
it trying to address an issue (as in trying to solve it), or is it merely sharing
information for folks to start investigating and deliberating on a question.
This is critical to not wasting people's time and energy.

4. *Clear and Concise Questions*. These are necessary for the Assembly to
sufficiently address a social question, engage in clear deliberations
regarding it, and make sound decisions on how to address it. Bad
questions can and will lead to run on discussions and inconclusive
deliberations.

5. *Strong, but Even-handed Facilitation*. We recommend that each
Assembly event have multiple Facilitators, playing mutually supportive
roles. The Facilitators must be prepared to move the agenda, move the
process(es), and intervene when and where necessary to ensure that
everyone is abiding by the Assembly Norms and Codes of Conduct.

6. *Detailed Note Taking*. It is critical that detailed notes are taken and
disseminated. These are essential not only for detailing what deliberations
and decisions have been made, but to hold the Assembly as an institution
accountable to itself and to the community.

7. *Next Steps and Follow Up Procedures*. At the end of each Assembly
event the Facilitators should reiterate what decisions have been made and
which body or group of the Assembly is responsible for carrying it out,
how, and by when. The Facilitators should also move the group to ensure
that each committee or working group has the capacity to fulfill the task
or help it add to its capacity by recruiting more participants in the
Assembly to get involved. The People's Task Force is also tasked with
making sure that each committee is clear about what its task is, that it has
the resources it needs to accomplish its task, reiterate when it is expected
to accomplish it, and aid it by organizing more support to the committee
should it require it.

Key Components of the Assembly as a "Process"

Although the authority of the Assembly is expressed to its highest extent during the mass "events", the real work of the Assembly, which enables it to exercise its power, is carried out through the organizing bodies and processes of the Assembly. The People's Task Force and various Committees and Working Groups are the primarily organizing bodies of the Assembly. These bodies execute the "work" of the Assembly—the outreach, networking, fundraising, communications, intelligence gathering, trainings, and campaigning of the Assembly.

In our People's Assembly model, the People's Task Force serves as the Coordinating Committee of the Assembly. The Task Force is a body directly elected by the Assembly, serve at its will, and is subject to immediate recall by the Assembly (meaning that they can be replaced, with due process, at any time). The primary function of the Assembly is to facilitate the work of the Committee's and the Working Groups. Which includes, ensuring that the Committee's and Working Groups regularly meet, or meet as often as is deemed necessary; ensuring that each body has as a facilitator, an agenda, and note takers (if not provided by the Committee or Working Group itself); facilitating communication between Committee's and Working Groups; ensuring that all of the actions of the Committees and Working Groups are communicated thoroughly to the Assembly; and coordinating the logistics for the Assembly gatherings.

Committee's are standing, meaning regularly constituted bodies of the Assembly to deal with certain functions and/or operations of the Assembly. The basics include: Outreach and Mobilization, Media and Communications, Fundraising and Finance, and Security. Working Groups are campaign or project oriented bodies. They emerge and exist to execute a decision of the Assembly to accomplish certain time limited goals and objectives. Examples drawn from our experience include Working Groups that successfully campaigned for the release of the Scott Sisters, forced the Federal government to provide more housing aid to Internally Displaced Persons from New Orleans and the Gulf Coast after Hurricane Katrina, and successfully organized public transportation workers in alliance with the Assembly to save JTRAN (Jackson's Public Transportation) and provide its workers with higher wages. All Committees and Working Groups operate on a volunteer principle, and for the most part, Committee and Working Group members participate on a self-selecting basis.

The Assembly "Institution"

Most People's Assemblies are relatively short-lived bodies, existing only for weeks or months, which does not allow or enable them to become "social" institutions. The Jackson People's Assembly, in its present iteration (NAPO/ MXGM organized a People's Assembly in the early 1990's that fought the Klu Klux Klan and designated human rights veteran Henry Kirksey to be first major Black candidate for Mayor), has been in continuous operation since 2005. Unlike many other models or examples of People's Assembly's, our model is focused on building an ongoing process and an enduring base of power. Sustainability is one thing that makes our Assembly an institution. But, it is not the only thing. What validates the Assembly as an institution more than its staying power is its social weight, which is its ability to act as a "dual power" or counterweight to the policies and actions of the government and local and regional business interests (i.e. capital).

It is the combination of staying power and attained social weight that makes the People's Assembly a social institution in its own right. But, it should be noted that becoming a counterweight or a dual power was not by accident, it was by design, and required strategic thought, detailed planning, intensive education, capacity building, trust building, persistence and determination. We mention this because we want to encourage all those who are considering building a People's Assembly to take the task of building an institutional vehicle of "dual power" seriously, as we think this is the primary reason to build this type of social movement vehicle.

What an Assembly Can Accomplish

When we look at the experiences of various people's and social movements throughout history and throughout the world, we see that People's Assemblies can and do wield different types of power (all contingent on factors of space, time, conditions, and balance of forces). Throughout the world today, People's Assemblies have been and are used to revolutionize people's daily lives, change the balance of power in societies, and in some recent (meaning the last 5 years) instances have toppled governments and ushered in revolutionary change. Some examples include: Nepal, Greece, Spain, Tunisia, Egypt, and Burkina Faso to name a few.

What follows is a brief breakdown of what People's Assembles have and can accomplish, based on the aforementioned and many other historic examples.

1. During periods of stability within the capitalist-imperialist nation-state system when the markets and the government (i.e. the state) are able to project and maintain the status quo operations of the system, an Assembly can push for various "positional" reforms and low to mid-level autonomous projects. Positional reforms include things like advancing various policy reform campaigns (offensive or defensive) such as the implementation of local Citizens Review or Police Control Boards. [1] Examples of low to mid-level autonomous projects include things like

building "self-reliant" oriented cooperatives, as we are currently working on in Jackson through Cooperation Jackson and initiatives it is pursuing like the Sustainable Communities Initiative (see http://www.cooperationjackson.org/sustainable-communities-initiative/).

2. During periods of progressive or radical upsurge an Assembly can push for structural reforms and engage in mid-to scalable autonomous projects. One of the best examples of the exercise of this type of power are how the various Assemblies in Venezuela were able to push and enable the progressive administration of President Hugo Chavez to make radical changes to the nation-states constitution between 1998 and 2010. Venezuela during this period is also a good example of what scalable autonomous projects can look like, such as the numerous cooperatives that were built, the housing developments that were constructed, and the significant land transfers that took place. Argentina during and after the crisis of 2000—2001 offers another critical example, of how the Assemblies there encouraged workers to seize numerous factories and turn them into cooperatives.

3. During pre-revolutionary periods an Assembly can function as a genuine "dual power" and assume many of the functions of the government (state). Perhaps the best example of this over the past 10 years comes from the revolutionary movement in Nepal, where the revolutionary forces stimulated and organized Assemblies to act as a direct counterweight to the monarchial government and the military. Ultimately, resulting in the establishment of a constitutional democracy and a more "representative" legislative body. Another recent example comes from Chiapas, Mexico from 1994 until the mid-2000's when the Zapatistas were able create extensive zones of "self-rule" and "autonomous production" that was governed by Assemblies.

4. During revolutionary periods an Assembly can effectively become the government (state) and assume control over the basic processes and mechanisms of production. There have been few experiences or examples of Assemblies commanding this much power since the 1980's in places like Haiti, the Philippines, Nicaragua, Burkina Faso, and Grenada. The recent experiences that come closest are Egypt in winter 2011 and summer 2013, and Nepal during stretches between 2003 and 2006.

5. During periods of retreat an Assembly must defend the people and the leadership that has emerged and developed, fight to maintain as many of the gains it won as possible, and prepare for the next upsurge. The experiences of the Lavalas movement in the early 1990's and mid-2000's is perhaps the best example of how Assemblies and other people's organizations can weather the storm of counter-revolutions and defeats.

Leadership of an Assembly should be able to make clear distinctions between these periods and understand how, why, and when to act as a counter-hegemonic force during stable and pre-revolutionary periods of the current social system, and how, why and when to act as a hegemonic force during revolutionary periods. It must also be able to make distinctions during each period between acts of positioning (i.e. building allies, assembling resources, and changing the dominant social narratives, etc.) and acts of maneuvering (i.e. engagements of open confrontation and conflict with the repressive forces of the state and capital).

"Do not be afraid of the people and persuade the people to take part in all of the decisions which concern them—this is the basic condition of revolutionary democracy, which little by little we must achieve in accordance with the development of our struggle and our life."

—Amilcar Cabral

"...we're trying to get ourselves organized in such a way that we can become inseparably involved in an action program that will meet the needs, desires, likes or dislikes of everyone that's involved. And we want you involved in it...We are attempting to make this organization one in which any serious-mined Afro-American can actively participate, and we welcome your suggestions at these membership meetings...We want your suggestions; we don't in any way claim to have the answers to everything, but we do feel all of us combined can come up with an answer... With all of the combined suggestions and the combined talent and know-how, we do believe that we can devise a program that will shake the world."

—Malcolm X

Notes

1. As promoted by the Every 28 Hours Campaign see https://mxgm.org/the-black-nation-charges-genocide-our-survival-is-dependent-on-self-defense/ or https://mxgm.org/operation-ghetto-storm-2012-annual-report-on-the-extrajudicial-killing-of-313-black-people/).

6.

The Jackson Rising Statement: Building the City of the Future Today

Kali Akuno for the Mayoral Administration of Chokwe Lumumba

Perspectives and priorities of Mayor Chokwe Lumumba on the development of Jackson, Mississippi

Jackson, Mississippi, is a city on the move. On June 4, 2013, the proud city of Jackson elected me to serve as its mayor to bring change to the city in the form of transparency, deep civic engagement, and economic reform and justice. By electing my administration, the people of Jackson made a clear statement that they are desiring fundamental change, are prepared to see it administered and, most importantly, want to play the leading role in implementing it.

Over the next four years, my administration will govern in accordance with human rights principles and standards. Our goal is to create equity for all. Through broad civic engagement, participatory and transparent governance and sound fiscal management, we will build a sustainable future for Jackson.

This future will be grounded in the highest provision of public services in public works administration, city planning, economic development, education, health care, transportation and public safety. We also aim to build a dynamic "new economy" rooted in cooperative development and anchored by green jobs, living wages and strong worker protections. The development of this new economy will be driven by the emerging human rights, workers, youth, immigrant and green social movements in partnership with my administration and socially responsible businesses, investors and philanthropies.

Contextualization: Where we stand

Jackson, like many urban centers, is struggling to overcome decades of economic divestment, deindustrialization, suburban flight, a declining tax base, chronic under- and un-employment, poorly performing schools, and an antiquated and decaying infrastructure.

While addressing all of these interrelated issues is important, the one that will receive the greatest attention during my administration is the infrastructure crisis. In order to ensure the health of our residents and rebuild our infrastructure to revitalize the economic foundations of our city, we must improve our sewage, water treatment and drainage systems, repave and rebuild our roads and bridges, expand our transportation systems and modernize our energy systems.

The *Jackson Rising* Conference will be held at Jackson State University on May 2-4, 2014. Come be part of participatory democracy. Help Jackson rise!

The most urgent infrastructure needs are our sewer and water treatment systems. In November 2012 the City of Jackson signed a consent decree with the Environmental Protection Agency (EPA), the Department of Justice (DoJ), and the Mississippi Department of Environmental Quality (MDEQ) to improve the sewer and water quality systems in the city.

The Consent Decree gives the City of Jackson 17 years to overhaul our water treatment and sewage systems. The critical improvements to these systems will require hundreds of millions of dollars to properly address. If the city is unable to make these improvements at scheduled intervals, the consent decree may result in Jackson losing control of its sewage and water treatment systems. My administration is determined to ensure that Jackson will retain its control over these life sustaining systems.

Crises often present new opportunities. Jackson's infrastructure crisis can be a major catalytic opportunity for our city and our residents. Over the course of the next 15 to 20 years, the City of Jackson will have to spend an estimated $1.2 billion to repair and upgrade its infrastructure. These infrastructure expenditures could potentially generate a short-term economic boom for the city.

However, the challenge is how will we finance these critical infrastructure expenses? The lion's share of the expense will be financed through bonds and other forms of debt financing. But relying on these means of finance alone will place an undue burden on future generations that my administration is determined to avoid.

Privatization is also not an option, under any circumstances. Therefore, we are going to have to be very creative and innovative in our approach to solving this critical issue.

How we will govern

We believe that the creativity and innovation will come from the genius within our own community. We will stimulate and catalyze this genius by our practice and methodology of participatory and transparent governance. This methodology is grounded in my firm belief and grounding in human rights advocacy and promotion.

Human rights implementation

To ensure that the full complement of our residents' human rights are respected, protected and fulfilled, my administration intends to implement the following policies and programs:

1. *Human Rights Charter.* The charter will establish the legal standing, policy framework and institutional support of our municipality for the promotion and protection of our residents' human rights. We seek to institute the charter with the support and approval of the City Council, through the passage of an ordinance establishing its full standing under the law.

2. *Human Rights Commission.* The commission will serve as the implementing, enforcement and monitoring body for the charter and the general programs it commissions. The commission will specifically address issues of compliance, accountability, monitoring and documentation pertaining to how the government fulfills its human rights obligations. The commission will work in consultative status very closely with civil society and the social movements of the city to fulfill its mission.

3. *Human Rights Institute.* The institute will operate as a quasi-governmental but independent institution dedicated to human rights education and the broad promotion of human rights. The institute will focus on providing human rights education to all city employees and the community at large.

Jackson, Miss., made history during the Civil Rights Movement and is making history again today—this time to strengthen, not destroy, human rights.

To design and develop these institutions, policies and programs, my administration is working closely with various local partners, including the Jackson People's Assembly, the Malcolm X Grassroots Movement, the Mississippi NAACP, One Voice, the Veterans of the Mississippi Civil Rights Movement, the Mississippi Workers Center for Human Rights, the Mississippi Association of Cooperatives and Mississippi Immigrant Rights Alliance, amongst others. On a national level, we are partnering with the Praxis Project, the Fund for Democratic Communities, the Human Rights Institute of Columbia Law School, the National Economic and Social Rights Initiative, the Human Rights Commission of Eugene, Oregon, and the U.S. Human Rights Network.

Participatory and transparent governance

There are numerous ways my administration will strive to elicit the broadest and deepest participation of our residents to resolve the challenges confronting our city. Our aim is to turn our challenges into opportunities for the empowerment of our residents and the revitalization of our city.

Two prominent ways my administration will foster and encourage broad civic participation amongst our residents are through "participatory budgeting" processes and "people's assemblies."

Our aim is to turn our challenges into opportunities for the empowerment of our residents and the revitalization of our city.

> 1. *Participatory budgeting.* Participatory budgeting is a process of democratic decision-making that encourages residents to directly deliberate upon and determine budgetary allocations for the municipality. Our objective in engaging the participatory budgeting processes is to place more power in the hands of our residents and to deepen democracy in our community by making governance more participatory.

My administration is beginning to collaborate with organizations like the Fund for Democratic Communities, the Democracy Collaborative and the Participatory Budgeting Project, preparing to introduce the participatory budgeting process to the city and to educate the government and the community on various ways it can be applied in Jackson. Our objective is to initiate the process in early 2014 to help us determine a portion of our 2014-2015 annual budget that will be more directly controlled by our residents via their direct determination on how these resources should be allocated.

> 1. *People's Assemblies.* People's Assemblies are self-organized instruments of people's agency and power. As a human rights promoter and community organizer, I have always advocated and supported the development of People's Assemblies as a means to give voice and power to those who have systematically been denied them in our society.

Over the years, as a member of community organizations like the Malcolm X Grassroots Movement, I have participated in organizing assemblies to elect the first Black mayor of Jackson, to give voice to those internally displaced by Hurricanes Katrina and Rita, and to give voice to the residents of Ward 2 and be directly accountable to them on an ongoing basis.

As mayor I fully intend to support the efforts of the Ward 2 People's Assembly, the People's Task Force, and the Malcolm X Grassroots Movement to build a citywide People's Assembly. In addition to supporting People's Assemblies, my administration will consistently consult the Neighborhood

Associations and other institutions of civil society in our community as part of my commitment to build a more vibrant and participatory democracy in Jackson.

Good governance through human rights advocacy and protection, we believe, will encourage and mobilize our city to unite as a community and create the long-term solutions needed to solve our critical problems. In addition to human rights implementation and participatory governance, we believe that the implementation of our core campaign agenda will lay the foundation for the long-term revitalization of Jackson.

My vision for the future

"Building the city of the future today"—this is the prime directive of my administration. Through the practice of participatory democracy and transparent governance, we will establish the foundations for equity and prosperity that will sustain the city for the generations to come by concentrating on these four fundamental programmatic objectives for the redevelopment of Jackson.

Rebuilding and redeveloping Jackson's infrastructure

As noted above, Jackson must overhaul and rebuild its infrastructure if the city is going to revitalize itself. It is imperative that we rebuild our water management and waste treatment systems, become more efficient in our energy consumption, diversify our sources of energy, overhaul our streets, highways and bridges, and create a comprehensive public transportation system.

> 1. *Water management and waste treatment.* We aim to completely overhaul these systems by removing all of our antiquated pipes, pumps and refineries and replacing them with the most sustainable equipment and materials that we can access. We also aim to reduce water consumption by installing newer, more accurate and efficient meters and by engaging in extensive community education campaigns to reduce extraneous consumption. We will also reduce hazardous runoff into our drainage systems by creating more stringent policies and penalties.

> 2. *Energy efficiency.* We aim to simultaneously diversify our energy sources and significantly reduce our consumption. We will start by retrofitting all of the city's buildings and facilities to ensure that they are energy efficient. We will also convert all of the city's light pole fixtures to ensure that they use solar power energy converters and efficient bulbs.

We aim to utilize as much solar and wind power as we can harness by supporting the building of solar power stations in several strategic locations throughout the city that are currently vacant or underutilized. We also aim to utilize several of these spaces to create wind farms to harness electricity. Further, we also aim to develop programs that will incentivize and subsidize the extensive cultivation of solar power in residential areas, businesses and governmental properties.

We aim to utilize as much solar and wind power as we can harness by supporting the building of solar power stations in several strategic locations throughout the city that are currently vacant or underutilized.

1. *Repaving our streets and rebuilding our highways and bridges.* We aim to repave all of the major thoroughfares, arteries and highways of our city (excluding interstate highways) that need repaving. In doing so, we will use the most eco-friendly and sustainable products currently available. We also intend on retrofitting all of the bridges in our city, all of which are vital for transportation and trade in our metropolis.

2. *Creating a comprehensive public transportation system.* We aim to lay the foundation for the development of a comprehensive public transportation in our city, based on a fleet of clean energy buses, an energy efficient metro-rail system, and a comprehensive system of bike and walking trails.

Making Jackson the greenest, most sustainable city in the Southeast

My administration is fully committed to building a sustainable future for our city and communities. Greening our infrastructure and transforming how we generate and consume energy is the critical first step. But it is only the first step.

Additional steps we are committed to taking include creating a comprehensive recycling system, developing a "zero" waste management system, eliminating the use of toxins in our community, creating a network of urban gardens and farms, and modernizing the city's policies and codes for procurements, contract bidding and departmental operations to achieve this overall goal.

1. *Recycling and zero waste.* We are going to design and implement a comprehensive recycling program for the city. The program will address not only government facilities but all of the city's residential and commercial facilities. We will also incentivize waste reduction at the source—in our households and businesses—by extensive education campaigns and policy change, such as "pay as you throw" legislation.

2. *Urban gardening and farming.* To effectively utilize our abundance of land, ensure the food security of our community, encourage and promote healthy eating habits and create long-term employment opportunities in impoverished communities, my administration is promoting the growth and expansion of urban gardening and farming. We are strongly

encouraging the development of urban farming cooperatives to produce "to scale" agricultural yields and serve the health and employment needs of our community.3. *Policy alignment.* In order to make Jackson the most sustainable city in the Southeast, we have to align our policies to meet our goals. In collaboration with the City Council, my administration intends to overhaul all of our zoning, permitting, procurement, contracting, and bidding processes to ensure they reflect our vision and priorities and establish the means for my administration to accomplish (its?)our goals.

Jackson is located on several major trade routes and, with improved infrastructure, has ample opportunity for all its people to enjoy prosperity.

Redeveloping West, South, Northwest and Downtown Jackson

To build equity in our marginalized and underserved communities, we are committed to concentrating our redevelopment resources (in?)to these strategic areas. Our objectives are to rehabilitate considerable portions of the existing housing stock in these communities to make them sustainable structures.

We are also going to develop new green, energy efficient housing complexes in these communities. We also aim to incubate and attract businesses to provide jobs and serve these communities. To retain and attract more youth and talent to our city, we are committed to building a dynamic network of arts and entertainment venues to enhance and highlight the talents and gifts of Jackson's residents.

1. *Housing.* My administration is fully committed to improving the overall housing stock of the city to retain our existing population and attract new young, creative and enterprising residents. We aim to create thousands of new affordable housing units in our target communities, utilizing the most sustainable and energy efficient methods and products available. We also aim to rehabilitate a substantial portion of our existing housing stock for historic preservation and affordability.

2. *Business incubation and employment.* In order to revitalize our target communities, we have to attract and create new industries to provide employment for the residents in these communities and offer new retail and service businesses to serve their consumer needs. We are strongly encouraging the development of cooperative enterprises to serve these needs but are also aggressively recruiting businesses nationally and internationally.

3. *Arts and culture.* Jackson is deeply connected to the Delta Blues and the artistic craftsmanship of the African American community. It is also steeped in the history of African American people for civil and human rights. My administration fully intends on celebrating and promoting our

culture and honoring the contributions of those who sacrificed for the fulfillment of many of our fundamental human rights as no Jackson administration ever has. Our aim is to use this cultural capital as an engine to spur economic growth via tourism and the creation of "creative zones" to support artists and cultural workers and encourage them to produce social and economic value for our community.

Building a dynamic 'new economy' based on cooperative development

A central component of the economic development vision and strategy of my administration is the promotion and development of various cooperative enterprises. In alignment with our vision of sustainability and to address our employment and economic equity issues, we are particularly looking to stimulate and incubate green manufacturing industries.

We are also looking to encourage the growth of cooperatives in the health services, recycling, waste management, hauling, warehousing, retail, hospitality and housing industries. My administration is developing the institutional capacity to promote, incubate and develop cooperatives by committing a division of our Department of Planning and Development to this task.

We are also creating a strategic cooperative fund and developing technical assistance partnerships with organizations and institutions like the Fund for Democratic Communities, the Democracy Collaborative, the Federation of Southern Cooperatives, the Malcolm X Grassroots Movement and Mondragon—USA amongst others.

A central component of the economic development vision and strategy of my administration is the promotion and development of various cooperative enterprises.

The broader aspects of our work to develop a "new economy" for Jackson, will encourage the growth of the private sector in manufacturing, retail and entertainment sectors and foster the development of various public-private partnerships with cooperatives, labor unions, credit unions, private enterprises, socially responsible banks and investors, and philanthropies.

1. *Cooperative development.* Cooperatives are rapidly becoming engines of economic growth and employment stabilization in several urban centers struggling with historic divestment and deindustrialization that are comparable to Jackson, such as Cleveland, Cincinnati, Reading, Pa., and Richmond, Calif. Jackson in many respects is poised to become the Mondragon of the United States, given its industrial infrastructure, strategic location along several trade routes (including I-20 connecting Atlanta to Dallas-Fort Worth and I-55 connecting New Orleans to Chicago), and historic knowledge and association with cooperative

development from the mutual aid societies, credit unions and farmers cooperatives developed in African American communities throughout the state.

2. *Cooperative incubator.* As noted, the incubator will be housed in the Department of Planning and Development and will operate in partnership with numerous academic and nonprofit organizations from Jackson and throughout the United States and the world in order to aid our communities and socially conscious entrepreneurs with the technical support they need to build sound businesses. These technical skills include business planning, market research and analysis, sustainable financing, financial and asset management, and worker-owner management and democracy.

3. *Cooperative fund.* My administration is committed to creating this fund utilizing city and CDBG (Community Development Block Grant) funds. Given the infrastructure challenges we have noted, these funds will not be as substantial as we would like. However, our aim is to use these funds as strategic leverage to attract additional financial resources from philanthropies, credit unions, banks, socially responsible corporations, various types of capital funds, and individual donors and investors.

One of our first major initiatives promoting cooperative development is the "Jackson Rising: New Economies Conference." The *Jackson Rising* Conference will be held May 2-4, 2014, at Jackson State University and focus on educating our community about cooperative enterprises and how to start and run them effectively, in addition to addressing how cooperative development can benefit the city of Jackson and how we will build cooperatives in our community to build wealth and equity. We encourage all of the participants of the Neighborhood Funders Group Conference to join us again for this conference in May 2014.

You can now register, apply for a workshop, make a donation, or become a sponsor or endorser of the conference through the website, www.JacksonRising.org. Visit our Facebook event page too, and follow the initiative on Twitter at @JacksonRising.

Moving forward: Developing strategic partnerships to our needs

To address our infrastructure crisis and accomplish this ambitious vision, broad unity and critical alignment will have to be achieved in our city. As stated before, we believe we can and will achieve the unity and alignment needed through the practice of good governance. Through this, we believe that we will be able to produce the majority of the resources we need to revitalize our community. But we won't secure all of the resources needed on our own.

We are going to have to secure some resources from the state of Mississippi and even more from the federal government. Given the growing political divisions at the state and federal levels, we doubt if we realistically will receive enough resources from these sources to meet our projected expenditures of $1.2 billion for our infrastructure overhaul, let alone the resources needed to redevelop our communities and improve our public education system.

To become the city of the future, the sustainable, cooperative city we envision, the City of Jackson must form strategic partnerships with philanthropies and other non-governmental entities that promote and support human rights, social responsibility, transparency, civic engagement, participatory governance, community empowerment, sustainability and cooperative development. We encourage all those who share our commitments and support our vision to join us in a strategic partnership on this trailblazing effort to make Jackson rise!

This article was first published at https://jacksonrising.wordpress.com/ local/jackson-rising-statement/

7.

Seek Ye First the Worker Self-management Kingdom: Toward the Solidarity Economy in Jackson, MS

Ajamu Nangwaya

We have to make sure that economically we're free, and part of that is the whole idea of economic democracy. We have to deal with more cooperative thinking and more involvement of people in the control of businesses, as opposed to just the big money changers, or the big CEOs and the big multinational corporations, the big capitalist corporations which generally control here in Mississippi.— Chokwe Lumumba[1]

"Always bear in mind that the people are not fighting for ideas, for the things in anyone's head. They are fighting to win material benefits, to live better and in peace, to see their lives go forward, to guarantee the future of their children." – Amilcar Cabral[2]

I am happy to be a participant at the Eastern Conference for Workplace Democracy 2013 and to be in the presence of worker cooperators, advocates of labor or worker self-management and comrades who are here to learn about and/or share your thoughts on the idea of workplace democracy and workers exercising control over capital.

Worker self-management or the practice of workers' controlling, managing and exercising stewardship over the productive resources in the workplace has been with us since the 19th century. Workers' control of the workplace developed as a reaction to the exacting and exploitative working condition of labor brought on by capitalism and the Industrial Revolution. Many workers saw the emancipation of labor emerging from their power over the way that work was organized and the fruit of their labor distributed.

I believe we are living in a period that has the potential for profound economic, social and political transformation from below. It might not seem that way when we look at the way that capitalism, racism and patriarchy have combined to make their domination appear inevitable and unchallenged. But as long as we have vision and are willing to put in the work, we shall not perish. We shall win!

On June 4, 2013, the people of the City of Jackson, Mississippi, elected Chokwe Lumumba, a human rights lawyer and an advocate of the right to self-determination of Africans in the United States, as their mayor. That is a very significant political development. But that is not the most momentous thing about the election of Chokwe Lumumba. The most noteworthy element of Lumumba's ascension to the mayoral position is his commitment to economic democracy, "more cooperative thinking" and facilitating economic and social justice with and for the people of Jackson.

The challenge posed to us by this historical moment is the role that each of you will play in ensuring a robust programme of worker cooperative formation and cooperative economics in Jackson. We ought to work with the Jackson People's Assembly, the Malcolm X Grassroots Movement and other progressive forces to transform the city of Jackson into America's own Mondragon. It could have one possible exception. Jackson could become an evangelical force that is committed to spreading labor self-management and the social economy across the South and the rest of this society—the United States.

The promotion of the social economy and labor self-management could engage and attract Frantz Fanon's "wretched of the earth" onto the stage of history as central actors in the drama of their own emancipation. By promoting the social economy/labor self-management and participatory democracy by civil society forces and structures (the assemblies), Chokwe and the social movement organizations in Jackson are privileging or heeding Cabral's above-cited assertion that the people are not merely fighting for ideas. They need to see meaningful change in their material condition. The development of a people controlled and participatory democratic economic infrastructure in Jackson would give concrete form to their material aspirations.

Amilcar Cabral was a revolutionary from Guinea-Bissau in West Africa and his approach to organizing and politically mobilizing the people could provide insights and direction to our movement-building work. In order to build social movements with the capacity to carry out the task of social emancipation, we need to organize around the material needs of the people. The very projects and programmes that we organize with the people should be informed by transformative values; a prefiguring of what will be obtained in the emancipated societies of tomorrow.

As an anarchist, I am not a person who is hopeful or excited by initiatives coming out of the state or elected political actors. More often than not, we are likely to experience betrayal, collaboration with the forces of domination by erstwhile progressives or a progressive political formation forgetting that its role should be to build or expand the capacity of the people to challenge the structures of exploitation and domination. I am of the opinion that an opportunity exists in Jackson to use the resources of the municipal state to build the capacity of civil society to promote labor self-management.

Based on the thrust of The Jackson-Kush Plan, which calls for the maintenance of autonomous, deliberative and collective decision-making people's assemblies and the commitment to organizing a self-managed social economy,[3] which would challenge the hegemony or domination of the capitalist sector, I see an opening for something transformative to emerge in Jackson. As revolutionaries, we are always seeking out opportunities to advance the struggle for social emancipation. We initiate actions, but we also react to events within the social environment. To not explore the movement-building potentiality of what is going on this southern city would be a major political error and a demonstration of the poverty of imagination and vision.

Primary imperatives or assumptions

There are four critical imperatives or assumptions that should guide the movement toward labor self-management and the social economy in Jackson. They are as follows:

1. Build the capacity of civil society

We should put the necessary resources into building the requisite knowledge, skills and attitude needed by the people to exercise control over their lives and institutions. In the struggle for the new society, we require independent, counter hegemonic organizational spaces from which to struggle against the dominant economic, social and political structures.

In any labor self-management and social economy project in Jackson, we must develop autonomous, civil-society-based supportive organizations and structures that will be able to survive the departure of the Lumumba administration. If the social economy initiatives are going to operate independently of the state, they will need the means to do so. Therefore, the current municipal executive leadership in Jackson should turn over resources to the social movements that will empower and resource them in their quest to create economic development organizations, programmes and projects.

2. Part of the class struggle, racial justice and feminist movements

When we talk or think about social and economic change in the City of Jackson, it is not being done in a contextless structural context. We are compelled to address the systems of capitalism, white supremacy/racism and patriarchy and their impact on the lives of the working-class, racialized majority. It is critically important to frame the labor self-management and the solidarity economy project as one that is centred upon seeking a fundamental change to power relations defined by gender, race and class.

The worker cooperative movement ought to see itself as a part of the broader class struggle movement that seeks to give control to the laboring classes over how their labor is used and the surplus or profit from collective work is shared. The solidarity economy and labor self-management will have to seriously tackle oppression coming out of the major systems of domination and allow our organizing work to be shaped by the resulting analysis.

3. Develop an alternative political decision-making process — an assembly system of governance

The system of assemblies that is proposed in The Jackson Plan is the right approach to creating alternative participatory democratic structures. It is through these political instruments that the people will set the community's priorities and wage a struggle of contestation with the powers-that-be in the liberal capitalist political system.

As we strive to build the embryonic collectivistic economic structures of the future just society, we need the political equivalent. The latter should be of a scale that allows for direct democratic participation of the people. The federative principle can be used to link the community-based assemblies into a unified city-wide, regional, or state-wide body, whose role would be a coordinating one. Power must reside at the base where the people are located.

4. Displacing economic predators who are currently located in racialized, working-class communities

In working-class Afrikan communities across the United States, there are economic predators that exploit and dominate the local business scene. These petty capitalists must be seen for what they are; business operators who do not normally employ the people in the local community but they live and spend the wealth generated elsewhere. We do not need to search hard for business ideas or opportunities because the existing capitalists and their businesses should become targets for replacement with worker cooperatives and other solidarity economy enterprises. If these existing owners would like to become worker-cooperators, they are free to join the labor self-managed enterprises.

The City of Jackson could contribute to worker cooperative development in a number of areas. It could make a material contribution in the areas of technical assistance provision, financing, procurement and contract set-aside for worker cooperatives, education and promoter of labor or worker self-management and the social economy.

Evangelical promoter of worker self-management and the social economy

The City of Jackson's Office of Economic Development is the chief organ that facilitates business development. Its mandate is "to maximize the city's potential as a thriving center for businesses, jobs, robust neighborhoods and economic opportunity for everyone in the Capital City.... supports business and the development community within city government and between city agencies. It also partners with other organizations to further economic development."

The terms of reference should be expanded and specifically states that it "promotes worker cooperatives, consumer cooperatives and other social economy enterprises as instruments to create economic security, jobs, livable wages, economic development and economic democracy."

Furthermore, the Office of Economic Development should be empowered to vigorously, strategically and relentlessly create the enabling condition for the development of worker cooperatives and other social enterprises in Jackson. A part of its worker or labor self-management agenda should include transforming the city of Jackson into a catalyst for this approach to workplace democracy, workers' control of the means of production and the producers of wealth being the ones who determine how the economic surplus or profit shall be distributed.

This new role for the Office of Economic Development will be startling to some and is likely to generate opposition. But Mayor Lumumba ought to borrow a play from the playbook of conservative governments; move with lightning speed in implementing his administration's policies in the first two years and keep the opposition dizzy, disoriented and playing catch up.

Lumumba has a mandate to include labor self-management by way of worker cooperatives. The economic development plank in the mayor's election platform stated that he is committed to "build[ing] co-ops and green industry" and ensuring "that Jacksonians are well-represented with jobs and business ownership."[4] Labour self-management, cooperatives of all types and social enterprises are the tools needed to give form to his electoral commitment. Colorlines' writer Jamilah King also interprets Lumumba's platform in a similar fashion:

> Larry Hales correctly asserts "In his campaign literature and in news media interviews, Mayor Lumumba stressed that his economic program will incorporate principles of the "solidarity economy." Solidarity economy is a[n] umbrella term used to describe a wide variety of alternative economic activities, including worker-owned cooperatives, cooperative banks, peer lending, community land trusts, participatory budgeting and fair trade."[5]

Larry Hales correctly asserts that "Lumumba's political history did not scare away voters, nor did the bold and progressive Jackson Plan, which is reminiscent of the Republic of New Afrika's program of the 1960s, calling for the establishment of an independent Black-led government in five former confederate states."[6] The City of Jackson should move ahead and start implementing the solidarity economy mandate. Mayor Lumumba should immediately hire a team of solidarity economy and labor self-management personnel, whose principal role would be to bring about the condition for the economic democracy take-off.

They would be embedded in the Office of Economic Development and at least one of the positions should be a senior leadership/management one. The latter is needed to communicate Lumumba's seriousness about the social economy thrust of his administration and to give the necessary clout to the economic democracy team to get the work done. Lumumba, the Malcolm X Grassroots Movement and the Jackson People's Assembly will have to get out into the community and in all available spaces to educate the people about labor self-management and the solidarity economy.

Education and conscientization for worker self-management

The people have been long exposed to the capitalist approach to economic development and it is quite fair to assert that the ideas of capitalism are dominant on the question of economic efficacy. The people might have critique of capitalism but it is generally seen as the only game in town, especially with the demise of the former Soviet Union and with it bureaucratic, authoritarian state socialism. In this context Marley's exhortation to the people to "Emancipate yourself from mental slavery / None but ourselves can free our minds" is very instructive.

The preceding verses from Marley's "Redemption Song" implicitly call on us to engage in critical education about oppression and emancipation. As worker self-management practitioners and/or advocates our educational programmes would also provide the necessary knowledge, skills and attitude to operate worker cooperatives, other social enterprises and the enabling labor self-management structures. Therefore, the educational initiatives would be directed at facilitating worker self-management and the social economy and political/ideological consciousness-raising.

In carrying out this educational programme, the method of teaching and learning should mimic the democratic economic development method that we are pursuing. We are not seeking to reinscribe authoritarian, leadership-from-above ways of teaching and learning. I believe ancestor Ella Baker, advocate of participatory democracy and an organizer within the Afrikan Liberation Movement in the United States, was onto something when she declared, "Give people light and they will find a way."[7]

We are not seeking mastery over the people. The goal is to engender in the laboring classes an appreciation and consciousness of the transformative possibilities and to move toward their realization.

Paulo Freire in his *Pedagogy of the Oppressed* reminds us, "Leaders who do not act dialogically, but insist on imposing their decisions, do not organize the people — they manipulate them. They do not liberate, nor are they liberated: they oppress."[8]

One of the admirable features of labor self-management is its commitment to placing the power of economic self-determination in the hands of the worker-cooperators. Education has long been an instrument for igniting the passion for emancipation within the radical or revolutionary sections of the labor self-management movement. Mayor Lumumba is very much aware of the educational task ahead in developing the social economy:

> And this will bring about more public education and political education to the population of the city, make our population more prepared to be motivated and organized in order to participate in the changes which must occur in the city of Jackson in order to move it forward. We say the people must decide. 'Educate, motivate, organize'.[9]

Mayor Lumumba and his civil society allies can carry out the following educational initiatives to advance worker cooperatives and the social economy:

- Hire worker cooperative educators and developers among the staff of the Office of Economic Development.

- Execute professional development education of all city personnel with economic and business development responsibilities.

- Educate institutional actors such as hospitals, educational institutions and the city's bureaucracy on the economic virtue of purchasing from worker cooperatives and other social enterprises that are located in Jackson.

- Organize labor self-management and social economy workshops for all relevant elected municipal officials and their staff.

- Develop a public education campaign to educate the people about worker cooperatives, labor self-management and the social economy.

- Enlist the support of the United States Worker Cooperative Federation, regional worker cooperative federations and cooperative educators in designing a worker cooperative/labor self-management education training manual and programme.

- Develop a three-year social economy and worker self-management education pilot project in an elementary, junior high and high school.

- Infuse materials on the social economy and labor self-management in all business and economics courses in the elementary and secondary school curricula.

- Engage in dialogue with the colleges and universities in the city of Jackson to add courses and programmes on the social economy and labor self-management.

- Work with colleges and universities and the state on workforce adjustment or retraining programmes that prepare workers for cooperative and labor self-management entrepreneurship

Technical assistance

Jackson's Business Development Division provides prospective business operations with advice on preparing their business plans, site selection and access to financial resources. Its role and that of other entities within the city's bureaucracy should be enhanced to provide business formation and development technical assistance to prospective worker cooperatives and other social economy businesses. The City of Jackson's technical assistance provision role could include the following:

- Work with civil society groups and the postsecondary institutions in the region to create a civil society-based technical assistance provider organization that would facilitate the formation and development worker cooperatives and other social economy businesses.

- Sell a city-owned building at the nominal price of $1 to a community-based labor self-management and social economy technical assistance provider.

- Aid the technical assistance provider to create a labor self-management and social economy incubator to increase the survival rate of these firms.

- Provide assistance and advice on the identification of business creation opportunities and the development of feasibility studies and business plans.

- Provide training and development opportunities to social enterprises that would allow them to bid for city contracts.

Financing labor self-management

One of the most serious challenges faced by small businesses is their limited access to investment and working capital. We have to find creative ways to build organizations that are able to mobilize capital for labor self-management and other social economy projects. The City of Jackson currently provides grants and incentives to businesses so as to attract investment dollars. It can expand the criteria to include worker cooperatives, other cooperatives and social enterprises. Some of the financial instruments that could be explored are:

- Encourage worker cooperatives and other cooperatives to apply for its matching business grants in the Small Business Development Grant Program and the Storefront Improvement Grant, which provides up to $15,000 to recipients.

- Create a Social Economy Development Grant Program that provides up to $30,000 to worker cooperatives and other social economy firms that employ at least seven employees, invest at least $100,000 (20 per cent of which can be sweat equity) and employ at least 75 per cent of the workers from within Community Development Block Grant eligible areas.

- Create a Social Economy Feasibility and Business Plan Grant that provides a 1:1 matched funding grant of up to $10,000.

- Create a credit union that is committed to facilitating cooperative entrepreneurship and community economic development.

- Collaborate with credit unions to expand their capacity to serve as agents for cooperative economic development.

- Work with civil society organizations to create a cooperative and social enterprise loan fund. The revolving loan fund Cooperative Fund of New England could be used as a model for the provision of start-up and working capital to social economy entities.

- Capitalize the cooperative and social economy loan fund with a $300,000 grant over four years that would be matched at a 2:1 ratio from foundations, trade unions and other social movement organizations and/or other levels of government.

- Procure funding for a labor self-management and social economy incubator that is operated by a civil-society-based organization.

- Seek funds to support the matched savings instrument called the Individual Development Accounts. Prospective worker-cooperators would use their accumulated savings to capitalize their labor self-managed enterprises. This matched savings programme would enable worker cooperators in developing the business plans through its accompanying educational component.

Procurement and equal opportunity programme

- Create procurement opportunities for worker cooperatives and other social economy businesses, including those with a few worker-cooperators or employees and a small annual turnover.

- Establish business or contracting set-asides that are exclusively directed at worker cooperatives and other social economy businesses.

- Include worker cooperatives in equal opportunity or affirmative action business programmes established by the city.

- Develop sub-contracting opportunities for cooperative businesses on the city's infrastructure development projects.

- Develop the creative capacity to ensure that labor self-managed and social economy firms are able to participate in business opportunities with the City of Jackson.

Conclusion

We have to build the road as we travel. All of our organizing work should be directed at developing the capacity of the oppressed to act independently of the structures of domination. The Lumumba administration, the Jackson People's Assembly and the Malcolm X Grassroots Movement have an opportunity to use the resources of the municipal state to advance labor self-management and the solidarity economy.

The worker cooperative movement and progressive entities across the United States should support the civil society forces in Jackson in their effort to build the supportive organizations and structures to engender labor self-management and the solidarity economy. The labor self-management and social economy work being advanced in Jackson ought to be geared toward the purpose of social emancipation and to place the people in the driver's seat in creating history.

I would like to close with a statement by the Italian anarchist Errico Malatesta who captures the spirit in which we ought to wage struggle and create a participatory-democratic culture within the movement for emancipation:

> We who do not seek power, only want the consciences of [the masses]; only those who wish to dominate prefer sheep, the better to lead them. We prefer intelligent workers, even if they are our opponents, to anarchists who are such only in order to follow us like sheep. We want freedom for everybody; we want the masses to make the revolution for the masses. The person who thinks with [her] own brain is to be preferred to the one who blindly approves everything.... Better an error consciously committed and in good faith, than a good action performed in a servile manner.[10]

First published: Pambazuka News, September 18, 2013, https://www.pambazuka.org/governance/seek-ye-first-worker-self-management-kingdom

Notes

1. Chokwe Lumumba, "Jackson, Mississippi, Mayor-elect Chokwe Lumumba on economic democracy," interview by Anne Garrison, San Francisco Bayview, June 20, 2013.

2. Amilcar Cabral, *Revolution in Guinea: Selected Texts*, New York: Monthly Review Press, 1969, 86.

3. Malcolm X Grassroots Movement (MXGM) and the Jackson People's Assembly, 'The Jackson Plan: A Struggle for Self-determination, Participatory Democracy and Economic Justice,' Malcolm X Grassroots Movement, July 7, 2012, http://mxgm.org/the-jackson-plan-a-struggle-for-self-determination-participatory-democracy-and-economic-justice/

4. Electlumumbamayor.com

5. Jamilah King, J. "Mayor Chokwe Lumumba wants to build a 'solidarity economy' in Jackson, Miss." *Colorlines*, July 2, 2013.

6. Larry Hales, "The political, historical significance of Chokwe Lumumba mayoral win in Jackson, Miss.," *Workers World*, June 25, 2013.

7. Barbara Ransby, Ella Baker, *The Black Freedom Movement: A Radical Democratic Vision*. (Chapel Hill: University of North Carolina Press, 2003), 105

8. Paulo Freire, *Pedagogy of the Oppressed*. 30th Anniversary Edition. New York: Continuum International Publishing Group, 2005), 178. Retrieved from http://libcom.org/files/FreirePedagogyoftheOppressed.pdf

9. Monica Moorehead, "People's Assembly's platform brings mayoral victory for Chokwe Lumumba," *Workers World*, June 11, 2013,http://www.workers.org/2013/06/11/peoples-assembly-platform-brings-mayoral-victory-for-chokwe-lumumba/

10. Cited in Michael Schmidt and Lucien van der Walt, *Black Flame: The Revolutionary Class Politics of Anarchism and Syndicalism*. Oakland: AK Press, 2009, 184.

III

BUILDING SUBSTANCE

8.

Free the Land: An Interview with Chokwe Lumumba

Bhaskar Sunkara

Chokwe Lumumba's dilemma was simple: how to be a revolutionary in a Mississippi the popular imagination would paint as anything but.

It was a mission that seemed bound to alienate and polarize long before he became mayor of Jackson, home to a State Capitol building that flies a defiant Confederate battle flag and a City Hall built by slave labor.

But when I went to Jackson to profile the newly elected Lumumba last year and in my conversations with Mississippians throughout this year, I was shocked at how hard it was to find someone who didn't like him. Mainstream politicians like Rickey Cole, chairman of the state Democratic Party, and his staff were keen to show solidarity with Jackson's new administration. They talked about Lumumba's honor and integrity, whatever their political differences. After the mayor's death in February at the age of sixty-six, Cole called him "a man by the people, of the people, and for the people."

Even city business leaders like Ben Allen, president of Downtown Jackson Partners, expressed surprise during Lumumba's administration about how clear, open, and efficient his first few months in office had been. Hampered by a lack of city revenue and hostility at the state level, Lumumba had just passed a one-cent local sales tax to fund Jackson's infrastructure. The taps ran brown and many roads were in disrepair when I visited the city, and the Environmental Protection Agency had threatened action if waste systems weren't upgraded. There was nothing especially radical about the tax, except for the fact that Lumumba took his case to the people, explaining the situation and winning consent for the measure in a referendum.

It gave a new resonance to the "sewer socialist" tradition that administered public office for generations in Milwaukee and elsewhere in the twentieth century. But there were signs that if the mayor and his Malcolm X Grassroots Movement stayed in power, the deepening of their revolution would attract something of a counterrevolution in response.

Lumumba was born in Detroit as Edwin Finley Taliaferro. He saw racism growing up, from all-white restaurants in Dearborn that wouldn't serve his family to housing and job discrimination in the inner city. It instilled a level of social consciousness in the young man, consciousness that would only grow as he absorbed the era's images: Emmett Till's battered teenaged corpse, street battles and sit-ins, and, most formatively, the assassination of Martin Luther King.

Like so many other Black youth, he was radicalized. Adopting his new name from a Central African ethnic group and slain Congolese revolutionary Patrice Lumumba, Chokwe put ambitions of becoming a lawyer on hold to join the fight. He was attracted to the Republic of New Afrika (RNA) movement, which had roots in Detroit but relocated to Jackson. They wanted a new nation in the African-American majority counties of the Southeast.

In 1971, Lumumba joined them in Jackson — where, as in other cities in Mississippi, blacks had little political representation and nostalgia for Jim Crow was still strong. In August of that same year, local police and FBI agents raided the RNA compound. In the ensuing gun battle, during which Lumumba was not present, a police officer was killed and another, along with a federal agent, was wounded. Eleven New Afrika members were arrested. In the aftermath, Lumumba moved back to Detroit, finishing law school at Wayne State University in 1975 before finding his way back to Jackson a decade later.

But Lumumba's was not the tale of a radical coming to terms with society as it exists, like so many from the New Left. His legal career was radical and often controversial. He took on a host of high-profile cases, including those of Fulani Sunni Ali, rapper Tupac Shakur, and former Black Panther Party members Geronimo Pratt and Assata Shakur.

He never renounced the goal of Black self-determination or apologized for his activism during his Republic of New Afrika years. Lumumba told me in the interview below that only his tactics had changed in light of the new political avenues now open to Black militants in the South.

"At that time, in the seventies, we were locked out of government completely," he said. "We were actually victims of government violence, so we protected ourselves against that repression."

Today, the situation is different. From Tunica, in northwest Mississippi, to Wilkerson County, in the southwest, there are eighteen predominantly Black counties in the state that have in the last few decades finally been able break the domination of white officeholders. Lumumba saw this as only the start of the deep transformation that the region needed.

"One of the routes to that self-determination," he told me, "is to use the governmental slots in order to accumulate the political power that we can, and then to demand more, and to build more." But he was quick to portray his movement as an inclusive socialist one. "This is not a 'hate whitey' movement. This is not some kind of a reactionary nationalist movement."

Lumumba and the activists who rallied around his campaigns hoped to establish two planks of political power: one based on people's assemblies and another on a solidarity economy, built on a network of worker-owned cooperatives. The assemblies were, for the moment, purely advisory. They started in Ward 2, while he was a councilman, but spread after his election as mayor.

Mississippi has had truly universal suffrage for only a little more than a generation. Yet Lumumba wanted to foster a democratic culture that was not just representative, but participatory. Inviting people to voice their grievances in town halls and have a say in the distribution of public resources was part of that commitment. But he had loftier ambitions: over time, he wanted the new organs of people's power, absolute and direct democracy, to replace existing structures.

He didn't even think that his government could be equated with "people's power." "That's still a struggle to be achieved; that's a goal to be reached. That's not where we are now," Lumumba cautioned.

The solidarity economy schemes were just as ambitious. While keenly aware of and open about the limits of political and economic experimentation on the local level — and seeing his new administration's efforts as transitional — Lumumba wanted to use city contracts and economic leverage to foster worker ownership. Invoking the Ujamaa concept of former Tanzanian president Julius Nyerere, he hoped to transform a full 10 percent of Jackson's economy into cooperatives by the end of his first term alone. The administration had been planning for months to debate and explore their options with activists and outside experts at a "Jackson Rising: New Economies Conference" in May.

It was less about spearheading a revolution from above than creating a climate of radical thought and experimentation that could take on dynamics of its own. In the meantime, even Jackson's moderates were won over by clean and efficient government and Lumumba's easy charm and humor.

That support would have been needed. Activists within the Malcolm X Grassroots Movement worried that if they went too far too fast, the state legislature could limit self-governance in Jackson, maybe even place the city under trusteeship. What's more, both sides knew that the honeymoon period with downtown developers couldn't last either. Real economic and political transformation requires taking power away from those not keen on relinquishing it.

◊

This interview was conducted with Lumumba in February 2014, several days before he died from heart failure. For the Left, a few lessons in particular should be drawn from it. Lumumba governed to inspire movements from below, not to administer austerity. There need not be a contradiction between holding office, even executive office, and building a radical opposition.

Lumumba navigated these waters successfully despite the fact that he ran as a Democrat. Utilizing open primaries — a peculiarity of the American system — may not be the best route for socialists in northern cities where liberal machines still dominate and neutralize insurgencies from within, but it can make tactical sense elsewhere.

Nowhere is that truer than in states such as Mississippi. One of the most progressive voting blocs in the country is in the so-called Black Belt: the African-American majority counties that stretch across the Southeast. Without sufficient progressive numbers statewide to swing states in the electoral college or to elect anyone but local officials, these constituencies are ignored by presidential-cycle-minded national liberals. They shouldn't be by socialists and all those committed to building militant currents among the most oppressed.

Success doesn't come easy. But Lumumba and the Malcolm X Grassroots Movement showed how years of disciplined work "serving the people," including politicized relief work after Hurricane Katrina, could pay off in the electoral arena and how those victories could expand rather than restrict popular power.

We'll need many more efforts like it in the years to come to end class and racial exploitation. And that's the only way fit to commemorate a comrade as astounding as Chokwe Lumumba.

Bashkar Sunkara (BS): You came to Jackson in the early 1970s — what was the political climate in the city like at the time?

Chokwe Lumumba: When I came to Jackson in March 1971, it was just about six to eight months after two Jackson State University students — James Earl Green and Phillip Lafayette Gibbs — had been killed on the campus.

The Civil Rights Movement rocked the foundation of the white-supremacist government and culture in the South. And across Mississippi, a lot of good work was spearheaded by Fannie Lou Hamer, Vernon Dahmer, Medgar Evers and others. In 1964, they helped organize the Mississippi Freedom Democratic Party. That party, in the early seventies, had a profound effect on the state Democratic Party. It was forced, for instance, to mandate that half of its delegates would have to be Black and half be women.

So the Civil Rights Movement had significant gains, but repression was still extreme. Discrimination on jobs was commonplace. Even though the Civil Rights Movement had pretty much nationally won acceptance of the idea that Mississippi apartheid, or Jim Crow, as it was called, had to go, in the state there was still resistance to it. It was clear that even where access had come to universities and to restaurants, that was not associated with access to power — economic or political — for blacks.

There were very few blacks that were political officials — none in Mississippi's major cities, and only some in small towns. Economically, it was still pretty much a white supremacist system. Rich whites owned production and blacks and others were relegated to the fringes.

At the same time, we still faced intimidation from right-wing forces. Klansmen populated police departments, and so on.

Around the country, a lot of Black people's movements had moved from the phase of just merely turning the other cheek in the face of attacks and egregious repression to actually declaring the right to self-defense, under the inspiration of Malcolm X. And that certainly was the position that we took, which inevitably led to clashes between those who were used to preying on blacks — and particularly movement blacks, like civil rights organizers — without any kind of response, and our determination to say that we weren't going to be victimized.

We came in peace, but we came prepared.

BS: Given this context, during the 1970s, you were a supporter of the Republic of New Afrika movement. How do you reflect on this period in your activism? Have your political views shifted at all in regards to Black self-determination and the methods in which it can be achieved?

Chokwe Lumumba: My view on self-determination is the same. First of all, it's a fundamental right for all people — not just Black people. I'd say that what has changed are the tactics, and somewhat the strategy, for reaching that goal.

In the seventies, we were locked out of government completely. We were actually victims of government violence, so we protected ourselves against that repression. But since that time, particularly in Jackson, where I am now the mayor, the population changed. The city is now 85 percent black. Many of those people have worked together with us as we fought for rights for our youth, political prisoners, the victims of racism, the prosecution of the murder of Medgar Evers, and so on.

We've been able to politicize the growing Black population in Jackson, and in the state. We now have not just an 85 percent Black population, but a Black population prepared to elect progressive leadership.

The tactical change here is that we now can elect Black people into government, particularly into local governments and county-wide governments. And we have a whole region called the Kush region, as we've named it, on the western part of Mississippi — everywhere from Tunica, which is the northwest, all the way down to Wilkinson County, which is southwest, and everywhere in between those two points. A contiguous land mass of 18 different counties; 17 of them are predominantly black. Only one of them, Warren County, is about 47 percent black.

In those areas, the population has been now for some time electing Black sheriffs, Black mayors, Black city council people, et cetera. So what we have determined is that one of the routes to that self-determination is to use the governmental slots in order to accumulate the political power that we can, and then to demand more, and to build more, and even to build more statewide as the leverage for our position so we can launch an effort for more statewide control and participation by the Black population.

I think it is important to say here, because I know some people will mischaracterize this, that this is not a "hate whitey" movement; this is not some kind of a reactionary nationalist movement. This is a movement that is geared toward winning the right of self-determination. It is our view that where you have a majority-Black population, they have the right to have the majority of political power, to exercise the majority of the economic power and social power, to build that kind of influence. And at the same time they have a responsibility to make sure that the resources of society are equally available to all residents, whether they be white, Hispanic, Indian, and so on and so forth — particularly Indian, I would say. But all folks.

BS: Last year, in an interview with the *Jackson Free Press*, Jackson's police chief, Lindsey Horton, inadvertently laid out a pretty vulgar Marxist view of policing. He said that policing goes back to the biblical days — you can't have a civilized society with haves and have-nots without the have-nots trying to take from the haves. Policing defends property.

How does administering these repressive parts of the state in Jackson clash with the movement's values? What, if anything, can be done to change the nature of policing in Jackson, considering we'll probably be living in a class society for a little while longer?

Chokwe Lumumba: There have been a lot of contradictions in our struggle, and this is just another one. There are many stages of struggle that have contradictions in them. As a lawyer, people used to call me the "revolutionary lawyer" because I served political prisoners, took on causes for resistance and helped the movement move forward in many different ways. But nothing could be more of an oxymoron than a "revolutionary lawyer," because the law itself is a reactionary thing in the United States, which has been set up, in many instances, by the people who keep us oppressed. There's no question about that.

But that doesn't mean that you can't be a lawyer, and it doesn't mean that you can't serve the people as a lawyer, and that you can't fight for people's rights as a lawyer, and that you can't do all you can in order to change the situation. It's the same thing in this position as mayor. And in fact, we think I can do more in this position than I could as a lawyer.

We've made sure that Lindsey Horton is in line with our vision that we are working to change the situation between haves and have-nots in order to bring up people who are have-nots and put them in a position where they will be equally respected in this society, where the social forces in this society will respect their equality and that, therefore, would reduce crime. Jobs and other programs reduce the need for crime. I don't think that Mr. Horton is where I am on the issue, and he doesn't have the background that I have, but I do believe that's one of the obligations I have, to try to teach those who are in my administration the points that are important to the transition of society.

So, yes, we still run into some behavior which is problematic in terms of our march forward to create a revolutionary culture down here, to create a culture that challenges all repression and all types of exploitation — and the struggle against that manifests itself in many different ways — but I think so far, we've been pleasantly surprised at the response that we've gotten from people.

However, just because the people were ready to step forward and say, "Oh, I want to make that change," does not mean that all the people who voted have a thorough understanding of what that change is, or how we've got to go about that change. And the same is true for all the people who work for the government.

BS: You just alluded to your work as a cofounder of the Malcolm X Grassroots Movement and the movement's role in your election. How do you see the relationship between the Malcolm X Grassroots Movement and your position now as mayor of Jackson? Have there been measures to maintain the independence of the movement? Is it hard to govern without demobilizing the activists and the energy that actually got you in office? Or do you not see a contradiction between having a grassroots movement and also holding executive power?

Chokwe Lumumba: Here again, you're good at asking questions that present contradictions, but you certainly identified one there. It was a contradiction that was raised in Detroit when they elected their first Black mayor, Coleman Young, who had some history of fighting for the labor movement and for the rights of our people. It raised itself in Chicago when Harold Washington was elected, and it's true for some cities. And it may be nowhere more manifested than right here in the city of Jackson. There is a tendency — this is what creates the contradiction — for movement groups and protest groups and other activists who are trying to get revolutionary change to put their movement on hold and to rely exclusively on the mayor and the mayor's staff to get things done for the people.

That's a mistake. Our administration has very little more control over the economic realities of our society than we did before we got in these positions. We have some technical control over those things — or technical influence, let's put it that way. But not real control — and especially in a city setting, as opposed to being in charge of the whole state. The contradictions exist. So what you have to do is, you have to tell the folks they have to be steadfast. You have to teach them that it's important to have someone in office who's trying to fight for the right things.

That's necessary, but not sufficient. It's not sufficient to win our struggle. We need to encourage the whole population to become involved in the movement for change.

BS: To foster that kind of involvement, you've encouraged the creation of people's assemblies. Do you envision direct democracy of this type just augmenting traditional representative offices, or one day replacing them?

Chokwe Lumumba: The people's assembly is a body where the people challenge government, ask government questions, get informed by government, and protest government when necessary. And that's a movement that we support, and we to continue to support, to tell people that government is totally in their hands — and that's on all levels: federal, state, and local.

The assembly should represent all things that don't currently represent the people's authority. And in many instances, that will be some of the elected government. And some of the bureaucratic structures. So I think the people should become more and more involved in reforming and changing the structures that surround them and the people that surround them — determining who handles structures, and how they should be elected, and who should be elected — until the people's power becomes the same as, becomes simultaneous with, the development of government.

Now what does that mean? Does that mean that you have to have something different in terms of the name of the government, something different in structures? It's probably going to mean that. That's going to be for the people to decide. But right now, I don't think it would be truthful to say, even though we are building a people's government, that our government at this time is simultaneous with, and the exact same as, people's power.

That's still a struggle to be achieved; that's a goal to be reached. That's not where we are now.

BS: You described the type of economy you'd like to build in Jackson as a "solidarity economy." You've mentioned worker-owned co-ops and banks, community land trusts, and participatory budgeting. How is this progressing considering the fact that you are, as you mentioned, running a city where you can't deficit-finance like we could at the national level?

Chokwe Lumumba: Yes, there are limitations to what we can accomplish. We know that the problem is that too few people control too many of the resources that people live on, and that's why you have your big gap between haves and have-nots.

What can we do in order to change that situation? Well, from the mayor's position, a number of these companies want to get local contracts from us. We can create rules, and that's what we've done. Jackson's open for business, but if you're going to do business in Jackson, then we say, "Look, you're going to have to employ the people of Jackson." And we say that over 50 percent of your subcontracting has to go out to what they call minorities — I don't really agree with that term, but we'll use it for the time being. It could mean Native American contractors; it could mean various other people like that. So that's something to help begin some change.

However, that's not comprehensive enough, because it leaves out a lot of the private sector who do not come through government in order to get their contracts, and the people employed by these businesses. We are a city, and I don't want you to mistake us, yet, for a revolutionary state or some other place. We can't seize corporations and turn them over to the people. We can't do that. So that's one of the limitations.

And secondly, we can have influence on trying to stop these corporations from discriminating on various different levels, because we can make it uncomfortable for them. But we don't have the ability to police that completely, because we're just a city.

BS: What did the movement look like before you were elected, either during the campaign or before it, in terms of community work building some sort of presence in the city?

Chokwe Lumumba: That's a good question. The Malcolm X Grassroots Movement was created here in Jackson in 1990, and it was predated by some other work you have already referred to — the Republic of New Afrika — that started here back in 1971. So over the years, a lot of work has been done. But more importantly, since 1990, we have been engaged in a lot of youth programs. We have literally been involved in helping hundreds of youths go to college who would not have gone to college, and probably would not have finished high school, had it not been for us. We have run programs where they've learned about their cultural heritage, where they've gotten aid and assistance in the academic world, where they've had a chance to learn drama, and so many other things — and where they really became stand-up figures in their community.

We've also defended a lot of people who were the victims of racial abuse. We've done that all over the state. And that helped our situation. We helped thousands of Hurricane Katrina survivors. We literally sent tons of material aid to Gulf Coast survivors of Katrina, and we created political programs, political projects, and political organizations in order to fight the abuses that the Katrina residents were suffering.

As you know, Katrina happened in 2005. My first election to anything was in 2009, when we ran for City Council. We were also engaged in a lot of work to straighten out specific communities — building a garden, for instance, to help food flow for some people, and really for the idea of bringing people in the community together.

And we aligned ourselves with a lot of the civil rights organizations here who are working on many projects. A lot of them had to do with the so-called criminal justice system. So many people going to prison — not only those who are being wrongly convicted, but those who became sensitive to the problem that America wasn't really providing, and that Mississippi's system wasn't providing, the opportunity for a number of young people to grow up in a healthy social environment.

We united with a very progressive ACLU movement in Mississippi at the time, with the NAACP, who worked on many of these projects, and with a number of other people and organizations that were dealing with the prison situation. Fifty prisoners had been killed in jail over a five-year period in the state. So we got involved in that project and exposed that in several instances they were not all victims of suicide as had been claimed. There was some skullduggery going on.

Those are some of the things, off the top of my head, that I can tell you about that we were working on at the time of our election. And of course we were building the people's assembly before I got elected mayor.

BS: Do you see your success in Jackson as being indicative of a model that could work nationally? I know the Malcolm X Grassroots Movement organizes across the state, and elsewhere in the South, but have you sought national alliances with other left groups?

Chokwe Lumumba: The Malcolm X Grassroots Movement definitely seeks alliances with other groups, and the idea of the Malcolm X Grassroots Movement is to build a movement of what we call a new Afrikan people. And a new Afrikan people is the same thing as Black people, or so-called "African-American people." But it's also to build a movement of people, period. In other words, to create a positive, progressive movement across the borders of the United States and internationally.

We fully understand that there's no freedom for us unless there's freedom for everybody. Martin Luther King said that at one point, and I think it's very true. So we seek different kinds of relationships, and we want to spread the things that we are doing, which we think are useful and can help people in other places. Of course, people are going to have to organize and plan based on the conditions in their own areas.

But the people's assembly is something we recommend, and actually, the people's assembly is something we borrowed from elsewhere. Our use of the assembly really comes from Katrina, with the destruction of New Orleans. There was a survivors' assembly created in order to try to help folks in the New Orleans area and in the Gulf Coast area to reclaim their land and their jobs and their educational status. We facilitated that from Jackson, which is about two and a half hours away from the Gulf Coast. But we later decided that we would create an assembly for ourselves in order to advance our political objectives, so we wouldn't wind up in a situation like the folks did down in New Orleans and other parts of the Gulf Coast.

But yes, we certainly think that's a model that can be exported and work for others across the country.

BS: What has the response been from the Right in Jackson and Mississippi as a whole? Obviously, you're contending with a hostile and very conservative state legislature.

Chokwe Lumumba: The New Afrikan Independence Movement — which the Malcolm X Grassroots Movement is a part of, and is preceded by the Republic of Afrika and others — has been hated by the Right. We may be the most hated group by the Right, historically. And that was reflected in the way we got elected. During the election process, those communities that are more identified with the right wing voted almost unanimously for the other candidate.

I didn't get many of those votes at all. In fact, there was one precinct where I got three votes. But fortunately, we got overwhelming support from the majority of the city, from people who benefited from our long struggle against repression, as opposed to people who felt threatened by that long struggle. However, I would like to suggest something: since I've been elected, even though those forces still exist which would oppose us, we have been getting overwhelming support, initially, from all sectors of the community.

I'm sure we're not getting it from the Tea Party, or the extreme right — don't get me wrong. But I'm saying that clearly there are white people in the city who were persuaded by Tea Party right-wingers and others that we were the devil, who are now realizing that is not true. And they see the logic in what we're talking about, and we seem to be getting their support.

Now, there's a lot to that, and some other time we can both talk about it and dissect it, and I'm sure there are going to be some strains in that relationship from time to time as people have difficulty understanding the sacrifices that they have to make in order to get a really revolutionary, changed society, and the other things that are involved in our transition. But as of right now, we're actually in a period where we're getting overwhelming support from across the city.

As an example, we just put a referendum on the ballot and got 91 percent support. That means that we got support from every segment of the community, and the referendum had to do with work that we need to do to repair the infrastructure of our city. That's good for us, because we're going to march on ideas which ultimately do help everybody, not just the Black population. So I think we're on a little bit of a honeymoon still, and I'm sure there will be a lot of political struggle in the future.

But as long as we can stay on the right side of it, keep the good ideas, and not get politically reactionary, then I think that ultimately — I'm sure that ultimately — we will win.

Reprinted with the permission of Jacobin. Jacobin is a leading voice of the American left, offering socialist perspectives on politics, economics, and culture.

9.

Jackson Rising: An Electoral Battle Unleashes a Merger of Black Power, the Solidarity Economy and Wider Democracy

Carl Davidson

Nearly 500 people turned out over the May 2-4, 2014 weekend for the 'Jackson Rising' conference in Jackson, Mississippi. It was a highly successful and intensive exploration of Black power, the solidarity economy and the possibilities unleashed for democratic change when radicals win urban elections.

The gathering drew urban workers and rural farmers, youth and the elderly, students and teachers, men and women. At least half were people of color. About 50 were from the city of Jackson itself, and most were from other Southern states. But a good deal came from across the country, from New York to the Bay area, and a few from other countries—Quebec, South Africa, Venezuela and Zimbabwe.

The major sponsors included Malcolm X Grassroots Movement, the Federation of Southern Cooperatives, Praxis Project, Southern Grassroots Economies Project, US Solidarity Economy Network, and the US Social Forum. Funding came from Community Aid and Development, Inc., Mississippi Association of Cooperatives, Coalition for a Prosperous Mississippi, Fund for Democratic Communities, Ford Foundation, Wallace Action Fund, Surdna Foundation, and the Rosa Luxemburg Foundation.

But to grasp the meaning and significance of this meeting, a step back to see how it began—and why it almost didn't happen—is required.

The conference was the brainchild of Jackson's late Mayor Chokwe Lumumba and one group of his close supporters, the Malcolm X Grassroots Movement (MXGM) soon after he was elected on June 4, 2013 and had placed his people in a few key city positions. They had initiated the conference, which was then endorsed by the city council, to help shape and economic development plan for the city and the outlying Black majority rural areas, known as the 'Kush'—hence the name of the overall project, the 'Jackson-Kush Plan.'

Chokwe Lumumba was rooted in the Black revolutionary organization, the Republic of New Afrika (RNA), which claimed the Black majority areas of several states in the Deep South. He was one of its leading members, and a widely respected civil rights attorney. The RNA also had an economic outlook, a form of cooperative economics through the building of 'New Communities'—named after the concept of 'Ujamaa', a Swahili word for 'extended family,' promoted by former Tanzanian President Julius Nyerere. The new mayor connected this core idea with the long-standing role of cooperatives in African American history, the experience of the Mondragon co-ops in Spain, and the solidarity economy movement that had emerged and spread from the Third World in recent decades. Together, all these ideas merged in the mayor's project, 'Cooperation Jackson.'

Lumumba's election had taken Jackson's political elite off guard. Making use of the Mississippi Freedom Democratic Party to run as an independent in the Democratic primary, he defeated the incumbent and forced a runoff. Given that Jackson is an 80% Black city, he then won overwhelmingly. So when he died suddenly of heart failure on February 25, 2014, with his supporters in a state of shock, his opposition moved quickly to counterattack. The MXGM, the Peoples Assembly and other pro-Chokwe groups now had two tasks, trying to get Chokwe's son, Chokwe Antar Lumumba, elected mayor while continuing to plan the conference, but with city support on hold.

Lumumba, 31 years old, lost to Tony Yarber, 46% to 54%. Chokwe Antar received over 65% of the Black vote, but the turnout had dropped. The Yarber team immediately moved to fire all the Choke sympathizers from city government, and tried to sabotage the conference. Local rightwing web publications attacked it as "thinly veiled communism."

A Tale of Two Cities

What is behind this antagonism? Jackson is indeed a tale of two cities, on the cusp of two competing visions. Given its demographics, any mayor is likely to be Black, but what that can mean is another matter. Just driving around the city gives you a quick glimpse of the problem. While the largest city in the state and the Capitol, replete with major government buildings, the city is eerily quiet and empty. There are a few upscale areas, but also large areas of older, wood-framed housing of the unemployed and the working poor. There are huge fairgrounds, but little in the way of basic industry.

So two paths emerged. One was neoliberal, and aimed at exporting as much of the Black poor as possible, in order to open up wider areas for gentrification attracting the better-paid servants of the businesses that served government. The other was progressive, the Jackson Cooperation plan, which aimed at growing new worker-owned businesses and new housing co-ops that worked in tandem with the Black farmers of the 'Kush.' It also stressed democratized city services, while creating new alternative energy and recycling startups and also taking advantage of the city's position as a major regional transport hub. It's a conflict not unique to Jackson and shared by many cities around the country. Here's the four points summing up 'Cooperation Jackson':

- Cooperation Jackson is establishing an educational arm to spread the word in their communities about the distinct advantages and exciting possibilities of mutual uplift that business cooperatives offer.

- When Mayor Chokwe Lumumba was still in office, Cooperation Jackson planned to establish a "cooperative incubator." providing a range of startup services for cooperative enterprises. Absent support from the mayor's office, some MXGM activists observed, a lot of these co-ops will have to be born and nurtured in the cold.

- Cooperation Jackson aims to form a local federation of cooperatives to share information and resources and to ensure that the cooperatives follow democratic principles of self-management that empower their workers. We've always said "free the land," observed one MXGM activist. Now we want to "free the labor" as well.

- Finally Cooperation Jackson intends to establish a financial institution to assist in providing credit and capital to cooperatives.

The conference project thus found itself in the eye of a storm. But with luck and some judicious tactics, one key figure, Jackson State University President Carolyn Meyers, decided to stick with MXGM and allowed the conference to continue its plans on her campus, using the huge Walter Patton Center and two classroom buildings. A last minute fundraising blitz pulled in enough resources to squeeze through and make it happen.

When the hundreds of registered participants poured into the huge hall Friday evening and saw it filling up, one could sense the excitement and rising spirit of solidarity amidst diversity. The opening plenary keynote speakers included Jessica Gordon Nembhard of the US Solidarity Economy Network (SEN), Wendell Paris of the Federation of Southern Coops/Land Assistance Fund (FSC/LAF), Cornelius Blanding, Special Projects Director of the FSC/ LAF, Ed Whitfield of the Southern Grassroots Economies Project based in North Carolina, and Kali Akuno of Jackson's MXGM.

Gordon-Nembhard started off. A professor at John Jay College in New York, she recently published *Collective Courage: A History of African American Cooperative Economic Thought and Practice*, a groundbreaking study on the topic.

> Courage is a word I had to use,' she explained. 'Everywhere I turned, from the early efforts of free Blacks to buy others in their family out of slavery, to the Underground Railroad, to burial societies and other clandestine forms of mutual aid; it took courage to motivate all these cooperative forms of resistance to slavery and white supremacy, from the beginning down to our own times.

She gave the example of Fannie Lou Hamer in the battles in Mississippi in the 1960s, well known as a founder of the Mississippi Freedom Democratic Party. "But do we know her as a coop member, a group that sustained her when she was denied an income. As Ms. Hamer put it, 'Until we control our own food, land, and housing, we can't be truly empowered.'"

Wendell Paris who, as a young SNCC [Student Nonviolent Coordinating Committee] worker mentored by Ms. Hamer, continued the theme: "Land is the basis for revolution and it is important for us to hold on to our land base." He described the workings of the Panola Land Buyers Association in Sumter County, Alabama. "Freedom isn't free. In the training to run co-ops successfully, you learn more than growing cucumbers. You learn organizing and administration, the training ground for taking political offices."

At different times during introductions, or even in the remarks of speakers, the chant, 'Free the Land!' would rise from the participants, accompanied by raised fists. This came from the RNA tradition, referring to an older battle cry of self-determination for the Black areas of the Deep South. It clearly still had resonance, and was often followed with 'By Any Means Necessary!'

The opening session was closed out by comments from Ed Whitfield and Kali Akuno. "All successful enterprises produce a surplus," said Whitefield, "and our empowerment runs through retaking the surplus we have created, and putting it to uses that best serve us. We're not here making excuses. We're here making history. As long as we accept the current economic structures and approaches to development that flow from those structures and paradigms, we can't get out of bondage."

> It's an uphill climb here in Mississippi," added Akuno. "The Republican Tea Party government we have on a state level is not in favor at all of what we're trying to push through cooperative development. There was a bill supporting cooperatives that they killed earlier this year. On a municipal level, we are looking to transform all of the procurement policies of the city, all of the environmental regulations and standard policies within the city, and particularly all of the land-use policies in the city, that will support cooperatives. On the more practical side, we are launching a new organization from this conference called Cooperation Jackson, and it is going to be the vehicle by which all of the follow-through is going to be carried out.

But the municipal battle, Akuno concluded, would be difficult, given the neoliberal, repressive and pro-gentrification policies of the new team in charge.

All the items presented by the opening speakers expressed the common theme of the conference organizers—political power in the hands of the Black masses and their allies, then anchoring and using that power to shape and grow a cooperative economic democracy that would serve the vast majority. It was both a tribute to Chokwe Lumumba and an expression of his vision. Winning it, however, would not come easy.

The next day, Saturday, was a different story. Here space was opened up for more than 30 diverse workshops, spread out over three time slots, with two more plenary sessions. Topics included the influence of Mondragon, community land trusts, Black workers and the AFL-CIO, the communes in Venezuela, mapping the solidarity economy, co-ops on a global scale, waste management and recycling, working with legislatures, and many more. No one report can cover them all, but here's the flavor of a few.

Mondragon and the Union Coop Model

What were the nuts and bolts of Spain's Mondragon Coops (MCC), and how could unions serve as allies in creating similar enterprises in the U.S.? This was the question posed at an excellent workshop with three presenters: Michael Peck, the U.S. representative of Mondragon; Kristen Barker of the Cincinnati Union Coop Initiative; and Dennis Olson, of the United Food and Commercial Workers.

Peck began with a brief overview of MCC and its 120 co-ops and their accomplishments. The key point: In MCC, workers own their labor, but rent their capital, rather than the other way around. "But sometimes," he noted, "you can tell more about something by look[ing] at one of its failures than all its successes."

He was referring to the fact that a major MCC coop, FAGOR, which made kitchen appliances, recently closed down. "The housing market in Spain and Europe collapsed, and without new homes, new appliance sales sink Plus there was tough price competition from Asia." MCC had carried FAGOR for several years, but could no longer justify it. Despite anger, "the vote of the workers to close it was unanimous." In the regular world, the workers would get their pink slips, and be on the street.

But Mondragon was different. "MCC first set up a solidarity fund with every worker donating 1.5% of their salary, adding up to some 15 million Euros," he explained. "This was to cushion the transition. Then it worked to reassign all the FAGOR workers to other co-ops, which it has now accomplished for the large majority." Peck added that Mondragon would continue creating new co-ops both in Spain and around the world, and the true test was not that some would eventually close, which was natural, but what happened when they did.

Kristen Barker then gave the workshop an enthusiastic account of how a small group in Cincinnati, armed with only a few good ideas, had over four years moved to a point where three substantial co-ops were opening in the city and several more were in the works.

We were really inspired when we heard of the agreement between Mondragon and the United Steelworkers," said Barker. "Our effort also stands on the shoulders of the Evergreen Coops in Cleveland. To date, Evergreen has launched three co-ops, Evergreen Laundry, Ohio Cooperative Solar that offers energy retrofits and solar panel installation, and Green City Growers that grows high end lettuce for hotels and restaurants in Cleveland. They have dozens of potential cooperatives in the pipeline. We are partnering with the major players of this initiative including the Ohio Employee Ownership Center for our unique project.

The first three co-ops in Cincinnati, Barker added, were Sustainergy, a building trades coop to retrofit buildings to better environmental standards; the Cincinnati Railway Manufacturing Cooperative, which will make undercarriages for rail cars, and partnered with both the United Steel Workers and the local NAACP; and Our Harvest, a food hub coop which starts with local farms and takes their produce to a central site for packaging and marketing. It's partnered with the UFCW union and other agricultural groups. Dennis Olson explained how the UFCW was particularly helpful in connecting growers through the distribution centers to the unionized grocery chains, as opposed to Wal-Mart.

We only had a small study group to start—some community organizers, some Catholic nuns, a few union people," concluded Barker. "But we did a lot of research, made partners and got the word out in the media. Soon we had more people calling with more ideas, like coop grocery stores in 'food desert' areas, jewelry makers' co-ops and so on. We started getting some interest from the city, and now things are taking off.

Starting Coops in Jackson and the 'Kush'

This session was chaired by John Zippert of the Federation of Southern Cooperatives. He started with an excellent short summary of 'Cooperatives 101,' but quickly turned to drawing out the workshop participants on their concerns. Most were Black women from Jackson—one was interested in whether an African hair care products and services was possible; another wanted to start a coop of home health care workers. One man from Memphis said he had a small business distributing African products to small Black stores in the surrounding states, but he was getting on in years. How could he turn it into a coop that would live after him? Everyone shared ideas and legal options

As the session ended, I ran into Ben Burkett, a Black farmer who is locally active in the Indian Springs Farmers Association, part of the 'Kush.' I knew he was also president of the National Family Farm Coalition, but asked him more about his local operation.

"Well, I don't do cotton anymore, not much cotton in Mississippi these days," he explained. 'I do many vegetables, and sweet potatoes are a good crop. But it's one thing for a farmer to grow and dig sweet potatoes. It's quite another to have the equipment to scrub them, cut them into French fries, and then bag and store them, while getting them quickly to your markets. That's where the value of the coop comes in. We can pool our resources for these things, and it makes a big difference. We'd be in bad shape without the coop."

Waste Management, Recycling and City Politics

The politics of garbage was the main topic here. Chaired by Kali Akuno, this workshop gave the most insight into what was going on in Jackson as a new and backward regime was replacing that of Chokwe Lumumba. "Waste Management serves the city poorly," said Akuno. "It often ignores our neighborhoods. It does no recycling; it dumps the waste in a landfill in a small city to the North of here, gives them a payment, and that's the end of it."

Akuno explained they had a different plan. Since a large part of the city budgets deal with services like these, they wanted to break them into smaller pieces so local contractors or co-ops could bid on them, then recycle the waste into a revenue stream. In addition to helping the environment and employment, it would keep the money circulating locally.

Another piece was setting up an incubator to foster the development of cooperatives," Akuno added. "The government can't run the co-ops. It won't build them, but it can set the table. For most of the past 20 years, even though there has been a succession of Black mayors, 90-95 percent of contracts to people who don't live in Jackson. It was all about hiring people in Jackson.

Now everything is going to be a fight,' he added. "Even if your plan is reasonable and sustainable, it won't matter if it's stepping on the wrong toes."

Saturday also included two mealtime plenary sessions, one, at lunch, featuring the diverse organizations taking part, and the other, at dinner, giving everything an international dimension.

The lunch plenary included Omar Freilla of Green Workers Cooperatives, Steve Dubb of the Democracy Collaborative, Michael Peck of Mondragon USA, Ricky Maclin of New Era Windows, and Saladin Muhammad of Black Workers for Justice and MaryBe McMillan, Secretary Treasurer of the North Carolina AFL-CIO.

"Community cooperatives," said Steve Dubb, "can be considered part of a long civil rights movement that fights for both racial and economic justice. For example, Dr. Martin Luther King in the last year of his life helped launch the Poor People's Campaign for an Economic Bill of Rights. The return of cooperatives to the movement, as illustrated by what's happening here, is a welcome development."

MaryBe McMillan stressed the importance both of labor and the concentration of forces in the South. "Why organize in the South? Because what happens in the South affects the entire nation." Speaking for Black workers, Saladin Muhammed added, 'We need power not just democracy; we need power that shapes what democracy looks like. When plants shut down workers, should seize control and turn them into cooperatives."

The evening session started with a tribute to Chokwe Lumumba by his son, Chokwe Antar Lumumba. "We are victorious because we struggle. I'm not afraid of the term revolutionary. We need to be as revolutionary as the times require. Free the land! The struggle my father started is not over, but only beginning. It continues, by any means necessary."

Also featured were Francoise Vermette of Chantier in Quebec, Pierre LaLiberte of the International Labor Organization in Switzerland, Mazibuko Jara of Amandla! Magazine in South Africa, Elbart Vingwe, Organization of Collective Cooperative in Zimbabwe, Omar Sierra, Deputy Consul General of Venezuela-Boston, and Janvieve Williams-Comrie, Green Worker Coops in the U.S.

"Freeing the land has given our people a new sense of belonging," said Omar Sierra, of Venezuela. "Chokwe Lumumba extended his solidarity to us in a time of need. Our people are saddened by his passing, and will not forget him."

William Copeland, a cultural organizer from Detroit, summed up the spirit of the crowd: "These presentations demonstrate the international significance of the Black Liberation Movement and Southern movement building."

On Sunday morning, those who hadn't have to leave early for the airport, gathered in a large session of the whole that closed out the weekend. One after another, people stood up and testified to how their consciousness had been altered by their discussions and new experiences over the weekend. Emily Kawano of the Solidarity Economy Network made the point of understanding that the projects ahead, while including co-ops also reached beyond them to other forms, such as participatory budgeting, public banks and alternative currencies. Finally, at an auspicious moment, an African American women rose and in a strong church choir voice, began singing an old civil rights anthem, "Organize, organize, organize!" Everyone was on their feet, hands clapping, fists raised, and interspersing 'Free the Land! with the chorus. It couldn't have had a better closing moment.

This article first appeared at http://portside.org/2014-05-15/jackson-rising-electoral-battle-unleashes-merger-black-power-solidarity-economy-and-wider

10.

Jackson Rising: Black Millionaires Won't Lift Us Up, But Cooperation and the Solidarity Economy Will

Bruce A Dixon

...The hundreds gathered at Jackson Rising spent the weekend exploring and discussing how to fund, found and foster a different kind of business enterprise—democratically self-managed cooperatives....

For a long time now we've been fed and been feeding each other the story that uplifting Black communities means electing more faces of color to public office and creating more Black millionaires. Those wealthy and powerful African Americans, in the course of their wise governance, their normal business and philanthropic efforts can be counted on to create the jobs and the opportunities to largely alleviate poverty and want among the rest of us. The only problem with this story is that it's not working, and in fact never really did work.

It was a myth, a fable, a grownup fairy tale which told us nothing about how the world and this society actually functioned.

In the real world, we now have more Black faces in corporate board rooms, more Black elected officials and more Black millionaires than ever before, alongside record and near-record levels of Black child poverty, Black incarceration, Black unemployment, Black land and wealth loss. The fortunes of some of our most admired Black multi–millionaires, like Junior Bridgeman and Magic Johnson, rest firmly on the continued starvation wages and relentless abuse of workers in his hundreds of fast food and other restaurants.

Over the first weekend in May about 320 activists from all over the country, including 80 or more from Jackson and surrounding parts of Mississippi converged on the campus of Jackson State University for *Jackson Rising*. They came to seek and to share examples of how to create not individual success stories, but stories of collective self-help, collective wealth-building, collective success and the power of mutual cooperation.

The hundreds gathered at *Jackson Rising* spent the weekend exploring and discussing how to fund, found and foster a different kind of business enterprise—democratically self-managed cooperatives. They reviewed future plans for and current practices of cooperative auto repair shops, laundries, recycling, construction, and trucking firms. They discussed cooperative restaurants, child and elder care co-ops, cooperative grocery stores, cooperative factories, farms and more, all collectively owned and democratically managed by the same workers who deliver the service and create the value.

Participants at *Jackson Rising* learned a little of the story of Mondragon, a multinational cooperative enterprise founded in the Basque country, the poorest and most oppressed part of Spain. That country now has about a 25% unemployment rate, but in the Basque country where Mondragon cooperatives operate factories, mines, retail, transport, and more, the unemployment rate is 5%. When a Mondragon factory or store or other operation has to close because of unprofitability, Mondragon retrains and relocates those workers to other cooperative enterprises. Mondragon's cooperative ethos makes it so different from other enterprises, one representative explained, that they're about to have to offer their own MBA program, to guarantee they get trained managers without the bloodsucking, predatory mindset taught and valued at most business schools. They heard that Mondragon is now partnering with the UFCW and local forces to establish cooperative grocery stores and enterprises in Cincinnati.

Those attending *Jackson Rising* heard about the concept of a solidarity economy, an economy not based on gentrification or exploitation or the enrichment of a few, an economy based on mutual cooperation to satisfy the needs of many, to stabilize neighborhoods and communities, to provide needed jobs and services.

Cooperation, or as it's sometimes called, "the cooperative movement" is a model that is succeeding right now in tens of thousands of places for tens of millions of people around the world. It's a model that can succeed in the United States as well. The dedicated core of activists in the Malcolm X Grassroots Movement, MXGM, after deeply embedding themselves locally in Jackson, Mississippi, and briefly electing one of their own as mayor in the overwhelmingly Black and poor city of 175,000 people, are determined to show and take part in a different kind of Black economic development.

To that end, they've formed what they call "Cooperation Jackson," with four short term objectives:

1. Cooperation Jackson is establishing an educational arm to spread the word in their communities about the distinct advantages and exciting possibilities of mutual uplift that business cooperatives offer.

2. When Mayor Chokwe Lumumba was still in office, Cooperation Jackson planned to establish a "cooperative incubator." providing a range of startup services for cooperative enterprises. Absent support from the mayor's office, some MXGM activists observed, a lot of these co-ops will have to be born and nurtured in the cold.

3. Cooperation Jackson aims to form a local federation of cooperatives to share information and resources and to ensure that the cooperatives follow democratic principles of self-management that empower their workers.

We've always said "free the land," observed one MXGM activist. Now we want to "free the labor" as well.

4. Finally Cooperation Jackson intends to establish a financial institution to assist in providing credit and capital to cooperatives.

The MXGM activists are serious thinkers and organizers. They conducted door to door surveys of entire neighborhoods in Jackson, complete with skills assessments to discover how many plumbers, plasterers, farmers, carpenters, construction workers, truck mechanics, nurses and people with other health care experience live there, and how many are unemployed. You'd imagine any local government that claimed it wanted to provide jobs and uplift people might do this, but you'd be imagining another world. In Jackson, Mississippi, local activists are figuring out how to build that new and better world. The US Census Bureau gathers tons of information useful to real estate, credit, banking and similar business interests, but little or nothing of value to those who'd want to preserve neighborhood integrity and productively use the skills people already have.

In the short run, new and existing cooperatives in Jackson or anyplace else won't get much help from government. Mike Beall, president and CEO of the National Cooperative Business Association pointed out that the federal budget contains a mere $7 million in assistance for agricultural cooperatives, and that the Obama administration has tried to remove that the last two years in a row. There was, he said, no federal funding whatsoever to assist non-agricultural business cooperative startups or operations.

By contrast, Wal-Mart alone receives $7.8 billion in tax breaks, loophole funds and public subsidies from state, federal and local governments every year, and according to one estimate, about $2.1 million more with each new store it opens. Another single company, Georgia Power is about to receive $8.3 billion in federal loan guarantees and outright gifts for the construction of two nuclear plants alongside its leaky old nukes in the mostly Black and poor town of Shell Bluff. When it comes to oil companies, military contractors, transportation infrastructure outfits, agribusiness, pharmaceuticals and so on there are hundreds more companies that get billions in federal subsidies. Cooperatives get nothing. In the state of Mississippi, according to one *Jackson Rising* workshop presenter, non-agricultural cooperatives are technically illegal.

All these traditional corporations have one thing in common. Unlike democratically run cooperatives which share their profits and power, traditional corporations are dictatorships. Their workers don't, in most cases, have the freedom of speech at work or the opportunity to form unions, and certainly don't get to share in the wealth their labor creates for their bosses. To normal capitalist corporations, those workers, their families and communities are completely disposable. Detroit used to be a company town for the auto industry. When that industry grew and consolidated enough to disperse production in lower wage areas around the world it quickly abandoned Detroit and its people leaving a shattered, impoverished polluted ruin behind.

The new mayor of Jackson, (Tony Yarber), who ran with developers' money against the son of the late Chokwe Lumumba and narrowly defeated him, locked a number of city employees affiliated with the old administration out of their offices immediately after the election, before even being sworn in. The city removed all sponsorship and assistance to the *Jackson Rising* conference. There was a campaign in the local press branding its organizers as communists, terrorists, unpatriotic and unfit to discuss the serious matters of job creation and building local economies. But the conference ran smoothly anyway, with invaluable assistance from the Federation of Southern Cooperatives/Land Assistance Fund, an organization that has help save the land and land rights of more Black farmers over the last forty years than any other, and the Praxis Project, the Fund for Democratic Communities, the Highlander Research and Education Center, and several others.

> At *Jackson Rising*, hundreds of movement activists from around the country discovered, rediscovered, began to visualize and explore cooperation and the solidarity economy...
>
> This new mayor of ours made a big mistake. What would it cost him, even if he imagines cooperatives cannot succeed, to give his blessing to this gathering?" asked Kali Akuno of Cooperation Jackson. "As an organizer I can now ask why he's against job creation? He's got no answer to that.... It's hindsight of course, but maybe we should have paid attention to this piece first, and the electoral effort only afterward. Who's to say that if we'd done it that way we would not have been more successful in retaining the mayor's seat.

This past weekend was the 50th anniversary of the first freedom rides which kicked off the youth-led phase of the southern Freedom Movement. Something of similar importance happened in Jackson, Mississippi, last weekend.

At *Jackson Rising*, hundreds of movement activists from around the country discovered, rediscovered, began to visualize and explore cooperation and the solidarity economy. They met with their peers from North Carolina, Ohio, Zimbabwe, South Africa, and of course Mississippi already engaged in pulling it together. It's an economy not based on gentrification as Black urban regimes in Atlanta, New Orleans and other cities have and still are doing. It's not based on big ticket stadiums or shopping malls or professional sports teams, none of which create many permanent well paying jobs anyway. It's not based on fast food and restaurant empires that follow the McDonalds and Wal-Mart model of low wages and ruthless exploitation. It's about democracy and collective ownership of business, collective responsibility and collective uplift.

It's coming. Jackson Mississippi is already rising, and your community can do the same. Black Agenda Report intends to stay on top of this story in the coming weeks and months.

This article first appeared at http://www.blackagendareport.com/content/ jackson-rising%C2%A0black-millionaires-wont-lift-us-cooperation-solidarity-economy-might

IV

CRITICAL EXAMINATIONS

11.

Why the Left Should Look to Jackson, Mississippi

Michael Siegel

A new political and economic model is emerging, and it is not appearing where we might suspect it would. In the heart of the South, in a city named after one of the most racist presidents in United States history, in a landscape that resembles parts of Detroit and other decaying industrial centers, an impressive intergenerational collection of community organizers and activists have launched a bold program to empower a Black working-class community that 21st -century capitalism has left behind.In the last two months, I have traveled twice to Jackson, Miss., first for the memorial of Mayor Chokwe Lumumba, and most recently, between May 2 and 4, 2014 for the Jackson Rising: New Economies Conference held at Jackson State University. On both occasions, I have been struck by the amazing individuals and families who have dedicated themselves to developing economic democracy in Jackson.

A Black revolutionary mayor in the heart of the South

Jackson Rising is the brainchild of a coalition of local and national political forces, including the Malcolm X Grassroots Movement (MXGM), the Jackson People's Assembly and Lumumba's office. Part of the initial vision was for the conference to catalyze some of the mayor's economic initiatives, including the goal of helping local workers win government contracts. Unfortunately Lumumba, who won election by an overwhelming majority in June, held office for only a brief period before dying Feb. 25 of unexplained causes.That Lumumba won the election at all is a testament to his sustained radical human rights work and to the group of community organizers he worked with over many years. Even during his campaign for mayor, Lumumba made no apologies for his revolutionary background, including his commitment to the New Afrikan People's Organization (NAPO) and its claim to a homeland in the predominantly Black regions of the South (described as the "Kush"), including broad swaths of Louisiana, Mississippi, Alabama, Georgia and South Carolina. Lumumba's history also included decades of experience as a civil rights and criminal defense attorney, with past clients including freedom fighters and political prisoners such as Mutulu Shakur, Geronimo Pratt and Assata Shakur.

Despite his radical background, Lumumba was embraced by the people of Jackson, where he had long been an active community advocate and youth mentor. Lumumba and MXGM also utilized innovative organizing tactics to activate the local population. They went door to door to recruit participants for the Jackson People's Assembly, an independent formation that began as a response to Hurricane Katrina. The Assembly now meets quarterly to discuss community concerns and debate issues including participation in the U.S. Census and the curriculum in the Jackson Public Schools. Hundreds of residents have participated in the Assembly, and locals who are unaffiliated with Lumumba or MXGM lead working committees on topics such as economic development, education and public safety. Perhaps even more important than his impressive history and tactics, however, the conditions on the ground provided the opportunity for Lumumba because the large community of poor and working people in Jackson truly need a radical politics. As I learned in an MXGM workshop at the Jackson Rising conference, the city is 85 percent black, the student body of its public schools is 98 percent Black and the surrounding Hinds County is 75 percent black, yet out of the total of approximately $1 billion of annual public expenditures in the region, only 5 percent goes to Black employees and black-owned businesses. The vast majority of government contracts are awarded to businesses outside of Jackson and even outside the state.Lumumba's administration promised to address entrenched economic inequity through a new approach to government spending. One of the mayor's key initiatives was to secure a billion-dollar bond measure to rebuild Jackson's infrastructure, including repairs to roads, water lines and sewage facilities. And although the passage of a sales tax increase was not a revolutionary act standing alone, Lumumba's goal for the use of the funds was to incubate local worker cooperatives that could win contracts to rebuild the city.

Cooperative enterprise as a vehicle for economic self-determination

The South is often derided as a place of destitute poverty, but the Lumumba administration was acutely aware of the tremendous wealth in the region. Today the South, standing alone, would constitute the fourth largest economy in the world. International capital has recognized this fact, and multinational corporations including Siemens and Nissan are expanding in Mississippi. The challenge for a progressive local government is to ensure that the outside investment does not lead to a drain of local resources.

As Jessica Gordon Nembhard chronicles in *Collective Courage: A History of African American Cooperative Economic Thought and Practice*, the Black cooperative movement can be traced back to times of slavery and the Underground Railroad, when some pooled their savings to buy one person's freedom and when others pooled resources to support the escape network. In the early 20th century, Nembhard writes, cooperative activity enabled Black people "to achieve a level of economic independence that contributed to their later success in achieving voting rights and other civil rights."At the Jackson Rising conference, a variety of panelists and speakers, including Nembhard, spoke to the utility of the worker cooperative as part of a larger strategy to support the health of the Black working class. In a time of Right to Work laws, attacks on worker centers, massive and underreported unemployment and a pitiful federal minimum wage, the worker cooperative appears to be a tool to prevent the extraction of surplus value from the backs of labor. A leading international example of the cooperative movement is the Mondragon cooperative from the Basque region of Spain. Founded by a young Catholic priest and students of a technical school in 1956, Mondragon is now a cooperative of cooperatives, encompassing nearly 300 distinct businesses and employing over 80,000 people. Mondragon cooperative enterprises include banks, manufacturing, skilled and unskilled labor, public schools and a university. Consistent with a broader international movement to define and promote ethical cooperative enterprise, the pay differential between the highest and lowest paid workers at Mondragon is generally between 3-to-1 and 5-to-1, and the CEO of the entire Mondragon Corporation earns only nine times as much as the lowest-paid worker (this compares with an average ratio of 600-to-1 at large U.S. corporations). The organizers in Jackson aim to build their version of Mondragon in the South. The Jackson Rising conference brought together nearly 500 interested participants, including dozens of local would-be cooperative organizers along with representatives of political and co-op organizations from around the country. New cooperatives springing up in Jackson include a recycling business, a five-acre urban farm, a laundry business and a construction firm. Regional and national organizations are providing support, including the Federation of Southern Cooperatives/Land Assistance Fund, the Southern Grassroots Economies Project, and the Fund for Democratic Communities.

The hub of a new human rights movement

On March 8, over a thousand people attended Lumumba's memorial service. The Jackson Convention Center was packed to overflowing. Individuals from every part of Lumumba's life came to honor his legacy, including leaders from NAPO, MXGM, the National Conference of Black Lawyers, the Mississippi Immigrant Rights Alliance, the Jackson City Council and even the Bolivarian Republic of Venezuela. Lumumba had been responsible for liberating the unjustly imprisoned—including the Scott sisters, who were notoriously imprisoned for nearly 20 years for stealing $11 in merchandise—and for helping develop a new generation of political organizers in places including Detroit, Atlanta and Jackson. Every speaker at Lumumba's memorial committed him- or herself to the continued work of fulfilling his revolutionary legacy in Jackson. When a caravan of cars and buses followed the hearse from the Jackson Convention Center to Lumumba's gravesite, hundreds upon hundreds of residents parked their cars, stood by the road, shouted Lumumba's favored slogan—"Free the land!"—and gave the Black Power salute to the procession. The people of Jackson are ready for the continued fulfillment of Lumumba's vision. The Jackson Rising conference represents a critical next step in the work to turn Jackson into a national model for how a poor and working-class community can rebuild itself despite the pressures of our current economy. The organizers have invited support from all corners, and some groups have already answered the call. The 2015 U.S. Social Forum will be held at three sites, and on April 4, 2014, the national planning committee announced that Jackson would serve as the convergence point for the South. As the committee noted:

> The organizing in Jackson and legacy of Mayor Lumumba show how people can build and are building a better world using people's assemblies to facilitate participatory democracy and unity in action. This demonstration of people's power to transform the city from below offers to the nation a model for how to transition from what is to what must be through autonomous collectives, electoral strategy, and alternative economic models that liberate people from exploitative forms of capital and build communities of mutual respect and collectivity.

The world is starting to take notice of the work in Jackson. We should all figure out how to support the critical work there, and also bring cooperative and liberatory economic endeavors to our own communities.

This article was first published at http://www.truthdig.com/report/item/ why_the_left_should_look_to_jackson_mississippi_20140521

12.

The Jackson-Kush Plan: The Struggle for Land and Housing

Max Rameau

"Revolution is based on land. Land is the basis of all independence. Land is the basis of freedom, justice and equality. —Malcolm X, *Message to the Grassroots,* November 10, 1963

While the land relationships that dominate this society have implications for every relation in society, the recent crisis of gentrification and forced removal in low income Black communities, along with the volatile boom-bust real estate cycles, has made the struggle for adequate housing the most pronounced battleground in an increasingly intense war over the vision for the future of how we relate, prioritize and manage access to land.

The current regime of land relationships renders housing and community development fatally flawed in at least two respects: first, houses serve dual social functions in this society, but those functions are contradictory and at odds with each other. And second, decisions about land use is fundamentally undemocratic, rendering people unable to make basic decisions about how to improve their own communities. Left unresolved, these two contradictions conspire to perpetuate poverty, destabilize societies and provoke social unrest.

As things stand, a house simultaneously serves two starkly dissimilar functions: the first function is housing as the shelter required for human survival. A place to live, rest, raise a family and contemplate the meaning and direction of one's life. The second function is housing as an investment. Generally speaking, real estate is regarded as a solid investment specifically because human beings cannot survive without it. The quality of that investment improves as housing prices increase beyond the reach of low and middle income people. That is to say, the more difficult it is for average people to access basic housing they can afford, the greater the likelihood of a substantial return on investment.

This dual function, housing as both shelter and investment, creates a perverse incentive for banks, corporations, developers and individual investors to support gentrification, which constitutes in essence the forced removal of low-income people from targeted communities. The aforementioned actors profit directly from this economic phenomenon, setting the stage for an inherent conflict of interest that pits two opposing rights directly against each other.

It is easy to see how those rights—the right to housing and the right to make profit—can come into conflict with one another: if the right to housing means everyone gets a home they can afford, then how do banks, developers and landlords make a profit? Conversely, if banks, developers and landlords have the right to profit maximization by increasing prices, how do the human beings who do not have a lot of money access housing?

When the economic stakes are sufficiently high—such as during a housing 'boom' where hundreds of millions of dollars in profit are on the line—the drive to expand the supply of housing and increase profit margins intensifies, making the competition even more cut-throat. At this point, the core issues of land and housing exceed the corrective powers of regulation or other types of legislation. At this point, a house can no longer effectively function as both a home, of which every human being has a right, and an investment vehicle, through which investors have a right to derive profit, which might come at the expense of human beings seeking life sustaining shelter. At this point, the fundamental role of land and housing in that society is in full contradiction.

The second fatal flaw in the current regime of land relationships is the undemocratic nature of decisions made about land usage. Under the existing economic order, residents of a racialized low-income neighborhood may collectively decide, in a democratic manner, that their community is in great need of decent and affordable housing, access to fresh food, local shops, playgrounds and activity areas for children and space for public meetings and access to internet connected computers. In order to meet these needs, the community may identify local land, the land upon which they have lived their lives, worshipped, worked and been educated, to set aside as space for housing, farm land, commercial activities, recreational areas and the commons. Residents may determine such land usage will improve their individual and collective lives, allowing them to build a sustainable and thriving community.

Instead, however, the land is converted into high end lofts, a high end art gallery specializing in post-modern impressionistic sculptures and a chain shop offering $5 cups of coffee while pimping the stylistic renderings of white artists providing their own interpretations of Black music genres.

The difference between the vision and the reality is not rooted in best practices, but in the dominance of those who have money—even if they lack good ideas —over those who endure marginalized social and economic real life conditions. This situation—where people with a deep stake in the outcome of their long time neighborhood have less of a voice in how their community is developed than someone who has never visited and whose interests primarily lie in extracting dollars from that community—is an insurmountable contradiction that is incapable of developing human beings and more closely resembles a colonial relationship than a functioning democracy.

Of course, contradictions exist in every system and their existence alone is not necessarily indicative of systemic failure or crisis. Contradictions escalate to the level of crisis not only when the contradiction is sufficiently deep, but when the area of contradiction is central to the survival of the group involved.

For example, a family might be forced to confront the contradictions associated with limited resources and prioritization when, at a particular time on a specific night, the single television set in the home is tasked with the triple functions of simultaneously broadcasting a presidential debate, a high stakes playoff game and a troupe of stuffed animals who sing, dance and recite a series of base-10 integers in correct sequence. While this contradiction is real, it is not rooted in an issue area that is central enough to challenge that family's very existence in the same way as contradictions over access to food or housing. Therefore, even though contradictions themselves are inherent in any system, the depth and issue areas of those contradictions determine if the situation devolves into full-blown crisis.

During the so called 'real estate boom,' from approximately 2003 to 2007, land and housing prices across the country skyrocketed to unprecedented levels at break-neck speeds. While rapidly rising real estate prices resulted in tremendous profits for banks, developers and other speculators, the underbelly of the 'boom' was nothing short of devastating for Black communities. Long-time residents—who were only residents because they were segregated into those neighborhoods in the first place—found themselves forced out by a combination of rapidly rising prices, a sudden interest in the government in enforcing housing codes resulting in huge fines, changes in the local support system (cheap corner store replaced with less centrally located and higher priced organic food store) and stepped up harassment by local police interested in protecting the new residents from the natives.

The gentrification and forced displacement of low-income Black communities is always a devastating process, but given the nature of finance capital during the era of neo-liberalism, is a entirely predictable consequence of the predominant land relationships in this society. The preceding outcome in 2007-2008 highlighted to a new generation the way the investment function of houses squeezed out the housing function. This state of affairs exposed the undemocratic nature of housing or community development.

As the real estate boom turned into a bust, middle class whites were, often for the first time, forced to confront the impacts of some of those same contradictions, albeit in entirely different ways. Even as the 'home' aspect of millions of houses were undamaged by storms, fires or even the ravages of time, millions of middle class whites lost that home because the 'investment' aspect of the house was adversely impacted by the real estate bust.

Even when there was nothing wrong with the 'home,' tens of millions of people faced foreclosure related eviction because of the house's function as an investment. In order to maximize those investments, financial institutions designed and implemented complex and risky financing mechanisms that maximized profit when it worked, but led to a full collapse of the house of cards as foreclosures increased.

Consequently, the number of families without homes, from gentrification and foreclosure, skyrocketed while, simultaneously, the number of vacant houses—each representing a failed investment—also skyrocketed. Due to the risky investment schemes employed, the foreclosures had a multiplier effect, triggering even more investment losses and causing an economic recession.

The only way to prevent a full global economic collapse was to force low and middle class people to use their future earnings to bailout a hand full of financial institutions that made and lost billions by defrauding the same low and middle income people who were now bailing them out.

In order to realize proper levels of profit, big banks and other speculators asserted their right to use the investment function of a house, not just as a priority over the home function of the same house, but at the very expense of that home function.

Equally as bad, house investors, even the demonstrably fraudulent ones, rather than the residents of the house or the impacted communities, had full authority to determine what to do with all of those vacant foreclosed homes as well as the hundreds of billions of dollars the banks received in exchange for them.

In case the point has not been adequately underscored, the contradictions associated with land relationships – particularly how the investment function of a house is incompatible with the housing function of a house – directly causes gentrification and other displacement and has reach full crisis level.

In response to the growing crisis, an aggressive and robust social movement emerged to defend families from forced removal, whether in the form of gentrification or foreclosure related eviction, and redesign the system in order to resolve the underlying contradiction.

One of the early entrants in that movement was Take Back the Land (TBtL), which was formed in Miami, Florida in 2007. Take Back the Land helped create a national, Black-led Land and Housing Action Group (LHAG) in the fall of 2009, that was initiated and anchored by the US Human Rights Network (USHRN), and consisted originally of the Malcolm X Grassroots Movement (MXGM), Survivors Village in New Orleans, the Chicago Anti-Eviction Campaign (CAEC), and Picture the Homeless (PTH), a full two years before Occupy Wall Street (OWS) took over Zuccotti Park in New York City. The Land and Housing Action Group initiated the national Take Back the Land campaign in 2010, which itself became a national network in early 2011.[1]

The national Take Back the Land campaign made at least three major contributions to the burgeoning movement: first, as a Black led and populated organization, it came with a clear line on the importance of Black self-determination, political leadership and perspective on common social issues. Second, the Take Back the Land campaign modeled a form of civil disobedience

– called Positive Action (after the theory and practice developed by Kwame Nkrumah and the Convention People's Party)[2]—that was appropriate for this particular issue and historical moment. And, third, the national Take Back the Land campaign developed a political theory that framed the underlying contradiction as one of land and land relationships, not just gentrification or foreclosures.

The theory and framing proved critical in distinguishing the way in which the Take Back the Land campaign analyzed the underlying contradiction at the root of the crisis.

For example, the primary argument adopted by most organizations engaged in anti-foreclosure work was that foreclosure was caused by high mortgages (the result of the real estate boom) and, therefore, families should benefit by getting new mortgages that reflected the housing prices of the real estate bust, not the boom.

The demand inherently cultivated a base limited by two essential factors: income and status. While a reduced mortgage could prove helpful to an individual family in an 'underwater' property—where the amount of the mortgage is greater than the market value of the house—the broader economic recession significantly swelled the ranks of the unemployed. Consequently, dropping the mortgage by $50,000, $100,000 or even $200,000 had little practical value to a family with no income.

Potential movement members were also limited by historic social and economic realities. While roughly 58% of whites live in a family owned home, in the history of the United States, the number of Black people living in a home owned by a family member has never exceeded 49%. For those organizing in Black communities that meant that even if their anti-foreclosure campaign succeeded beyond their wildest imaginations and helped 100% of homeowners, it would still fail to help the majority of Black people.[3]

A movement fighting for the human right to housing cannot be based on economic distinctions such as homeowners, renters, squatters and people without homes.

Additionally, campaigns designed to win mortgage principal reduction for a single homeowner proved too transactional in nature to serve as the basis on which to organize over the long term. Without a broader vision, members left after the 'victory' of a new mortgage. The campaign failed to include a mechanism through which members would remain engaged over the long term.

Most importantly, winning a new mortgage, based on the investment function of the market value of a house, did nothing to change the underlying causes of either gentrification or foreclosures. In fact, giving everyone new and lower mortgages only increases the chance that prices will skyrocket again soon, repeating the entire cycle in record time.

So, while most anti-foreclosure campaigns framed the issue of foreclosure in terms of ... foreclosure, the limitations of that framing were quickly revealed in practice. Ending foreclosures by only looking at foreclosures was a logical dead end.

Take Back the Land ventured to answer the fundamental question facing all social movements: how do we resolve the underlying contradiction that gave rise to this movement in the first place?

The Malcolm X Grassroots Movement (MXGM) played a central role in organizing the national Take Back the Land campaign and developing the political theory and analysis that informed the movement's ground breaking work.

While we were clear that the only way to end gentrification and foreclosure related displacement was to look beyond gentrification and foreclosure and fundamentally re-imagine and re-structure land relationships, we struggled to clarify what that meant in terms around which campaigns could be built.

In an early campaign document, Kali Akuno of MXGM argued the recent boom-bust cycle demonstrated the unsustainability, danger and inhumanity of the investment function of housing. Therefore, Akuno argues that housing can only serve a single function: that of a home. In order to advance this bold vision, our general strategy must be to end the investment function of housing by protecting housing from the forces of the market forces. In short, because it is an essential human need, housing cannot be a commodity subject to profiteering.[4]

As long as housing remained a commodity subject to the whims of market forces, we can never realize either the human right to housing or democratic control over resources owned by corporations or individuals. In order to ensure the human right to housing and democratic control over land in our communities, we must ensure that housing is a protected public good, not just another commodity. Akuno called this 'the decommodification imperative."[5] From that moment onward, Take Back the Land's clarion call was the decommodification of land and housing.

◆

In a direct and congruent way, the initiatives of the Land and Housing Action Group and the national Take Back the Land campaign paved the way for the land-centered organizing of Cooperation Jackson. Pursuant to the Jackson-Kush Plan, over the past 3 years, Cooperation Jackson has secured nearly 40 properties in West Jackson, that constitute over 4 non-contiguous acres of land. The land is not individually owned for the purpose of resale at profit, but collectively controlled for the purpose of sustainable development with equitable benefit.

And while the dual crises of gentrification and foreclosures have focused attention on housing, Cooperation Jackson has clearly understood that housing is but one function of land. As such, land has been set aside for farming, commercial space, recreational space, nature conservancy, natural resource exploration, and the development of a new "commons" in Jackson.

At a time when economies of scale are causing the displacement of Black families and communities off of their farms, out of their homes and from their long-standing neighborhoods, Cooperation Jackson's fulfillment of the decommodification imperative through the collective acquisition of land is protecting those areas from the next round of land speculation because these properties are being held in a community land trust (CLT), dubbed the Fannie Lou Hamer Community Land Trust, and per the organization's covenant agreements will not and cannot be put up for sale and, therefore, will not be directly subject to market forces.

As decommodified land, those properties are liberated to serve out their more important social functions of housing human beings, growing food and providing common space from which to build community.

Further, organizing those properties democratically- instead of consolidating them in the hands of an individual or family – advances the cause of social transformation by fundamentally redefining the meaning of ownership and power in the tradition and reality of the collective African experience in the South.

In this society, property ownership is an overwhelmingly individualistic concept. A business has at least one owner in whom power is concentrated and profits or rewards disproportionately appropriated. This setup is bad enough in the broader society, but inside an exploited and oppressed Black community, mimicry of structures of power often leads to confusing, if not disastrous, results.

Following the end of legal segregation, Black communities, understandably, rallied behind the idea of building Black owned versions of businesses traditionally dominated by whites, as a means of advancing the race. As Black owned magazines, restaurants, radio stations, cable television stations and even hotels came into their own, the limitations of the 'Black owned' version quickly became evident. In spite of the obvious benefit of a business that did not discriminate based on race, the decision making power and the distribution of wealth associated with the business was concentrated in the hands of a few, albeit Black ones. There was little accountability to or broader benefit (aside from racial pride) for the larger Black community.

The results were predictable on a number of levels: first, the campaigns that fought for the Black business were demobilized once the campaigns were successful as there was little else for them to do. The organizing effort dissipated with the victory instead of continued. Second, any wealth generated by the venture was concentrated in the hands of a small number of Black families and individuals, a class which grew increasingly isolated and estranged from and even disdainful of the masses that made their wealth possible in the first place. And third, the conditions of the Black community as a whole did not improve as a result of victories of individual ownership.

Cooperation Jackson, as a Black-led force of human-centered economic development is working diligently to flip this script and create a new paradigm. It is critical that as part of the legacy of the national Take Back the Land Campaign, that the leadership of Cooperation Jackson has internalized the many lessons of the campaign from 2009 through 2013, and applied them in new dynamic ways in a particular grounded context. All those seeking to advance a modern program of decommodification and decolonization would do well to learn from the organizing program and strategies of Cooperation Jackson, as there is plenty to digest and assimilate in our ongoing quest for liberation.

Notes

1. See, "Take Back the Land" https://www.scribd.com/document/226197384/Take-Back-the-Land-National-Campaign-Launch-Announcement-2009.

2. See "What I mean by Positive Action", by Kwame Nkrumah https://www.democraticunderground.com/discuss/duboard.php?az=view_all&address=277x471. For more background on Kwame Nkrumah's theory of "Positive Action", see *Consciencism: Philosophy and Ideology for Decolonization*, Monthly Review Press, NY, NY, 1964.

3. For more information on the racial disparities in the housing market and home ownership see, "Homeownership in the United States" https://en.wikipedia.org/wiki/Home-ownership_in_the_United_States#cite_note-US_Census_Bureau.2C_homeownership_by_race_and_ethnicity_of_householder-11.

4. See, "Reclaiming TARP, Reclaiming Public Housing" at https://www.scribd.com/document/226198635/Reclaiming-TARP-Reclaiming-Public-Housing-Land-and-Housing-Action-Group-Work-Group-Paper-1-2009 and "Identifying, Occupying and Transforming Un-indentified Public Housing" https://www.scribd.com/doc/226199196/Identifying-Occupying-and-Transforming-Unidentified-Public-Housing-Land-and-Housing-Action-Group-Working-Paper-2, and "The Meaning of the Slogan, the Meaning of the Movement" https://www.scribd.com/document/226199934/The-Meaning-of-the-Slogan-The-Meaning-of-the-Movement-Land-and-Housing-Working-Group-Paper-3, and "Beyond Foreclosure Fraud" https://www.scribd.com/document/226201216/Beyond-Foreclosure-Fraud-Moving-to-Take-Back-the-Land-through-Strategic-Action.

5. See specifically "The Meaning of the Slogan, the Meaning of the Movement" at https://www.scribd.com/document/226199934/The-Meaning-of-the-Slogan-The-Meaning-of-the-Movement-Land-and-Housing-Working-Group-Paper-3.

13.

The City as Liberated Zone: The Promise of Jackson's People's Assemblies

Makani Themba-Nixon

"Hey, uh, we didn't get our forty acres and a mule
But we did get you, CC..."
    —Lyrics from *Chocolate City* as recorded by Parliament

Jackson, MS, is the site of an important political project: to build a people-centered democracy based on the principles of self-determination and cooperative economic and social relations. It was literally centuries in the making, drawing from African systems and African American social experiments dating before the 18th century. The People's Assembly is an important component of this project as it is the primary forum for resident engagement. Yet, to simply refer to the People's Assembly as an engagement strategy would belie its important political purposes as well as the deep philosophical framework from which it grew.

Local Governance as Black Self Determination: A Rich Legacy

The Jackson effort is rooted in a long tradition of the city as a site of struggle for Black liberation. The concentration of Black people in urban areas during the 20th century, peaking at more than 80 percent in cities by 1970, necessarily made cities (especially northern cities) a critical site for organizing Black people. Even prior to the "Black Power" era of the late 1960s and 1970s, there were several important experiments in Black governance in the early 20th century. These projects were often post slavery havens created by and for Black people: Allensworth, California; Eatonville, Florida; Blackdom, New Mexico; Hobson City, Alabama; Greenwood, Oklahoma; and Mound Bayou, Mississippi. There were more than 100 Black communities in all, bound together by shared dreams of Black Power and community control. Most of these places did not survive the constant assault of legal, economic, state sanctioned and vigilante violence. Yet, they left a powerful legacy that informed local organizing in the context of Black liberation.

In the 1970s, there was a second wave of local self-determination "projects" as a number of places specifically incorporated as cities in order to create spaces of Black power and control. These include Soul City in North Carolina (NC), an interesting collaboration between longtime civil rights leader Floyd McKissick, then Charlotte mayor and later NC gubernatorial hopeful Harvey Gannt; and East Palo Alto (aka Nairobi) in California. Accompanying this wave was an insurgent Black Power movement (mostly located in cities) where grassroots resistance and civil unrest forced the federal government to increase public investments in Black urban centers including revenue sharing, Head Start, and community action programs.

The Republic of New Afrika (RNA) and the New Afrikan People's Organization (NAPO) led a critical set of organizations that took up the mantle of Black self-governance as self-determination. Founded in the late 1960s, RNA has been advocating for an independent New Afrikan nation in what is now the southeastern part of the United States known as the Black Belt South. RNA and NAPO helped lead struggles for Black independence in the North and South and were influential in ushering in a "second wave" of local self-governing efforts in Black communities.

A number of factors, including aggressive state violence, deep cuts to social programs and the discontinuation of revenue sharing dramatically shifted how cities would be financed and governed. Amidst this backdrop of public and private divestment, the crack cocaine crisis and a significant rise in Black unemployment, Black people began what came to be known as the "reverse migration" as millions of Blacks moved to the South in search of jobs, a lower cost of living and a better quality of life.

Jackson Rising

The Black population in the south was on the rise and NAPO was positioned to accelerate its southern organizing efforts. Chokwe Lumumba was a part of a group of seasoned organizers that included Dr. Safiya Omari and Lumumba's wife Nubia Lumumba (both venerable leaders and cadre in their own right) to help build out organizing efforts in Jackson, Mississippi. Jackson's high percentage of Black residents, high rates of poverty alongside its colleges and location as Mississippi's capital made it an important site of struggle. Jackson was also hard hit by private sector divestment and public sector budget cuts. Unemployment was rising. There was a need for a more radical response to the city's crisis. NAPO and its mass organizing vehicle, the Malcolm X Grassroots Movement (MXGM), built on local radical traditions while helping to grow a progressive multiracial organizing community.

It was these organizing efforts, beginning in earnest in the late 1980s, that laid the foundation for the Jackson People's Assemblies. The Peoples Assembly drew its inspiration from a number of sources including Mississippi's century-old National Negro Convention Movement that started in 1831 and ended in 1864. The assemblies were created as a vehicle for engaging residents—especially grassroots residents—in the practice of self-determination and governance.

Prior to the Assembly, Jackson's resident engagement was mostly in the form of neighborhood associations that were mostly focused on crime, beautification and the interests of property owners. A number of association members were absentee land owners whose primary stake in the city was the protection of their property. It was not until the advent of the People's Assemby that Jackson's large low income and mostly renter population had a forum for addressing their issues.

People's Assemblies are a part of a long democratic tradition in progressive movements worldwide. They are essentially forums for mass engagement to address the issues that affect a community's life. Assemblies can focus on issues or projects that are independent of government action and they can act as advocates to influence and make demands on government in their interests. The Jackson People's Assembly did both.

The meetiangs of the Assembly were significant in at least five ways:

1. *They provided clear, formal venues for listening to the issues of local residents.* This was particularly important given the significant number of organizers who were not Mississippi natives.

2. *They served as a training ground and leadership pipeline.* Everything from outreach to meeting logistics provided opportunities to test new leadership, mentor new members and build skills. The assemblies were also intergenerational engaging a significant number of youth and elders providing yet another opportunity for learning and skills exchange.

3. *They provided a vehicle for coalition building around a broad agenda.* As a vehicle for mass organizing, the assemblies allowed for engagement around a much broader set of issues and, as a result, attracted a diverse set of partners. As assemblies (pushed by residents) took on critical bread and butter issues like wages, land use and budgeting, they also took on their own political life.

4. The focus on public policy pushed members into deeper engagement with governance structures—at the local and state level. Residents were trained on local budgeting and tax policy and the role of state agencies, the legislature and the governor in the decisions that affected Jacksonians quality of life. It also built a cadre of activated residents who learned how to conduct research on policy issues and make independent proposals to policymakers.

5. Assemblies took on independent projects to improve quality of life which served as concrete examples of the power of self-determination and collective action. Assembly projects included the establishment of food gardens, clean up and beautification efforts.

The first assembly was organized in Ward 2, the home ward of Chokwe Lumumba. Based in North Jackson, Ward 2 is a mix of homeowners, stable working class renters as well as Tougaloo College. Although students played an important role in the development of the Assembly, (they volunteered to do outreach and other forms of support) much of the organizing was done by senior leadership with Lumumba playing a primary role.

Lumumba's charisma, wit and sharp systemic analysis was an important factor in engaging residents. After decades of work in the community, Lumumba was a known quantity to residents. A number of the early NAPO organizers were still in the city organizing at various levels; however, there were no paid organizers whose focus was building the assemblies. In fact, it was primarily organized by NAPO/MXGM members some of whom served as staff working out of Lumumba's law firm. These members essentially did double duty—helping to organize residents and working as part of Lumumba's progressive legal practice.

Faith communities also played a critical role. For example, collaborators New Hope Baptist and Anderson South United Methodist were among the spaces where assemblies were convened. Churches not only hosted assemblies, they helped promote them and church members (including leadership) participated in assemblies. These partnerships were important because they helped to extend the limited infrastructure of MXGM and helped more strongly root the process with local leadership.

Into the Belly of the Beast

Originally conceived as an "outside" strategy to provide a space for resident engagement in building alternative, community serving forms of governance, the People's Assembly quickly became a force to reckon with on city government issues as well. The Ward 2 Assembly was gaining momentum and residents from other wards expressed an interest in taking the People's Assembly citywide. In the meantime, Lumumba's active leadership in the Assembly as well as his extensive knowledge of municipal functions were increasingly in the spotlight. Residents made it known that they wanted a progressive leader like Lumumba on Jackson's City Council and the base built through Assembly outreach turned to work to elect one of their own.

When Lumumba was successfully elected to represent Ward 2 in 2009, MXGM refocused efforts on building the People's Assembly as a platform for resident voice and reshaping municipal policy. With a strong ally on council, the Assembly kicked off its *Deepening Democracy* campaign to organize low and moderate income Black communities. The goal was to develop progressive policy initiatives "around community/economic development, food security and health issues"—priorities identified in assemblies. By 2010, the People's Assembly was the fastest growing organizing force in Jackson with more than 300 members citywide.

Training and political education was important to this process—both in terms of building hope and belief in people's own ability to govern and make decisions together and in terms of residents' understanding of the issues and what can be done to address them. Political education took place during the large assemblies, in the task forces (smaller groups charged with developing strategies for implementing priorities surfaced in the assemblies), and even during outreach efforts. Perhaps the most ambitious effort of the Assemblies was the engagement of residents in a participatory budget process—a process where large numbers of residents would collectively identify budget priorities for the city.

The process was modeled on best practices from the growing participatory budget movement with resident leaders working with MXGM organizers to develop the process. Lumumba participated in the political education process providing participants with information on city mechanisms and potential targets for change. Budget priorities were identified and delivered to the Council. Lumumba played a leadership role in advancing the issues on the Council by leveraging the fact that it was the only policy agenda developed directly by residents.

Over time, resident energies were increasingly split between independent, "self-determination" projects—like its cooperative garden projects and solidarity economy work—and its "reform" work to change municipal policy. Policy work was drawing more of the Assembly's resources. And while residents were encouraged by the real and potential impact of policy work, they knew that they were going to have to build more power if they were to going to win their policies on Council.

By 2011, Assembly leaders were starting to focus on the next mayoral election. Many were frustrated with Jackson's third term mayor, Harvey Johnson. Jackson's first African American mayor, Johnson was perceived as a "safe" candidate firmly entrenched with business and other powerful interests. When Johnson announced that he was seeking a fourth term, there was growing sentiment that enough was enough. Residents actively recruited Lumumba to run for mayor as MXGM weighed the issues in the context of their long term organizing vision. By 2012, the Assembly network was in full swing working to build the citywide infrastructure necessary to support Lumumba in a mayoral run. Lumumba was elected in 2013 receiving 90 percent of the vote. The People's Assembly agenda had moved from an outside campaign to the official platform of the mayor.

The People's Assembly was now faced with the challenge of supporting the Lumumba Administration, which was leading efforts to advance its agenda, and maintaining an independent, "outside" presence in order to hold officials accountable (much less maintain its work to create alternatives). This challenge was exacerbated by the need to staff the Administration with people who shared the People's Assembly vision and had the skills to help implement it. Virtually all of the organizers working on the People's Assembly were called into service for the Administration with MXGM even recruiting organizers and staff from outside of Mississippi.

As the People's Assembly and the Lumumba Administration infrastructure become increasingly interlinked, the work of the Assembly focused on moving its policy agenda through City Council. A critical challenge was funding. Jackson did not have the kind of tax base that allowed for the kind of resourcing the People's Assembly agenda required. It was decided that Jackson should hold a referendum to raise the sales tax by 1 percent in order to generate additional revenues for infrastructure and other public improvements.

The People's Assembly played a pivotal role in the successful referendum in 2014, holding educational forums and mobilizing people to get involved in the campaign. It also helped organize residents to push the state legislature to grant the city Jackson permission to hold the January 2014 referendum and continues to work to defend the increase and focus resources on the priorities surfaced in the People's Assembly participatory budgeting process. This work is critically important in the wake of Mayor Lumumba's untimely death a month after the referendum.

Reflections for the Future

The Assembly continues to play a vital role in the community's life as it rebuilds in a post-Mayor Lumumba Jackson. They have focused more energies on the development of alternative structures through the launch of Cooperation Jackson—an initiative to help address the material needs of Jackson's low income and working class communities through cooperative economic efforts. They have also pulled back some on their policy work but certainly not completely. Looking ahead, the Assembly faces some critical questions including: How can the People's Assembly process more effectively engage local residents—especially Jackson's working class and poor Black folk—as leaders and organizers in the Assembly structure? What will be the balance between its "inside" policy focus and its "outside" independent, alternative institution building? And what will Black Power look like in the context of Jackson's class issues—especially addressing how a number of Black middle class leaders have opposed initiatives that address the needs and concerns of poor Black people?

Of course, there are no easy answers. What is certain is that the organizers will continue to draw on their rich legacy and emerging practice to forge new local, liberatory models.

This article first appeared at https://mxgm.org/the-jackson-plan-a-struggle-for-self-determination-participatory-democracy-and-economic-justice/

14.

A Long and Strong History with Southern Roots

Jessica Gordon Nembhard

African Americans, as well as other people of color and low-income people, have benefitted greatly from cooperative ownership throughout the history of the U.S., similar to their counterparts around the world. My recent book, *Collective Courage: A History of African American Cooperative Economic Thought and Practice* (2014), documents these experiences, and particularly the efforts—successes as well as challenges—of African American-owned cooperative enterprises, and analyzes the lessons learned. I explore a variety of cooperative economic models for contemporary community economic development, particularly in communities of color.[1]

The African American Cooperative Movement was a silent partner in the long civil rights movement. Throughout the efforts for Civil Rights, from when we first set foot on North American soil, African Americans have resisted enslavement and oppression and fought for their own freedom. Pursuit of economic alternatives and solidarity economic relationships were part of this struggle and resistance. Even in the face of sabotage and violence we practiced cooperative and collective economics.

African American Cooperative Economics Message

Several African American scholars and leaders have advocated for economic cooperation as an important strategy for Black economic development and increased quality of life. Some leaders have actually practiced cooperative economics in their communities. Although all of them are well known for achievements in other areas (and not for their involvement in the cooperative movement), examples include scholar/activist William E.B. Du Bois (1907, 1933a, 1933b, 1975); activist Marcus Garvey (Shipp 1996: 87-88); businesswoman Nannie H. Burroughs (Hope 1940: 46); activist and organizer Ella Jo Baker (Grant 1998: 30-36; Ransby 2003:75-90); writer, journalist and satirist George Schuyler (Schuyler 1930 and 1932; Calvin 1931; Ransby 2003: 80-90); historian E. Franklin Frazier (1923, 228-229); former Jackson State College (now University) President Jacob Reddix (1974, 117-121); and Black labor leader and organizer A. Philip Randolph, and the Ladies Auxiliary of the Brotherhood of Sleeping Car Porters, (Cohen 2003: 49; Chateauvert 1998). Maulana Karenga (1989) included both Ujima—the collective work and responsibility of African Americans toward their community—and Ujamma—cooperative economics—in addition to self-determination among the seven Kwanzaa principles. Kwanzaa is an African American holiday created by Karenga.

W.E.B. Du Bois proposed economic cooperation as the only effective and practical solution throughout his life. Du Bois argued that African Americans must become the masters of their own economic destiny. Blacks could position ourselves at the forefront of developing new forms of industrial organization that would free us from marginal economic status. He advocated using "intelligent [consumer economic] cooperation" as an important approach. He advanced the concept and strategy of "racial economic cooperation" combining cooperative industries and services in a "group economy," through which African Americans could use their sense of solidarity, gain control over their economic lives, and assert themselves as equals into, even leaders in, the mainstream economy.[2]

"We can by consumers and producers cooperation, ... establish a progressively self-supporting economy that will weld the majority of our people into an impregnable, economic phalanx" (W. E. B. Du Bois 1933b, 93-94).

Schuyler (and co-founder of the Young Negroes' Co-operative League) advocated similarly,

"As I have pointed out again and again ... there is only one thing that can immediately get the Negro group out of the barrel and that is consumers' cooperation, the building up of a Negro cooperative democracy within the shell of our present capitalist system of production and distribution" (1930: 9).

He called on African American youth to lead the movement (Schuyler, 1930 and 1932; and Calvin 1931)). W.C. Matney (1930), manager of the co-op store at Bluefield Colored Institute, West Virginia, was articulate about how cooperatives offer a solution to "the economic riddle confronting the Negro" (p. 49). President of the Ladies Auxiliary to the Brotherhood of Sleeping Car Porters, Helana Wilson, reminded that:

"No race can be said to be another's equal that cannot or will not protect its own interest. This new order can be brought about once the Negro acknowledges the wisdom in uniting his forces and pooling his funds for the common good of all. Other races have gained great wealth and great power by following this simple rule, and it is hoped some day that the Negro will do the same" (Halena Wilson, ALetter to Lucille Jones,@ January 26, 1942 (1942: 1-2)).

Philip Randolph argued that cooperatives are "the best mechanism yet devised to bring about economic democracy" (Randolph 1944).[3] Three decades later in his memoir, Jacob Reddix (1974), co-founder of Consumers Cooperative Trading Company (Gary Indiana) and former president of Jackson State College (now University), also concluded that a "nationwide system of [African American] cooperative businesses" ... "could lift the burden of economic exploitation" from the backs of African Americans (p. 119).

African Americans often followed this advice and engaged in cooperative economic practice throughout our history (see especially Woods 1998, and Reynolds 2001). According to Clyde Woods:

> Generation after generation, ethnic and class alliances arose in the [Delta] region with the aim of expanding social and economic democracy, only to be ignored, dismissed, and defeated. These defeats were followed by arrogant attempts to purge such heroic movements from both historical texts and popular memory. Yet even in defeat these movements transformed the policies of the plantation bloc and informed daily life, community-building activities, and subsequent movements (Woods 1998: 4).

African American Cooperatives in the South

The South was well represented in the African American cooperative Movement. The Colored Farmers' National Alliance and Cooperative Union officially started in Texas in 1886, and grew to establish chapters in every state in the South. By 1891 the CFNACU become the largest African American organization in its time with an estimated 1 million members or more (Gordon Nembhard 2014, 55). The first African American association to demand reparations, National Ex-Slave Mutual Relief, Bounty and Pension Association, was founded in 1896 in Tennessee as a mutual aid society (Berry 2005, Gordon Nembhard 2014). The Colored Merchants Association, a marketing cooperative of independent African American grocery store owners, is founded in Montgomery Alabama in 1925. Chapters of the Young Negroes' Co-operative League, co-founded by George Schuyler and Ella Jo Baker in 1930 and headquartered in New York City, were organized across the country, including New Orleans, Columbia SC, Portsmouth VA, and Washington, DC (Gordon Nembhard 2014, 116).

After the Civil War, Blacks in Baltimore, Maryland, turned to cooperation to try to improve their lot in life. One cooperative was formed in 1865 to hire Black shipyard workers and stevedores. White workers in the shipyards agitated to get free Blacks fired, and so they formed their own shipyard, the Chesapeake Marine Railway and Dry Dock Company, which operated successfully for 18 years, until the owner of the land used by the shipyard doubled the rent (Du Bois 1907, Gordon Nembhard 2014).

In August 1918, a "Mr. Ruddy" returned home to Memphis, after attending a meeting of the Negro Cooperative Guild called by Du Bois to discuss ways to spread the adoption of cooperatives among African Americans, and organized a study group (The Editor, 1919). In February 1919, the group incorporated as the Citizens' Co-operative Stores to operate cooperative meat markets. They raised more equity than expected, selling double the amount of the original shares they offered. By August 1919, five stores were in operation serving about 75,000 people. The members of the local guilds associated with each store met monthly to study cooperatives and discuss any issues. The Citizen Cooperative Stores planned to own their own buildings and a cooperative warehouse. The editor of the *Crisis Magazine* (presumably Du Bois himself) who reported this, notes that: "Colored people are furnishing their own with work and money for services received and the recipients are handing the money back for re-distribution to the original colored sources" (The Editor, 1919: 50).

The Commercial Department of the Bluefield Colored Institute in Bluefield, West Virginia, formed a student cooperative store probably in 1925 (Sims, 1925). The store's mission was to sell supplies the students and school needed and be a "commercial laboratory for the application of business theory and practice" (Sims: 93). A share of stock sold in the Co-operative Society for less than $1. After two years in business the cooperative paid all its debts and owned its own equipment and inventories (Matney, 1927). The store began to pay dividends of ten percent on purchases made. The student members voted to use profits to pay for scholarships to the Secondary School and Junior College (see Sims, 1925, and Matney, 1927). Members of this cooperative were the first African Americans to attend the National Cooperative Congress, when they attended the one in Minneapolis in 1926 (Matney). They had became members of the Co-operative League of America in 1925.

There was extensive cooperative activity among African Americans in rural areas of the state of North Carolina in the 1930s and 40s anchored by Bricks Rural Life School and Tyrrell County Training School. These schools sponsored cooperative economics education and developed co-ops that joined together to organize the Eastern Carolina Council Federation of North Carolinian Cooperatives (Pitts 1950). Pitts documents that as interest increased among Blacks in North Carolina about cooperatives speakers from the Bricks and Tyrrell co-ops were asked to speak (Pitts 1950: 31). Efforts by the Eastern Carolina Council eventually led to the establishment of the North Carolina Council for Credit Unions and Associates (shortened to the North Carolina Council). The North Carolina Council, describing it as an organization of credit unions and cooperatives operated by Negroes to promote new credit unions and other cooperatives throughout North Carolina and to aid existing credit unions and cooperatives (Rosenberg 1950, 182). As a result of this activity to promote, develop and support credit unions and cooperatives among African Americans in North Carolina the number of credit unions and cooperatives among Negroes increased dramatically. According to Pitts (1950), in 1936 there were three Black credit unions in the state, and by 1948 there were 98, and 48 additional cooperative enterprises: nine consumer stores, 32 machinery co-ops, four curb markets, two health associations and one housing project (35). (From Gordon Nembhard 2014.)

The 1964-65 Black voter registration drives and the Selma to Montgomery "March for Freedom" contributed to the formation of the South West Alabama Farmers' Cooperative Association (Reynolds 2002: 12). The SWAFCA was formed in 1967 by a group of African American farmers whose families had farmed the same land for more than two centuries. The goal was to keep Black farmers and former sharecroppers in the region, on their land (de Jong 2005: 399). The means was to diversify their crops, create a marketing cooperative, and at the same time advocate for their political rights (Reynolds 2002; and de Jong 2005). The co-op was able to secure federal funding which allowed it to expand. Within a few years the SWAFCA included 1800 families, making it the largest agricultural co-op in the South.

In the first year the cooperative Association had saved its members an average of $2.00 per ton on fertilizer and to sell their crops for a total of $52,000 (de Jong 2005: 400). The SWAFCA worked with the Farmers Home Administration (similar to what Freedom Farm did in Mississippi) to help their members qualify for mortgages and loans (de Jong 2005). While the organization achieved significant marketing successes, despite white opposition, there were challenges with its management, cooperative education program, and access to markets (Reynolds 2002: 12). Overall, the cooperative increased members' economic security by working with them to reduce operating costs, encourage diversification, and raise incomes (de Jong 2005). Originally eight of the families were white. But harassment by racist politicians and businessmen; banks and suppliers refused to deal with them until the whites withdrew (Curl 1980).

Poor People's Corporation, Jackson MS was organized in 1965 in Jackson, Mississippi, by a former field worker of SNCC. Within four years they were running thirteen producer cooperatives and a marketing co-op, producing sewing, leather-and wood-crafts and candles. They had over 800 members, mostly former sharecroppers (Curl 1980, 45).

Freedom Quilting Bee was established in 1967, in Alberta, Alabama, to help share cropping families earn independent income. Some of the women in Alberta and Gees Bend, Alabama, came together to produce and sell quilts. In a few years they made enough money to buy land and build a sewing factory. They also provided day care and after school services (for members' children and others). The cooperative was a founding member of the Federation of Southern Cooperatives and is an example of women's leadership and control over their own work conditions and company; as well as an example of community solidarity in terms of the ways this cooperative supported and helped its community and members in its community. (See Gordon Nembhard 2014, 161-162.)

Federation of Southern Cooperatives

Founded in 1967 by Civil Rights groups to consolidate co-op development in the South, the Federation of Southern Cooperatives is a not-for-profit organization of state associations that promotes cooperative economic development as a strategy (and philosophy) to support and sustain Black farmer ownership and control, economic viability of farm businesses—especially small, sustainable and organic farming—and stewardship of Black land and natural resources in rural low-income communities in the Southern United States. After merging with the Land Emergency Fund in 1985, the organization became The Federation of Southern Cooperatives/Land Assistance Fund (FSC/LAF). FSC/LAF is a network of rural cooperatives, credit unions, and state associations of cooperatives and cooperative development centers in the southern United States. The FSC/LAF provides technical assistance, legal assistance, financial support, education and advocacy for its members and low-income populations in the south. In addition, the organization promotes and supports policy changes and legislation favorable to small farmers and low-income rural populations. In its almost 50 years in existence, the organization has helped to create and/or support more than 200 cooperatives and credit unions mostly in the seven states where is has state offices. Examples of cooperatives in the Federation are: Freedom Quilting Bee, North Bolivar County Farm Cooperative, Panola Land Buyers Association, and Shreveport Credit Union. The Federation owns and runs a rural training and research center that showcases sustainable forestry, provides co-op education, and helps to develop Black youth-run co-ops. The FSC/LAF also engages in cooperative development in Africa and the Caribbean. The organization has an important reach throughout the south, is connected to the larger U.S. cooperative movement, and has successfully advocated for important measures in U.S. farm bills to support Black farmers, Black land ownership, and Black co-op development.

Fannie Lou Hamer moved from advocating for voting rights to advocating for and creating cooperatives in her home county in Mississippi in the late 1960s and early 1970s. She began by working with Dorothy Height and the National Council of Negro Women in 1967 to establish a "pig banking" program in Sunflower County, MS, to help women farmers put meat on their tables and earn some extra income. She then raised money to buy a farm, and then more land. Hamer biographer Lee (2000, 147) summarizes that:

> "In 1969 Hamer laid the groundwork for an elaborate project to make poor folks economically self-sufficient. That project became the Freedom Farm Corporation. Through her work with the farm, Hamer broadened the meaning of civil rights activism to include addressing the economic needs of Black poor folks. Freedom Farm was to institutionalize a structure and process for low-income and destitute rural people (Black and white at first, and then with a focus on women and Blacks)

to feed themselves, own their own homes, farm cooperatively, and create small businesses together in order to support a sustainable food system, land ownership, and economic independence (which would allow for political independence)."

Hamer (1971) argued that "Cooperative ownership of land opens the door to many opportunities for group development of economic enterprises which develop the total community rather than create monopolies that monopolize the resources of a community." She had found that voting rights were not enough. White racists use economic retaliation, fire people from their jobs and/or evict people from sharecropping or housing for their civil rights activities. Without economic independence—owning our own land, growing our own food, owning our own homes- we can't gain political independence. Cooperative ownership allows a people to control their own economy and protect people from economic retaliation.

John Lewis, past president of the Student Nonviolent Coordinating Committee, former organizer for the Southern Regional Council's Community Organizing Project, and currently a member of the U.S. House of Representatives for Georgia, provides a similar analysis in his autobiography. "The civil rights movement was old news," with press coverage moving North to cover the Black Panthers, riots, campus unrest, and the Vietnam War, according to Lewis, when he started organizing in Alabama in the mid 1960s. People could vote, but did not have enough to eat. "My job was about helping these people join together, helping them help one another to fill those needs. It was about showing people how to pool what money they had to form a bank of their own, a credit union. Or how to band together to buy groceries, or feed, or seed, in bulk amounts at low prices – how to form cooperatives" (Lewis 1998: 399). John Lewis' main focus then was to establish "cooperatives, credit unions and community development groups" throughout the Deep South.

More recently two movements are of note: *Us Lifting Us*, and the *Southern Grassroots Economies Project*.

Us Lifting Us Economic Development Cooperative, LLC, describes itself as a "global economic enterprise designed to change the paradigm of how we do business with and among ourselves and with others." They aim to provide practical business models that "give us the capacity to gain significant control of the economics of our communities and to free us from the current state of economic exploitation by multiple forces in the world."[4] They practice Black Power cooperative economics in order to build a successful independent Black economy. The ULU Ten-Point Plan is listed as follows:

1) As Black People we take full responsibility for the economic destiny of our communities and nations.
2) Black persons and Black institutions (especially the Black Church) join together as Members in a large-scale Cooperatively Owned Business Enterprise to pool our resources.

3) This Cooperatively Owned Business Enterprise is reflective of our unique culture and interest in the world.

4) The governance and legal form of the Cooperative accommodate democratic principles; one member, one vote, with elected leadership.

5) Only members of the Cooperative (and not the public) have the opportunity to secure ownership units (equity) in the Business Enterprise, with the potential to amass billions of dollars for community development.

6) The Cooperative focuses on opening and operating businesses in local communities that (1) provide needed goods and services, (2) create new jobs, (3) stimulate additional business activity and (4) yield a fair profit.

7) The Cooperative is driven to duplicate and expand into hundreds and eventually thousands of businesses, all owned and controlled by the collective.

8) The net profits from overall Cooperative success are used to (1) reinvest, (2) for the distribution of grants and endowments and (3) direct returns (dividends) to Member/Owners of the Cooperative.

9) The large-scale cooperatively owned (group owned) Business Enterprise functions as a catalyst and central element in building and sustaining the new Black Economy; one that gives Power to our People.

10) Us Lifting Us Economic Development Cooperative, LLC serves as the aforementioned model.[5] .

The Southern Grassroots Economies Project

The Southern Grassroots Economies Project (*SGEP*) (http://sgeproject.org/about/) is building networks across the US South to promote and launch sustainable cooperative economies. Our work is inspired by the rich history of social justice struggle in the South and looks to the example of the worker-owned cooperatives of Mondragon, Spain, and Emilia Ramagno, Italy, for guidance. We are an association of southern organizations and national affiliate members: The Federation of Southern Cooperatives, The Fund for Democratic Communities, Highlander Research and Education Center, Cooperation Texas, Cooperation Jackson, Farmworker Association of Florida, with the U.S. Federation of Worker Cooperatives, Grassroots Economic Organizing (Ecological Democracy Institute of North America), and Working World. SGEP focus its work in three areas: education with the annual CoopEcon training conferences; policy analysis and development, and a loan fund.

The Southern Reparations Loan Fund (SRLF), a project of the Southern Grassroots Economies Project (SGEP), makes business loans to cooperatively owned businesses anchored in the most marginalized Southern communities. We especially focus our lending toward start-ups and expansions of democratically governed enterprises that meet the needs and elevate the quality of life of African Americans, immigrants, and poor whites. Our goal is to nurture the development of businesses that maximize community benefit, rather than the narrow concept of maximizing profit. The concept of reparations is at the heart of SRLF's mission: SRLF moves capital stemming from an economy rooted in extraction, exploitation, slavery, and land grabs to build Southern enterprises that are owned and democratically controlled by the very communities from which the wealth was stolen in the first place.

As part of of our commitment to the most marginalized communities, we target our lending to projects that other lenders might consider "un-bankable," because they are too small, not adequately collateralized, or, though profitable, not "profitable enough." Operating from a principle of "radical inclusivity," SRLF is interested in projects that are based on sound business ideas that meet real community needs, businesses built by people who know how to work together to get good things accomplished—regardless of their individual "credit-worthiness." If SRLF does its job according to its mission, the vast majority of our loans will go to poor people who have a direct personal and community-wide stake in building an inclusive economy that is democratic, just, and sustainable.

Concluding Remarks

In sum, African Americans have used cooperative economics for survival, but also to gain economic independence. African American cooperatives throughout history have provided livelihoods, land ownership, home ownership, savings opportunities, and other mechanisms for economic independence for their members—even if modest. Many of the cooperative businesses emerging in health care, child care and temporary services, for example, are leading their sectors in changing the nature of work and increasing the returns to such work and ownership—for African Americans, women, and youth.

They address market failure and racial discrimination. Cooperative businesses stabilize communities because they are community-based and locally owned. They distribute, recycle, and multiply all kinds of local resources, capital and expertise within a community. Co-op members pool limited resources to achieve collective goals. Co-ops generate income, and jobs, and accumulate assets; provide affordable, quality goods and services; and develop human and social capital, as well as economic independence for their members. In addition, co-op enterprises and their members pay taxes, and are good citizens by giving donations to their communities, paying their employees fairly, and using sustainable practices. (See also Gordon Nembhard 2013)

Cooperatives have longevity. Cooperative businesses have lower failure rates and higher survival rates than traditional corporations and small businesses, after the first year of startup, and after 5 years in business (Williams 2007). In addition, evidence shows that cooperatives both successfully address the effects of crises and survive crises better than other types of enterprises (Borzaga and Calera 2012, 7). Cooperatives enable their members to stabilize and increase their incomes, and to accumulate assets. Cooperatives also provide more stable employment levels than investor-owned firms which tend to adjust employment levels, in contrast to worker cooperatives that adjust pay or compensation to safeguard employment (Borzaga and Calera 2012, 9). As local businesses, cooperatives increase community economic development and sustainability, and recirculate resources. Cooperatives provide economic benefits but also social and health benefits. Cooperative ownership enables affordable housing and worker ownership. Cooperative enterprise ownership also enhances community relationships (community-business partnerships), well-being, leadership development, and women's and youth development.

References

Carlo Borzaga and Giulia Galera. 2012. *Promoting the Understanding of Cooperatives for a better world*. Summary, proceedings of "Promoting the Understanding of Cooperatives for a Better World" conference, sponsored by Euricse and International Cooperative Alliance, March 15 and 16, 2012, Venice Italy. September 28, Euricse. Retrieved from http://ica.coop/sites/default/files/media_items/Report_Venice2012_PRINT.pdf.

Cohen, Lizabeth. 2003. *A Consumers' Republic; The Politics of Mass Consumption in Postwar America*. New York: Alfred A. Knopf.

Du Bois, W.E.B. 1933b. "The Right to Work." *Crisis*, 40 (April 1933): 93–94. Reprinted in *W. E. B. Du Bois: Writings*, ed. Nathan Huggins, New York: Library of America, 1986, 1237.

Gordon Nembhard, Jessica. 2014. "White Paper: Benefits and Impacts of Cooperatives." With factsheet, executive summary and tables. *The Center on Race and Wealth*, Howard University, February.

Gordon Nembhard, Jessica. 2014. *Collective Courage: A History of African American Cooperative Economic Thought and Practice*. University Park, PA: Pennsylvania State University Press.

Hamer, Fannie Lou. 1971. "If the Name of the Game Is Survive, Survive." Speech given in Ruleville, Mississippi, September 27, 1971. Fannie Lou Hamer Collection, box 1, folder 1, Tougaloo College Civil Rights Collection T/012, Mississippi Department of Archives and History, Jackson.

Williams, Richard C. 2007. *The Cooperative Movement: Globalization from Below*. London: Ashgate Publishing Group.

Notes

1. This essay is based on Gordon Nembhard *Collective Courage 2014* and Gordon Nembhard *Cooperative Ownership in the Struggle for African American Economic Empowerment*. 2008

2. See in particular Du Bois 1907, 1933a, 1933b, and 1975; Joseph DeMarco 1974 and 1983; Haynes 1999; Haynes and Gordon Nembhard 1999; and Nembhard 2014.

3. At a Brotherhood of Sleeping Car Porters' Consumers Cooperative Buying Club rally, in Chicago in 1944. Quoted in Cohen, 2003, 49.

4. http://www.usliftingus.com/#!ulu-homepage/mainPage

5. http://media.wix.com/ugd/abf0d9_a7326989f2f844c1bce8e48070b09a95.pdf

15.

The Challenge of Building Urban Cooperatives in the South

Elandria Williams and Jazmine Walker

Jackson, Mississippi, is a city that sits in the Black belt south in the poorest state in the United States. Jackson has also some of the richest history in resistance and self-determination in the country and in the world. The city has also key institutions such as two Historically Black Colleges and Universities (one private and one public), and organizations of struggle that have been around since the 1950s. There are long-established cooperative enterprises in Mississippi that are supported by the Federation of Southern Co-operatives/ Land Assistance Fund and even cooperatives in Jackson that have been going on since the 1980s. Co-operation Jackson however is trying to accomplish what no institution or network of cooperative enterprises has done before which is to create an ecosystem of worker-owned cooperatives in an urban area of the Southern United States. This chapter sets the context for what Co-operation Jackson is aiming to do as well as laying out the challenges of building urban-based cooperatives in the South.

We will focus on four main areas of analysis. First, we use a loose definition of cooperatives that includes and incorporates worker owned enterprises that may or may not be legally incorporated. Secondly, we will focus primarily on Black or Afrikan led cooperatives. Thirdly, we view cooperative enterprises as political projects that live up to cooperative values. Finally, we will consider how 'urban' and 'cities' are to be defined.

There are many different ways of looking at urban centers in the South. The US South is made up of rural areas, small towns, mid-size urban centers and mega-cities. When we talk about cities or urban areas in the South, what comes to mind are places such as Atlanta, Miami, Charlotte, Birmingham, Jacksonville, Nashville, Dallas and a few others. However, all of these cities are between two to five-times the size of Jackson, and if one includes the panhandle of Texas that balloons to 12 times the size of the population. For that reason, we are going to discuss primarily midsize urban centers of between 100,000-200,000 people, which are the category in which Jackson falls. In addition, here we will focus on cities and urban areas with populations of less than 200,000 people which are at least 30% Black. Jackson, MS, is over 80%

Black.[1] There are only four other cities in the US South that have majority Black populations with a total population of between 100,000-200,000 people: Mobile, Alabama; Savannah, Georgia; and Shreveport, Louisiana.

The vast majority of cooperatives in the South are rural cooperatives that have formed to provide public utilities, financial or agricultural services. Utility cooperatives, especially electrical cooperatives, were created in the Great Depression by the Tennessee Valley Authority and, with the exception of Santee Electric Co-operative in South Carolina, almost all of the leadership is white and these institutions are mostly ran undemocratically. Producer cooperatives in the south range in size from four to five small growers to large producer and marketing cooperatives such as Florida's Natural Orange Juice. The latter began in the 1930s along with many other agricultural cooperatives in order to have greater control of the market and to compete effectively. Almost all of these cooperatives however did not allow Black and other people of color to become members. The only other cooperatives that have been around since in the 1930s are credit unions, which were also started by the Tennessee Valley Authority to support their workers in saving money. These rural cooperatives were started as initiatives to bring economic development to rural areas of the South and in many ways they worked hand in hand with the power elite. Most of the Black cooperatives started before 1965 were also rural, with only a small fraction being formed in urban centers with majority Black populations.

History of Urban Co-operatives in the South

While most of this article is about the current conditions and challenges of starting and sustaining urban cooperatives in the South, it is important to consider the history of cooperatives for two main reasons. First, the majority of cooperatives in the South that have survived have been in rural areas. Secondly, they were formed between the 1930s-1970s out of a political project that built economic power even if politics was not at the forefront. That has had an impact in terms of the politics and longevity of some of the cooperatives; however, many are still hanging on by a thread.

Co-operatives were needed originally for similar reasons as today: because people in urban areas needed ways to survive and be connected differently than working on a farm or sharecropping. Many families that left rural areas together went to the city to support one another. Support systems such as mutual aid societies grew out of this same need. Black urban cooperatives confronted multiple challenges from white businesses, which did not want Black businesses to succeed. As a result, most Black urban cooperatives remained strictly in the heart of the Black community. There were housing, consumer, producer, and other types of cooperatives such as the Black Co-operative Villages near Birmingham, Alabama, in the 1880s; Colored Farmer's Alliance Co-operative Stores/Exchanges in Charleston, Mobile, New Orleans, and Houston; Citizens'

Co-operative Stores in Memphis, Tennessee; Colored Merchants Society in Montgomery, Alabama; and Young Negroes' Co-operative League in Columbia, South Carolina and New Orleans, Louisiana.[2]

There have historically been cooperatives in Jackson, MS: two notable examples are the Poor Peoples Corporation (PPC) and the Brown-Tougaloo Exchange. The first was formed in 1965 by Student Nonviolent Coordinating Committee (SNCC) activist Jesse Morris and other SNCC and Delta Ministry members. The corporation was based in Jackson and intended *"to assist low-income groups to initiate and sustain self-help projects of a cooperative nature."* Membership was open to all poor people regardless of race. The PPC created a common fund and gave out seed money for new cooperatives and small businesses. Co-operative and small businesses training and marketing were provided as services. All members had to pay dues of 25 cents per year and members voted on decisions using a democratic process. The initial pot of money was $5,000 that was mostly donated by northern donors. The cooperatives and partners manufactured clothing, quilts and craft items. There were 16 PPC enterprises in 10 counties of Mississippi, and Liberty House stores in Jackson, New York, Boston and other cities that sold the goods.[3]

The 1964 Brown-Tougaloo Co-operative Exchange was started to increase Tougaloo's available academic and financial resources. Other colleges in the North and West started similar programs with Historically Black Colleges and Universities. These exchanges both supported funding but also laid the groundwork for students from the north and west coast to come south to support the civil rights movements of the day. The exchange paved the way for Title III, a federal funding program, which increased the amount of financial resources to Historically Black Colleges and Universities. Title III is still the most important funding program for education, federally.[4]

Challenges

Black workers and communities creating and sustaining cooperatives face numerous challenges. Many of these challenges mirror the challenges that confront nearly all Black businesses. Historically, Black urban businesses confronted pressure institutional racism, intimidation from the white business community and by white mobs.

Further, every business and cooperative operating within the capitalist system has to operate as a profit-making enterprise. Access to capital is therefore a necessity, and most poor people do not have funds or collateral to spare. Southern banks refused to give loans to Blacks and most commercial suppliers refused to extend credit that was routinely granted to white-owned businesses. Even federal government agencies that were supposed to give financial support routinely did not and, when they did, they refused to extend credit to cooperatives, whether in rural or urban areas. The credit was extended to white cooperatives and so the only money that most of these cooperatives were able to receive came from movement supporters in the North.

A key challenge that cooperatives faced historically is probably the most important one for us today: the skills, discipline, and techniques that work for registering voters and mounting protests are different from those required by a commercial endeavour and business training is hard to come by. So is mutual trust and confidence among co-op members who have often been competitors for scarce jobs and resources. Nevertheless, some co-ops manage to survive for a time, but those successes only illustrate the depth of the problem because the few members they are able to help are but a tiny fraction of those being dispossessed from their homes and livelihoods. Over the long haul, some of the farm-based co-ops manage to find corporate customers for their crops and continue into the '70s, '80s or longer. But most of the co-ops dependent on federal assistance or northern liberals for capital and marketing ultimately fail as funding is diverted to the Vietnam War and shifting political winds redirect social consciences towards other causes.[5]

It is important to note is that cooperatives in Jackson as well as in many other parts of the South could not survive without donors and support from the North, especially white people in the North. A similar model exists today in the form of grants or gift capital and this, oftentimes, is not a sustainable long-term practice.

Why cooperatives are needed now in urban areas

Creating cooperatives and building towards the Solidarity Economy is something we have to do because there is nowhere to go to the grocery store, to get a loan that doesn't take advantage of you for generations to come, and no place to get health care. Our communities and families have a legacy of making do and trying to figure out how to survive in these circumstances. Co-operative businesses have been created as a response to the failure of existing institutions to adequately meet the needs of the people. This form of businesses also helps people get together, entrepreneurially, with their values at the center alongside creating solutions to the repressions we are under as well.[6] The neoliberal capitalist and politically undemocratic system and world we are in requires a different way for our communities and enterprises to make it. This society is not set up for them to be successful.

Mississippi has the highest unemployment rate in the United States. Jackson's "official" unemployment rate is over 5.6% and the underemployment rate is much higher.[7] As a result, many people have opted out of the "mainstream" or formal economy. There is a tremendous amount of underground or Black people economies that happens out of necessity. Baba Chokwe Lumumba taught many comrades in Jackson that people are just waiting to be organized. People in Jackson are waiting for more cooperative models because there is this sense that "this is just how it is, this is just hopeless". Thus many have opted out and continue to not participate except as consumers in this mainstream economy.

The ideas that Baba Chokwe Lumumba articulated and what he was trying to do represented what could be and how this could be different. Jackson, like so many southern towns, has been impacted by a sustained brain drain. Many of the people doing good work in Jackson who have chosen to believe in Jackson are originally from outside the city. Such models are important to help encourage young people who are from Jackson to return or stay home to help support the creation of a different economy and a different city. There is growing interest in the concepts behind the cooperative economy, but many do not yet have direct experience of it.

Successful Co-ops in Urban Areas now

There are some successful cooperatives currently in urban areas in the South. It is important to analyze what has helped them become successful. This helps to better understand why other cooperatives have been hard to take off. Determining what is keeping the cooperative movement and cooperative enterprises from developing in urban areas of the South and especially in majority Afrikan or Black cities is essential. We are going to look at successful cooperatives in three mega cities, three midsize cities, and ones currently operating in Jackson, MS.

The three-mega cities in the South we consider are: Atlanta, Georgia; Birmingham, Alabama; and New Orleans, Louisiana. All of them have numerous credit unions and insurance companies but few that support low-income communities in these urban areas.

In Atlanta there are 11 cooperatives: Atlanta Homeschool Co-operative; Sevananda Natural Foods Market; a Housing co-op that was converted from traditional apartments; Southwest Atlanta Growers Co-operative; Partners Co-operative—hospital shared services cooperative; Sopo Bicycle co-op; Urban Recipe; Oakhurst Co-operative Preschool; and Us Lifting Us co-op marketplace and co-op network. Even though these co-ops were started in Atlanta, GA, white people started them all, except for Us Lifting Us. They are a mixture of producer cooperatives, housing cooperatives and consumer cooperatives. Us Lifting Us is the only one that is in the development stage and is working to develop a network of cooperatives.

Birmingham has a similar story: out of the ten cooperatives, there are only two Black-led cooperatives. The ten cooperatives are: Alabama Farmers Co-operative; Bici Co-op; Mannamarket organic food co-op; Central Alabama Electric Co-op; Alabama Homeschool Co-operative; Wandering Yoga Co-operative; Genius Co-op; National Housing Co-operative — solar powered home ownership; Artists Incorporated — an artists' cooperative; Magic City Agricultural Project and Black Star Academy.[8] All of the cooperatives, except for Artists Incorporated and Wandering Yoga Co-operative, are consumer, producer, or housing cooperatives. Artists Incorporated and Wandering Yoga are both worker cooperatives. Artists Incorporated has its own space, while Wandering Yoga members do not have a studio. Magic City Agricultural Project is the only one that is working on developing multiple cooperatives together with the Community Land Trust and others to support the Black community in Birmingham.

In New Orleans there are six readily accessible cooperatives and one cooperative development center that is in formation. These are: New Orleans Food Co-op; Veggie Farmers' Co-operative—a mostly Vietnamese farmers co-op in East New Orleans; New Orleans Co-operative Development Project—cooperative start-up and development of worker-owned cooperative business; New Orleans Scooter cooperative; New Orleans Co-operative Housing for university students; and Our School at Blair Grocery working to end hunger and engage high school and college students in service learning.[9] A similar story is evident in New Orleans with only consumer, producer and housing cooperatives. There is a worker development center that is forming but no worker cooperatives as such. The only cooperative that is majority people of color is Veggie Farmer's Co-operative and although it is located in a city it is based on the bayou for fishermen and farmers.

Midsize cities

There are only three other mid-size cities that are majority Black. All of these cities have credit unions whose primary focus is not in alignment with the development of the Black community.

- Mobile, Alabama, has two cooperatives: Alabama Farmers Co, and Evergreen Homeschooling Co-op.

- Savannah, Georgia, has four cooperatives: the Savannah Food Co-op, the Savannah Climbing Co-op, a Montessori Preschool, the Savannah Wedding Co-op, which is a worker cooperative unlike all the other cooperatives in Savannah.

- Shreveport, Louisiana, has two cooperatives and a community development credit union: a farmers cooperative; an electric cooperative and the Shreveport Federal Credit Union whose mission it is to support low income residents. It was started by the Black community to support the Black community.

Current day urban co-ops in Jackson

Currently in Jackson, MS, there are six cooperatives and one cooperative development center that support all of Mississippi.

The Mississippi Association of Co-operatives started out of the Federation of Southern Co-operatives and primarily supports the rural cooperatives of Mississippi but also helps the cooperatives in Jackson when necessary. The other cooperatives in Jackson were created after 1980. These are: the Rainbow Food Co-operative, Hope Credit Union, Stewpot, Computer Co-op, ACE Hardware Store, and Nationwide Insurance. All of these cooperatives are currently consumer or financial cooperatives although the Computer Co-op is currently in the process of shifting over to worker and investor ownership. The Mississippi Association of Cooperatives and Hope Credit Union are the only apex cooperative organization and coooperative, respectively, that were started by Black people to serve the mainly low-income Black communities of Jackson and Mississippi.

Reasons for Success

The success of urban cooperatives is to a large extent dependent on who is involved in starting them.

First, most cooperatives that are in these cities are producer, consumer, housing, and financial cooperatives. The producer and consumer cooperatives are focused on food either as restaurants or grocery cooperatives. The housing cooperatives are generally for college students or are focused on converting housing that are not for low-income communities. The financial cooperatives, whether they are insurance or credit unions, are generally larger credit unions or insurance companies. There are only a few Community Development Credit Unions that have been started to support low-income communities in the South.

Secondly, although there are cooperatives that support Black people there are only a few that have been designed and created by Black people for Black people or by communities of color as in New Orleans. White or majority white people who have easier access to credit through banks, investors, friends and government have established the majority of cooperatives that have survived. Many of these don't have to deal with the pressures of police harassment, poor schooling and other problems that poorer Black communities have to face. And they are often not involved in trying to build large-scale cooperative networks and cooperative development centers at the same time.

For urban cooperatives that are relevant and realistic for low-income communities, and especially low-income Black communities, they have to be both a political project and an economic one at the same time. The cooperatives have to be willing to do education in terms of cooperative values, business skills and collective ways of operating. They also need to be based on need and analysis of the city and what people are willing to do and create. Even though the challenges are great, and what is at stake sometimes appears to be almost unreachable, it is important for cooperatives to be established and run by and for the community. A combination of local and outside support both financial and otherwise is necessary, but without creating dependence.

Challenges or Must-Haves

Urban cooperatives must first deal with the challenge or necessity of building community in cities where community does not exist or where community is not strong owing to people moving in an out, or because they have been weakened intentionally in order to enable gentrification, or where communal spirit is low.

Co-operatives have to figure out a way to support the members while building the cooperative. Often, members are struggling to figure out a way to survive because, unlike in rural areas, there is no robust family support, rent/mortgages tend to be high, and many face difficulties in being able to grow easily accessible food to reduce their living expenses.

Another challenge is that many would-be members do not have the skills and financing necessary to start the cooperatives. In urban areas, prices for space and equipment are much higher—which means that financing needs are at a premium. A critical question is how to draw on the skills that people in urban areas have to propel cooperatives and cooperative development.

Urban co-ops are hard to grow in many ways because it is harder to build community. You are pushing against a variety of challenges: individualism, access to resources to buy materials, pressures arising from needing to have an income to survive, pressures of gentrification of the neighborhoods, and so on. When people are saying 'I don't have a home', 'my school is terrible', and 'I don't know where I am going to have enough to pay my bills and eat', the challenge of building cooperatives can be immense. The decks are stacked against people in communities because everything is coming against people at the same time. In order to sow co-ops people have to be willing not to get paid for a period of time: you can't make a large amount of money from the beginning even though people need money now. This is one reason that it is harder to start urban co-ops. In a rural space you can make money stretch farther because things are cheaper.

Jackson is a small to medium size city that for many people is economically depressed and so although money can go farther here, the challenges listed above are nevertheless substantial. These practical challenges as well as the need for strength, perseverance and imagination are all needed. This is mitigated if the urban community is smaller and everyone has lived there for much of their lives. However, most co-ops were built out of community struggle and the people who lived through these struggles don't always share the stories and history that cemented the relationships of the cooperatives founders. So, many second-generation cooperators are left to put the pieces together in order to sustain community. Those pieces do not often tell of the struggle of young people and the economic struggle is often totally left out. That economic struggle in urban areas of the South today is not that different from what was going on in the 1930s or the 1960s; just some of the players have gone underground or have changed stripes.

In urban areas it is harder to know your neighbor. Gentrification has multiple impacts, breaking up community and dissolving long-term connections. Gentrification also skews the amount of wealth that impacts which cooperatives, especially consumer cooperatives, end up in the area. This is why there are debates currently in the consumer cooperative movement about the role of cooperatives in the gentrification process. Gentrification is just one problem that causes harm to urban cooperatives forming as it relates to community. Key to cooperatives working and especially urban cooperatives is that you must have true solidarity within the group. It is important for the cooperative to be agile and on its feet. And critically you need the trust of the people who are co-owners or workers with you.

Every business, especially urban ones, all need staffing in some way, volunteer and paid, and all need some sort of investment. Co-operative businesses are no different. In the urban areas of the South, especially in the poor majority Black cities, there is no paid or part time technical staff or capital investment initially, which is in large part needed for these cooperatives to grow. For poor urban communities, you almost need someone to be able to quit their day job to focus on it and we don't have anyone with the technical know-how or freedom to do that. There is no technical assistance provider in our area and sometimes we are also are not linked up to the right people. Our communities need to see something tangible. Even for those people who are directly involved in cooperative building, most have not had previous experiences of cooperatives. It is important, therefore, to have a pilot co-op in our city, especially for community members who cannot leave the city.

Richard Rice in a personal interview said:

> "That is why we at Magic City Co-operative are putting all of our efforts towards that and we need one to legitimize our efforts. Getting people to buy into the idea because we don't have anything tangible on the ground. Farmer and consumer co-ops are the example and people have a hard time seeing how that translates to a worker cooperative."[10]

Creating a business that is sustainable is hard under any climate or situation even if you have technical assistance providers and the initial capital investment. One of the reasons why it is still hard to create urban co-ops is because they can be easily destroyed if the members and community are not vigilant. The leadership of the co-op can be distracted by petty arguments about financing and other issues. Prices can be increased and there can be no way around this. In an interview with Hollis Watkins he remarked that when he was younger,

> "If the price of bricks went up people just made their own bricks and if the price of concrete went up people just made their own concrete. One of the fondest memories of my Auntie Pearl is that when a brick would come off of her house of other houses on the family land she would gather the young people around and make us re-brick the houses that needed to be fixed alongside her." [11].

Owing to redlining, and the policies and practices of tearing down low-income homes and instead replacing them with housing projects, most people do not know how to survive and create their own businesses. We still have hair shops, cafes, and other traditional shops but on a large scale many of those skills and places are gone.

We are also living in a time where we are further removed from those raised in rural areas, which is why the creation of urban community gardens has become so important. In the 1960s, people would have just grown food in their yard and would have shared the harvest with each other. Today, most people don't have the space to do that.

One of the opportunities and challenges that was shared from the 1960s was about grant money being used to fund cooperative development or relying on Brown University to help get funding for Tougoloo. This challenge and opportunity around resources, especially financial, is no different today for Southern urban cooperatives. There is a large federal grant that supports rural cooperative development but nothing that compares to this for urban cooperatives. Most of the small business administration centers have very little knowledge about cooperatives, and what they do know is heavily weighted to agricultural or producer or marketing cooperatives. In most southern states, except for Alabama and Texas, non-agricultural and non-financial cooperatives are not legally sanctioned or provided for in legislation. And even if they do, anyone who is undocumented cannot access it.

Urban cooperatives ought to have members with cooperative values, a mentality of collaboration and trust within the group. Individual entrepreneurs often want their idea to produce results immediately, but it takes patience for people to work together and make a cooperative work. The group needs perseverance along with technical training and trust. For Black people, and in general for all people, trust has to be there. The relationship building has to happen, you still have to come sweep and do whatever is necessary for the cooperative to thrive. Everyone has to do the entire range of jobs – small to big tasks.

One of the main challenges in urban areas and potentially all areas of economic depression, but, especially in urban ones, is how do you honor the business models that people have been using to survive? The biggest growing cooperatives in urban areas are landscaping, mechanic shops, cafés, hair shops, bicycles, etc. because those are the jobs that people know how to do. In order for these, often small, enterprises to grow they need to create new co-ops or the existing co-ops need to get larger. It will take investment that is often hard to find. It is for this reason that the revolving or reparations loan funds are critical.

The biggest question or debate that we have to engage is what degree of balance are we comfortable with between institutionalized vs. non-institutionalized economies? That is the important question because everyone is engaged with the economy as both producers and consumers it is just a matter of what you are producing. So one of the challenges we are facing in urban communities is how does everyone produce and consume based on a value system that lifts up all members of our community?

In order for urban co-ops and urban cooperative economies to thrive we must engage in trade and bartering that is both large scale but also looks like the traditional hook-up system that we know. Urban cooperative ecosystems are going to have to be created so individual co-ops or co-op leaders cannot be targeted because that is the history of Black people and oppressed people working on economic self-determination. Many communities in urban areas in the South, but also in cities across the United States and across the world, are coming together in response to state-based violence and are trying to determine the best way forward. That best way forward, in our opinion, is leading people to explore cooperative models around economics and what community restorative justice models could mean. Urban cooperatives must be able to grow and withstand the repression of communities by the police state. So how does what the cooperatives create in the midst of this make the community and its people stronger?

Closing remarks

Creating urban-based cooperatives in the South is challenging and Black urban-based ones are doubly hard. There are some that have been created in the past, others that are going now and even more under development. Doing this work requires our communities to find that spirit of definition and a new definition of wealth. Most importantly it demands a digging into community and for urban areas that have been torn apart by gentrification, interstate highways, and displacement where it is even harder to build community. In many southern cities community has taken a new shape and the cooperative movement and cooperative enterprises have to take that new shape as well.

Part of that new shape means redefining what a cooperative is and also supporting the skills that members of our communities have either naturally or cultivated. Our community members are able to grind and hustle to make ends meet and sometimes these skills matter more than other technical skills that are often lifted up to make cooperative businesses work with sometimes a different value system.

Although the challenges are great, and where we have to go is so far in the distance, the first step is to just jump on the train and not lose what we have got. Richard Rice in his interview said that "People are interested in creating and joining a cooperative, but right now there is nothing to touch." There is nothing to grab hold of, people can't go inside, and they can't see it. The hope of the Renaissance Community Co-operative in Greensboro[12] is that people in a food desert can go inside a grocery store in their neighborhood. For Jackson it's going to be big because once the co-op ecosystem is created it will be more than just me walking to the Lumumba Center and having Brandon, a member owner, asking me if I want a watermelon and someone's face lighting up. It will be community members having the ability to experience life in a way that has never been around before.

Notes

1. American FactFinder". United States Census Bureau. Archived from the original on September 11, 2013. Retrieved 2008-01-31.

2. *Black Co-operatives in the United States*

3. Hartford, Bruce. "Poor People's Corporation, Co-operatives, & Quilting Bees". *Documents from Poverty and Economic Justice Projects*. Veterans of the Civil Rights Movement, www.crmvet.org/tim/tim65b.htm, Accessed 24 November 2016.

4. Doncan, Danny. "Funding Black Colleges: Title III of the Highlander Education Act." *Brown- Tougaloo Exchange, 2005* http://cds.library.brown.edu/projects/FreedomNow/themes/title3/index.html. Accessed 25 November 2016

5. Hartford, Bruce. "Poor People's Corporation, Co-operatives, & Quilting Bees". *Documents from Poverty and Economic Justice Projects* . Veterans of the Civil Rights Movement, www.crmvet.org/tim/tim65b.htm, Accessed 24 November 2016.

6. Rice, Richard. Personal Interview. 16 October 2016.

7. *Profile of General Demographic Characteristics: 2000* (PDF), United States Census Bureau.

8. Birmingham co-ops websites—Alabama Farmers Co-operative- http://www.alafarm.com/locations/storelist/; Bici Co-op- http://bicico-op.org; Mannamarket organic food co-op http://www.mannamarket.net; Central Alabama Electric Co-op; Alabama Homeschool Co-operative; Wandering Yoga Co-operative; GeniusCo-op National Housing Co-operative- https://gust.com/companies/geniuscoop; Artists Incorporated-http://artistsincorporated.com. Accessed 27 November 2016.

9. New Orleans co-ops websites—New Orleans Food Co-op -www.nolafood.co-op; Veggie Farmers' Co-operative-http://www.veggifarmcoop.com; New Orleans Co-operative Development Project-https://www.facebook.com/NewOrleansCooperativeDevelopmentProject/; New Orleans scooter cooperative http://www.nolascootcoop.com; New Orleans Co-operative Housing for university

students - nocha.org; and Our School at Blair Grocery- https://www.facebook.com/NewOrleansCooperativeDevelopmentProject/. Accessed 27 November 2016

10. Rice, Richard. Personal Interview. 16 October 16.

11. Watkins, Hollis. Personal Interview. 26 October 2016.

12. McColl, Sarah, "Co-op Offers Oasis in a Southern Town Food Desert," *Takepart*, October 23, 2016. Available online at: http://www.takepart.com/article/2016/10/23/food-insecure-neighborhood-gets-boost-new-co-op

16.

Coming Full Circle: The Intersection of Gender Justice and the Solidarity Economy

Sacajawea ('Saki') Hall interviewed by Thandisizwe Chimurenga

Thandisizwe: I see in one of your bios you talk about growing up in a solidarity economy, having a cooperative upbringing, what do you mean by that?

Sacajawea: My mother is from Haiti and my father is from St. Louis, Missouri. Since I lived in New York with my mom's side of the family, the Haitian side of my family predominantly raised me. So I have my Haitian family and then my extended family of friends I grew up with living in the Lower East Side of Manhattan. Both were tight knit communities. In both cases we didn't have a lot of money so folks creatively figured out how to meet their needs. I feel like I was raised in two cultures that actually taught me some of the fundamentals of what it means to care and share with each other, to be a cooperator, as they say in the cooperative world. Caring and sharing is a key dimension of solidarity.

My mom has told me a story several times of when my dad bartered a painting for bread. He had done a small oil painting of a loaf of bread with a wine bottle based on a local bakery. One day they were hungry and had no money, so he went to the bakery and in exchange for the painting the baker gave him the same daily baked long loaf of bread featured my dad's painting. At that time they lived on about $800 a month with only a VA pension and an SSI check.

In New York City, during the '80s we used subway tokens in place of dollars at bodegas – a corner store – and with street vendors. My best friend and I stretched our resources on Saturday's by going through together with one token each way on the subway and then we'd have two tokens to use for lunch. So, we could share a hot dog and a knish[1] from a hot dog vendor.

Another example that connects me to the work I'm doing now is the apartment building I grew up in on East 9th Street. My mother gave birth to me and my father delivered me in our apartment in 1978 with everyone from the building there pitching in. Our building went through a long coop conversion process. It was resident self-managed through the 80s and then formally became a low-income co-op in the early 1990s. I had always known we had a tenant association that governed and managed the buildings. I did not know that I lived in a "shared-equity cooperative" until two years ago at a Community Land Trust conference I went to for Cooperation Jackson. After college I learned of the strong housing, homesteading and squatting movements that the Lower East Side had, along with other boroughs like the Bronx. My building was a product of the successful actions and organizing. Now I'm learning the details of the process on a deeper level cause I'm one of the people leading our work to develop cooperative housing.

I feel like I've come full circle, and working with Cooperation Jackson to take it to another level. Housing is very important, land is critical. We are developing the Fannie Lou Hammer Community Land Trust. It's a tool that can make housing permanently affordable and put the development process in the hands of the community instead of corporate developers. Ultimately, we want to see land and housing no longer be a commodity to be bought and sold to the highest bidder.

What these personal stories mean for me in terms of our work in Jackson is that I've come to realize, remember really, that I have lived experiences that show what we are aiming for is possible. So it is totally possible for us to have quality, affordable housing, which is a human right. And even more importantly, *we can* collectively own and control the land and our housing. We are asserting that we have a right to the city here in Jackson.

From my childhood to now, I see the creativity of everyday working people and their organic practice of solidarity, especially women of color, immigrant women, single women, the women I grew up with including my mother. So we have a responsibility to: a) recognize and value that, and b) tap into the creativity and practices that already exist to strengthen and expand it. And connect it to a movement for transformative liberation.

I think our vision and goals resonate with people. I think a lot of people have a similar experience like I'm describing. So many of us have these roots that have been passed down, in most ways, informally. Black people would not have survived the brutality of chattel slavery and Jim Crow apartheid without practicing solidarity and cooperation in organized formal ways. So it is that sharing, caring and cooperation from the past with the ways we continue to do it now to survive that we want to very intentionally tap into and make them systematic with formal institutions like time banks, skill shares, bartering and have a dynamic solidarity economy.

Thandisizwe: You identify as a Black feminist.

Sacajawea: Right, a radical Black feminist.

Thandisizwe: How do Black feminist politics and the struggle for Black women's liberation connect with the work of Cooperation Jackson and the effort to build the solidarity economy?

So growing up in the hood, Black, a child of an immigrant, in a diverse multi-national, working class neighborhood, I formed a race and class analysis early on, my gender analysis did not get fully shaped until later.

For me, women have to be at the center of our efforts to build a solidarity economy. So when I talk about that organic solidarity I grew up with, the informal ways oppressed people around the world live and work cooperatively, even the so called informal economy, women are at the center of that.

Again, using an example from my childhood, I remember being sent downstairs to borrow milk, sugar or some other food on the regular. It's not borrowing cause you can't give what you put in some cereal and ate back [laughter]. We didn't have to pay anyone back because they came to our house just the same. And when I think about it, 9 times out of 10 it had to do with cooking and meals, and the majority of the time it was women doing that cooking. So I took part in that mutual aid, now what I didn't know and learned recently when my godmother passed away, was that they shared food stamps. And mind you I know people exchanged food stamps as a form of currency. When I heard that I was like wow, that's deep, I actually wrote it down on the, you know the program they have at wakes. Learning that women shared food stamps spoke volumes to me about women. We are creative about how to take care of our families and each other with very little resources.

I'm sharing that example because what I take from it is how central "care work" is to the practice of solidarity. And if we are going to truly build a solidarity economy that is transformative, women have to be at the center of that. In Cooperation Jackson we recognize this. As an organization we are working towards fully recognizing care work, and fully center it as much as we center the value of worker-cooperatives in building a solidarity economy.

Women pretty much still take on the primary responsibility for care work. This work holds the social fabric of communities together and labor goes into creating or reproducing this fabric everyday, social reproduction. Care work includes maintaining a household, parenting children, taking care of a grandparent, taking care of other people's family, social activities, healing, cooking, emotional support, even sex. A radical feminist lens recognizes social reproduction as labor and care work is critical to social reproduction. Capitalism and patriarchy separate social reproduction from economic production, it makes a false separation between public and private. Social reproductive labor is not valued, recognized. |Its unpaid, in some cases paid, but severely underpaid.

Disconnecting social reproduction from economic production marginalizes the people who do social reproductive labor, making their role invisible and easily exploited.

Any economy relies on social production. Capitalism would not survive without social reproductive labor, the unpaid labor that allows for immense profit. What would profit margins be if a company had to pay the husband for working in the office and his wife for the work she does to run their home? Or had to pay a single mom double for her 9 to 5 and her care work? Domestic workers, mostly non-white women, mostly immigrants, work for low pay, do unpaid care work at home, and with the sheer amount of hours taking care of someone's family and home, it limits the time they can provide for their family and community. Sex workers are in the public and private sphere, doing paid work that is criminalized because socially it's for the private sphere and morally only for married hetero men and women.

So social reproduction and the role of women, and some men, is solidarity based, and a solidarity economy can reflect and support the transformation of society. A solidarity economy in and of itself doesn't automatically end gender and sexual oppression. But, it does offer an opportunity unlike capitalism.

For Cooperation Jackson we believe we have to challenge ourselves and each other to actively struggle against patriarchy and heterosexism in our work and in our lives. Assigned gender roles and norms that dictate who is a woman, what being a man means, even the subtle things like what color is allowed for which gender, pink being for girls and blue being for boys. Violence that comes in different forms is used to enforce these made up concepts, especially towards people who do not conform to these standards like transgender people.

I see it as my responsibility as a member of Cooperation Jackson, as a mother, as a birth worker, to provide a Black radical feminist analysis for our work and to push us all towards practice that is beyond theory. And that is the hard part. The multiple systems of oppression and how they overlap limit us all.

Thandisizwe: Cooperation Jackson is working on participatory budgeting. What would it look like if Black women were in charge of the budget or had a say in the city budget? Is fighting for a participatory budget an intentional part of the work of Cooperation Jackson in terms of integrating Black women's knowledge and experiences into how to govern a municipality? Is that part of the plan?

Sacajawea: We've been talking about and studying participatory and human rights budgeting, which in simple terms is creating a budget that actually comes out of the community and reflects its needs, as opposed to a budget that is created by government officials and then we all deal with the consequences of it. In Jackson, Mississippi, if Black women, especially Black working-class women, were centered in the process of creating a budget I think it would look very different than the city's typical budget. What I mean by centered is that the development of a budget would be driven by the knowledge, experience, ideas and participation of Black women. For example, I think education and schools, things like affordable housing would be prioritized compared to police departments or tourism. So it would be important for families like mine that have a hard time or cannot pay at all for extra-curricular activities to have access to free afterschool programs, free arts programs. That could be included in a city budget. Going back to housing like I talked about earlier, the priority placed on urban redevelopment often means giving tax breaks to corporate developers. I'm sure for poor and working class women, bringing in money to help improve the city wouldn't mean displacing them from their homes. Protecting affordable housing with policy and the money to back it up would be my priority if I had a part in the planning.

The city of Jackson is in a budget crisis; so hard decisions have to be made about what gets cut, where money goes and how much goes where. If we were able to do things differently, these decisions would be based on the people most directly impacted. So, in our case setting priorities for Jackson's urgent infrastructure repairs would be done in a democratic participatory process set through the lens of Black and other working class people, particularly women and not the contractors and the corporations that typically dominate the process and its outcomes.

The important part is actually how decisions get made, not only about allocating resources through a budget, it is about who is there to make those decisions, how much power do they have and can use in the process. So, yeah there's a lot of things that are needed, that have to be changed on the municipal level for us to get to the goals we set outlined in the Jackson-Kush Plan that relate to human rights or participatory budgeting, and more. There are a lot of things that have to change to create a deep democratic system. Hnuman rights budgeting is just one of the tools that will go a long way towards advancing our goals. That is why we've been studying it and plan to relaunch mass education and trainings on human rights budgeting. Not only is there an opportunity to meet the economic and social needs going unmet when the decision makers don't have the same interest, imagine the impact of the process with practicing agency and collective power through the process.

Thandisizwe: When I hear people say women in leadership it makes me think of a woman, a female figurehead. When I hear about women's participation, what comes to mind are women doing the majority of the work, but not receiving the credit or acknowledgement of their work. So women already participate, women are in leadership. You know to me it's more than women and leadership or women's participation. How is this being practiced in Cooperation Jackson?

Sacajawea: Right, women's leadership has to be centered, it is not enough to have us in the room. To me there is a difference between women having roles in an organization and women having power in an organization. When I say power I mean decision-making power that sets the agenda and goals of every dimension of the organization.

Audre Lorde is quoted often saying we don't live single issues lives and there is no hierarchy of oppression. That highlights the intersectionality framework that informs our work. Cooperation Jackson understands that Black people's self-determination and liberation is not possible without ending heteropatriarchy just like it is not possible without ending capitalism and white supremacy.

Radical feminism recognizes the intersections of Heterosexism, Patriarchy, Capitalism, White Supremacy, and other systems of oppression. These systems of oppression privilege men, privilege heterosexuals, privileges whiteness, privileges the ruling class, English as a language, adults, etc. In Cooperation Jackson, we have a vision of a deep democratic, cooperative, sustainable community. For us that means we have to create a culture free of patriarchy and heterosexism. Our struggles are connected and our liberation is intrinsically connected and we are committed to moving us as close as possible in that direction.

Cooperation Jackson specifically, like every organization, at least that I'm aware of, we are struggling to create this liberated space in our organization and we all know we have a long way to go in our communities.

What we *have* done to this point is that we've institutionalized space for women's leadership and queer leadership. I'm excited that our membership and core leadership of the organization represents young queer people and women. That stands out in Jackson, Mississippi [chuckle]. At the same time, that is not enough. Heterosexist views and behaviors have to be struggled with and shifted. We attempt to make tasks non-gendered like taking notes at a meeting and cleaning. It is interesting how we all fall into defaults and have to remind ourselves and each other.

Sacajawea: Patriarchy is a- hell of a- [pause]

Thandisizwe: Well, hell of a drug

Sacajawea: [laughs] Yeah, and so you know, it rears its ugly head in the personal and political spaces. Even in radical, progressive, women friendly, queer friendly spaces, time and time again. And we've internalized it, so even women and queer folks perpetuate it ourselves.

We have been intentional in actively creating the space and environment that is truly open and conducive to women and queer folks coming in from anywhere and genuinely feeling like they can fully engage and participate in discussing the work and doing the work. And it is in subtle and overt ways. Like having a sign that says, "gender is a universe" on our bathroom door. We have a banner on our entrance wall outside that says, "All Our Family Welcomed", with the rainbow and gender equality symbols including a combined queer and Black power symbol. We have a room called the little people's society named by one of our members. She is a high school student and her family provides childcare at our gatherings. Little people (children) are welcomed in all spaces is a community agreement.

Thandisizwe: What do you see going forward?

Sacajawea: As a leader of Cooperation Jackson, I have to make sure that we create the time and space to engage in the struggle to dismantle sexism, patriarchy, and heterosexism. Because it takes time, it takes processing. It's about our relationships with each other. So, I'm not the only one doing this, but it can't only be a few of us. I do see it as part of my responsibility though, to point out when sexist language or behavior happens, or to highlight the impact on women if we are talking about an issue and that gets left out. And that can be uncomfortable and frustrating at times.

CJ has to systematize these things, document this analysis and integrate it into all of our writing more. We need to document how it is impacting our work and practice, both successes and challenges.

A challenge for me is how to encourage and push the younger women in the organization to be more visible and vocal in our overall work. But, I have to check myself sometimes because it can't only be about the way I define active leadership or challenging patriarchy. So, I am constantly learning and developing myself, which is a part of the process, unpacking our privilege and unlearning what we've been socialized to accept.

What I think we have done is create the space for this to happen, instead of sitting back and waiting for them to ask to step into a role. We are encouraging and asking them to facilitate a meeting, do a report back. Collective models of leadership and decision-making can provide a space for everyone to participate fully. But it has to be coupled with principles and practices like men stepping back and not dominating discussions, sharing power overall. So I see us getting stronger in our theory and practice.

Notes

1. Eastern European snack food consisting of a filling covered with dough that is either baked, grilled, or deep fried. Knishes can be purchased from street vendors in urban areas with a large Jewish population, sometimes at a hot dog stand or from a butcher shop. It was made popular in North America by Eastern European immigrants from the Pale of Settlement (mainly from present-day Belarus, Poland, Lithuania and Ukraine).

V

GOING FORWARD

17.

After Death of Radical Mayor, Mississippi's Capital Wrestles with his Economic Vision

Laura Flanders

On his way into work every morning, Chokwe Lumumba, the late mayor of Jackson, Mississippi, used to pass a historical marker: "Jackson City Hall: built 1846-7 by slave labor."

The building, like the city around it, came into being when African American lives didn't count for much. Unpaid Black workers created Mississippi's plantation fortunes; as recently as the 1960s, their descendants were still earning $3 to $6 a day as sharecropper farmers. Today, Black Jacksonians are almost ten times as likely as white residents to live in poverty or surrounded by it. There's no need for a historical marker to trace the roots of the city's enormous wealth gap. The question is how to narrow it.

Lumumba had the vision of a radical, but the manners of a movement-builder

Mayor Lumumba had a plan. Believing that history of a new sort could be made here in Jackson, he sought to use public spending to boost local wealth through worker owned cooperatives, urban gardening, and a community-based approach to urban development. His vision, developed over years in social movements, not only prized Black experience and drew on the survival strategies that Black Americans had come up with over the decades, but also set out to prioritize in the city's policies the very people who until now had been on the bottom of the state's list. The goal, he said, was "revolutionary transformation." In promoting what he called "solidarity economics," Mayor Lumumba was continuing a long tradition. "Name any famous African American leader, Ella Baker, [W. E. B.] Dubois, Marcus Garvey, A. Philip Randolph, they were all proponents of co-ops," says Jessica Gordon Nembhard, author of *Collective Courage*, a new book on the African American experience with worker-owned cooperatives. "I can't find any era when most of our leaders weren't talking about co-ops in one form or another," says Gordon Nembhard. "The most significant things happen in history when you get the right people in the right place at the right time, and I think that's what we are," Mayor Lumumba told me this February in Jackson. Less than two weeks later, on Feb. 25, he died after just seven months in office. Now Jacksonians are working to keep his vision alive, not just for the sake of their city, but as a model of alternative development for the nation.

The solidarity economy

The capital city of Mississippi, population 175,000, Jackson is home to some of the poorest citizens in the nation and a higher percentage of African Americans than any other city except Detroit (just under 80 percent).

The racial wealth gap is extreme—laid down, like the city's infrastructure, decades back. A few years ago, the federal government stepped in, threatening the city with massive fines if the infrastructure crisis wasn't addressed. But no federal agency stepped in to address the inequality crisis.

Which is why the election last summer of a new mayor who took race and poverty seriously, was a big deal, not only in Jackson, but around the country. According to a 2013 study by the Economic Policy Institute and the Center on Budget and Policy Priorities, the gap between the rich and the poor grew more in Mississippi in the last few years than in any other state. (The top fifth of households saw a 19 percent gain in income from the late 1990s to the mid 2000s, while the bottom quintile of earners saw a 17.3 percent drop.) Lots of leaders talk about reducing poverty and inequality. But Mayor Lumumba ran on an innovative plan to do it and received 85 percent of the vote in June 2013, after beating out the incumbent mayor and a well-funded former businessman in the Democratic primary. A former public defender and longtime radical activist, Lumumba had the organizing support of the group he co-founded, the Malcolm X Grassroots Movement, along with the Jackson People's Assembly, a neighborhood-based participatory democracy group, and the Mississippi Disaster Relief Coalition, which he'd helped to convene after Hurricane Katrina. Short of funds, but rich in organizers, Lumumba advanced what he called "The People's Platform" to revitalize the city—not by chasing away the people with problems but by tackling the wealth gap's underpinnings: the asset and income disparities that drive populations apart. "Mayors typically don't do the things we're trying to do," he said. "On the other hand, revolutionaries don't typically find themselves as mayor." Typically, mayors attempt to increase their city's "assets" and reduce their "liabilities" through promising investors they'll provide high-quality services at low prices and cutting taxes and crime rates. This February, Lumumba said he'd be doing "some" of that, but he also had a larger goal. Not urban renewal through what he called "urban removal," but urban revival—for everyone. "The mission is to accomplish economic development together," he said.When it comes to oppression in America, said Lumumba, Mississippians had experienced the worst of it for a long time. In terms of exploitation, disinvestment, deindustrialization and so-called "white flight," he said:

> What's exciting to me is the prospect of going from worst to first ... to take groups of dispossessed Black folks here and others, and make us controllers of our own destiny.

The city's old infrastructure and its corroded pipes, he believed, could actually help.

Rebuilding infrastructure—and the economy

Two years ago, a consent decree signed with the Environmental Protection Agency and the Department of Justice committed the city of Jackson to raising and spending an estimated $1.2 billion over the next 17 years to repair and upgrade its infrastructure. Lumumba's first order of business after taking office on July 1, 2013, was raising water and sewer rates and building support for a 1 percent increase in the sales tax on certain items, to be spent specifically on the infrastructure project.

In a citywide referendum held this January, an astonishing nine of out 10 residents voted "yes." While he initially opposed the sales tax as regressive—and especially the special commission that the state set up to spend the sales-tax dollars—Lumumba eventually agreed to raise the people's taxes but pledged that his administration would put as many of those dollars as possible back into the people's pockets.

To accomplish that, he laid out clear principles: buy local and hire local people. According to the census, whites, who make up just 18 percent of Jackson's population, own nearly 70 percent of businesses in the greater metro area. Under Lumumba, major employers would be required to hire 60 percent or more of their employees from within the city limits.

To further expand the economic base of the majority population, he wanted half of project subcontractors and partners to be so-called "minority" developers. "We want the wealth that is going to be generated here to stay here," Lumumba often said in speeches. To ensure the commission's spending stayed local, he sought to change the city's laws. "We have to have rules," he said. "One of the rules is, if you come to Jackson, you have to hire the people of Jackson." As a first step, the city changed its own hiring practices. City data showed 635 nonresident city employees, whose salaries totaled more than $20 million a year.

Even as Lumumba replaced the city's leaky pipes, he planned to stop city money from draining away and supported legislation to change the residency requirements for city workers. This January, Jackson's City Council voted to ensure that the money the city pays in wages stays within the city limits. All new city employees will have to be city residents. It was to have been only a beginning. The city is now facing its future without Mayor Lumumba.

Chokwe Lumumba died of reported heart failure at the age of 66 on Feb. 25, less than two weeks after we talked. The next week, on April 8, Jackson will elect a new mayor. The crowded field of candidates includes Lumumba's son, Chokwe Antar, a graduate of Tuskegee University in Alabama and the Thurgood Marshall School of Law in Texas. Chokwe Antar Lumumba worked on both his father's campaigns—for Jackson City Council in 2009 and for mayor in 2013—and has the support of his father's grassroots political machine behind him, not to mention his name's deep resonance. But Lumumba's supporters aren't hanging their hopes solely on the next mayor. "The vision that he represented—the People's Platform and the solidarity economics, were all social movement pieces," says Kali Akuno, director of special projects in the late mayor's administration. "They weren't framed by him alone."

Lumumba's plan for economic democracy was backed by the Jackson People's Assembly, a self-organized process of local consultation that took off during Lumumba's 2009 run for city council. Attended by voters and vote-seekers alike, the assemblies were held across the district and are expected to spread citywide in 2014. "We started by going out into the community asking people, what do you want government to do for you?" Mattie Wilson Stoddard, vice chair of the Jackson People's Assembly, told me.

The Jackson People's Assembly is one of the sponsors of "Jackson Rising: New Economies," an international conference taking place in May which was to have been a launching pad for Lumumba's solidarity economy project. "Jackson Rising is more important than ever," says Akuno, the late mayor's point-person on the conference, which focuses heavily on education and organizing around the development and incubation of cooperative enterprises. "We can't build economic democracy alone."

In different hands, the city's infrastructure spending could trigger a development gold rush of the sort seen in New Orleans after Hurricane Katrina, which resulted in disastrous speculation and permanent displacement, especially of low-income residents. Jacksonians need to know their options, says Akuno. Members of worker-owned enterprises in Cleveland, Ohio, and the Basque region of Spain have been invited to come share strategies for creating and keeping wealth in the community. "We need to make sure we're not robbed again, but get something that's going to benefit our children and our grandchildren," Akuno says of the infrastructure fund.

The best way to do that, Akuno and the other organizers of Jackson Rising believe, is by capturing and concentrating wealth in the hands of local people through solidarity economics and worker-owned cooperatives. It is not a new concept in these parts. Far from it. When asked if co-ops were a "hippy" thing,

Mayor Lumumba's patrician face cracked a grin and he replied, "There's a little hippy in all of us. And I think the hippies probably got a lot of it from what used to happen in Africa."

The first Black cooperatives

"The community I grew up in, in a sense, was a co-op although we didn't use the name," recalls Lumumba supporter Hollis Watkins, co-founder and president of the Jackson-based movement support organization, Southern Echo, "If you needed work done on your farm before the rain came, we all stepped in. At some point you knew your turn would come."

Hollis was born to sharecroppers in 1941, the youngest of twelve children.

After graduating college, Watkins joined the Student Nonviolent Coordinating Committee, SNCC, a grassroots-based Black liberation organization that played a leading role in the 1963 March on Washington for Jobs and Freedom.

"When we talked about rights, economics was always part of the program," Watkins recalled. "Our people understood that education and jobs and political empowerment were all intertwined."

Jacksonite Melbah Smith, who worked with Watkins at Southern Echo, and before that with civil rights activist Fannie Lou Hamer, grew up on her grandfather's farm in Brandon, just fifteen miles east of downtown Jackson. She still remembers the good times—like "hog-killing time," when the community would pool skills and tools to butcher meat. But she also remembers the hard times: "Ours was the last home in the county to get electricity or a telephone."

Smith went on to serve as the Mississippi Director of the Federation of Southern Cooperatives, a regional nonprofit which has helped create or support more than 200 cooperatives and credit unions in 10 states, providing services and meeting needs that were going unmet.

"Cooperatives were born out of a need to bring services to underserved communities," says Smith. Co-ops were also as a way to survive discrimination.

Smith's grandfather collaborated with his brothers to buy farmland after emancipation. Her father, born in 1910, grew up under the system of de facto and de jure apartheid known as Jim Crow. Under Jim Crow, not only were impossible obstacles erected to deny African Americans the vote; Black farmers were also denied loans and credit from white-controlled local banks.

The first Black cooperatives date back to the colonial age and "beneficial and burial societies"—founded by slaves who gathered dues covertly to pay for one another's burials. Free blacks started insurance companies to pay for cemeteries and doctors' bills. The first [cooperative? Insurance company? Mutual?], according to a study by NAACP founder W. E. B. DuBois, was incorporated by the AME Church in Philadelphia in 1787.

In his 1907 study of Black economic cooperation, DuBois includes the Underground Railroad, which transported hundreds of thousands of refugees across thousands of miles, via cooperating networks of supporters, organizers, and sympathetic landowners.

After the Civil War, "freedom" for millions of formerly enslaved men and women turned on their ability to combine their means in order to purchase land and sustain themselves—or find themselves forced back into bonded labor on their former plantations.

"The wonder is not that so many, but that so few, have needed help," DuBois quotes a chief of the federal Freedmen's Bureau, which was set up to assist freed blacks in 1865.

Almost 100 years later, Black political rights were still tied to Black economic resilience. When the civil rights movement of the '60s started, recalcitrant whites responded by exploiting the economic vulnerability of the movement's base.

"The Selma to Montgomery marchers couldn't stay on sharecroppers' land" recalls Jackson Rising supporter Wendell Paris, who helped organize the historic 1965 voting rights march that took place some 250 miles to the east of where he now lives near Jackson. Hundreds of tenant farmers were evicted for standing up for their rights.

Economic power is political power

The land of the Mississippi River Delta is famously fertile; rich enough to capitalize the early U.S. economy. But the people who have worked that land have rarely been enriched.

From the founding of the United States through the Civil War to the modern era, the plantation class, with overwhelming power and resources, has fought to keep their advantage. In the civil rights era—along with lynching, firebombing, and assassination—farmers who joined the NAACP would lose their loans, and African Americans who registered to vote risked losing hard-to-come-by employment.

Wendell Paris remembers spending a week persuading an older domestic worker to register. He took the woman, named Catherine Jones, to the registrar's office every morning, starting on a Monday.

"She'd stay there all day too afraid to sign her name." Finally, that Thursday afternoon, she signed and by Friday morning, she'd lost her job.

"Reprisals were immediate," Paris recalls.

Known for her role as a voting rights activist and founder of the Mississippi Freedom Democratic Party, Fannie Lou Hamer also started a co-op, "Freedom Farm," to support civil rights activists punished for their work.

With Hamer, Watkins started buying clubs and selling co-ops as a way to help poor families he met through the Head Start program. "They needed some economic stability before they could even begin to change the political situation," says Watkins.

In the 1970s, Watkins went on to manage two large farms bought by the Nation of Islam in Mississippi. "As manager of the Nation of Islam's farms, Watkins was able to buy farming supplies in bulk and share costly farm equipment with poorer farmers. Paris was doing the same with SNCC in Alabama.

The white establishment was quick to react to the co-op push, fearing, presumably, that Black co-ops could shift the power-balance.

"At one point we bought cows and white folks poisoned the water and killed the cows," says Watkins.

Paris remembers finding a market in New York that would pay almost three times the price Alabama farmers could get locally for their cucumbers. The local growers' cooperative rented a truck. On just their second run to market, state troopers pulled them over. "We asked Governor (George) Wallace why he'd stopped our truck. He said he didn't have to tell us why. He could detain any vehicle for 72 hours," recalled Paris.

"Seventy-two hours later, we opened the door and the entire load poured out." The cucumbers had liquefied in the burning summer heat.

Having retired from the federation, Melbah Smith directs the Coalition for a Prosperous Mississippi, which works to change Mississippi's laws concerning cooperatives. Currently, only agricultural-based entities can incorporate in Mississippi. Any other type of cooperatives must be charted out-of-state. According to the coalition, 44 percent of the 162 non-agricultural co-ops in Mississippi report that they could not have opened their businesses had it not been set up as a co-op.

"Co-ops are part of how we grew up," says Smith. In her view, their future is bright.

Just as cooperation worked for rural Mississippians—providing electricity or loans or social services in poor communities—so too can city dwellers use the cooperative model to pool resources and share the risk of starting a business. Cooperatives provide a way for low-income communities to build assets and create wealth, the decisive factor in narrowing the racial wealth gap. They have a strong track record of raising wages for their members too, and of staying put. Indeed, the experience of working together on an equal footing with co-workers often leads to other sorts of civic engagement.

Which is part, no doubt, of what Smith will be telling participants at the Jackson Rising. Still not retired, she's helping to plan the conference.

Jackson rises

The immediate threat poor blacks face today in Jackson comes from outside developers and speculators with the resources to move in and take over their neighborhoods.

Nia Umoja belongs to the Malcolm X Grassroots Movement. She moved to West Jackson last year with her husband. For just $1,500 they were able to purchase a single family home a couple of blocks off Capitol Street (a major east-west thoroughfare), within walking distance of the city zoo and Jackson State University.

Like the majority of the homes around hers, Umoja's house needs work. When she moved in, the empty plots on two sides of hers were overgrown with high, scrubby trees and bushes. According to recent surveys, some 40 percent of the lots nearby are abandoned or vacant. Eighty-eight percent of the population lives in poverty. Payday lending stores outnumber groceries 10 to one.

"You have to start with what you have to get what you want," community organizers say. What West Jackson has is a lot of overgrown land, a lot of underemployed labor, and a good amount of (albeit rusty) farming experience.

"The people here have lost their voice, but they're not resource-less," Umoja told me. When she surveyed her neighbors about their assets, she found that while they may not have considered themselves "skilled," they had talents. "They grew up on farms," explained Umoja. "They know how to grow things."

In August 2013, Umoja helped establish the Cooperative Community of New West Jackson with the hope of establishing a cooperative farm. Under Mayor Lumumba, the group was able to clear 1.5 acres of vacant city-owned land just off Capitol Street. Near the north end of the plot sits an abandoned Dairy Queen whose forecourt would make a great green market, she says, if only she could get the long-absentee owner to agree to sell, or the city to take it over.

Umoja and her colleagues have grand plans for what they are calling the Grenada Street Folk Garden, but private developers are already coming around and just a few blocks away, lots are already selling for $40,000 to $80,000.

Some would like to see gentrification come to West Jackson, like it came to the city's North Midtown section. That area too, was a high crime, low income, low-property-price area not long ago. Now it's one of the city's leading neighborhoods, thanks to development funds from the U.S. Department of Housing and Urban Development as well as the American Recovery and Reinvestment Act of 2009. With help from Habitat for Humanity and private "green" developers, the Jackson Housing Authority demolished dilapidated houses, retrofitted others, and watched rents and property prices rise.

In 2012, a group of institutional stakeholders in West Jackson—a group including Jackson State University, the Center for Social Entrepreneurship, the Jackson Zoo, Jackson-Evers Municipal Airport, and the Voice of Jackson

Calvary Ministries (a church group)—hired Duvall Decker Architects, the same firm that worked on North Midtown, to draw up a master plan for West Jackson. Some are already calling it the "Capitol Street Corridor."

At a community meeting convened by architect Roy Decker this February, Umoja and Akuno were shown half a dozen colorful maps, detailing "assets" and "concerns" in the West Jackson neighborhood. On Decker's maps, the Cooperative Community of New West Jackson sits on plots featuring almost no assets and many "concerns," including homelessness, crime, a high proportion of vacant properties, and few businesses or public services. Still, when Umoja got a chance to describe her garden plan, the response was mostly positive.

"Sounds good. Like hog-killing time in the old days," said one resident.

"We just have to work harder to get the word out," Umoja said.

Whether change is driven by worker owned co-ops or outside speculators, it's going to take some doing to achieve "revolutionary transformation" in Jackson. Investment is driven by demand, says Mukesh Kumar, professor of urban planning at Jackson State University, and right now, Jackson has very little of that. Downtown is already circled by a big sticky suburban ring, sucking shoppers, contractors, and prime business out of the city's center.

The Greater Jackson Chamber of Commerce, which backed the North Midtown plan, is setting its hopes for growth on further development of the city's "medical corridor," the building of a 1,500-acre downtown lake, and an arts and culture expansion to "attract talent."

It's hard to see how any of those plans will work. Several major hospitals (including Baptist Health Systems, University of Mississippi Medical Center, and St. Dominic's) and as many major colleges have left the inner-city core poor up to this point. For tourists, Jackson's competing with Nashville and New Orleans.

At least Mayor Lumumba's plan to stimulate internal demand through local employment in public works has a proven track record. Federal public works programs helped recovery after the Great Depression, just as reconstruction projects helped rebuild the south after the Civil War (until they fell victim to Jim Crow). As civil rights organizers learned, for people to participate in the political process, their economic necessities need to be seen to. After years of ineffective government, Jackson needs both political, as well as economic revival.

Lumumba had the vision of a radical, but the manners of a movement-builder. He reached across political lines to build support for his plan. One of his first calls after his election was to Duane O'Neal, head of the Jackson Regional Chamber of Commerce.

Before Lumumba's death, O'Neal said he'd already had more and "more meaningful" meetings with the new mayor than he did with the preceding administration in all the 16 years they had been in office. Lumumba won respect because, as O'Neal put it to me, "he's shown himself to be a man of action."

Lumumba's mission was "development together." He understood his goal was, as much as anything else, to re-engage the city.

"The job is not a single individual affair but a collective affair, and the creation of jobs is not an individual affair but a collective [one.]"

Cooperation in the handful of urban gardens currently in Jackson, has already brought people together, says Akuno. What Jackson does not yet have are any worker, producer or housing cooperatives. Only a few cooperative Credit Unions operate within the city limits. Jackson Rising seeks to change that.

With only a few months to go, organizers of the Jackson Rising conference were struggling this February with how to appeal simultaneously to entrepreneurially minded students and Nia Umoja's hard-up neighbors. Charlotte and Luke Landemeaux, founders of Jackson's one existing food co-op, Rainbow Foods, (incorporated in Delaware), were feeling anxious about competition from Jackson's first Whole Foods, which has just opened its doors. But everyone's immediate problem was a good one. The first in a series of "Grassroots Economics" meetings, intended to build to the May conference, was filled to capacity.

In the 1960s, when they were fighting for bottom-up democracy, Fannie Lou Hamer and the members of SNCC used to say "The people must decide."

Chokwe Lumumba and the Jackson People's Assembly used this phrase over and over during his campaign. Even though he's gone, it's hard not to hear those words echoing around Jackson more loudly than ever.

As they ask themselves which way forward for Jackson and Jacksonians, the answer comes: "The people must decide."

18.

The Jackson Just Transition Plan: A Vision to Make Jackson a 'Sustainable City'

Cooperation Jackson

There's no Hispanic air, no African American air, or white air, there's just air. And if you breathe air, and most people I know do breath air, then that makes you part of the environment and if you are concerned about the quality of that air, I would consider you an environmentalist. And if you drink water, and most people I know drink water, and you are concerned about what's in the water, then I would consider you an environmentalist. And you eat food, and again most people I know eat food, and you are concerned about what's in the food, then I would consider you an environmentalist. If you answer two of the three, then I would say you are an environmentalist, you just might not know it.

—Dr. Robert Bullard

A City in Crisis

Jackson is a city in crisis. As noted in the "Jackson Rising: Building the City of the Future Today" statement of the administration of the late Mayor Chokwe Lumumba, "Jackson, like many urban centers, is struggling to overcome decades of economic divestment, deindustrialization, suburban flight, a declining tax base, chronic under and unemployment, poorly performing schools, and an antiquated and decaying infrastructure."[1] To this we must add that Jackson is also a city confronting numerous environmental racism challenges that constitute an ongoing health crisis and human rights violations for many of our city's residents, particularly in our most impoverished neighborhoods.

Some of these chronic problems and human rights violations include the air quality in parts of South and West Jackson created in large part by the problematic design of the city's highways and industrial areas, leading to chronic levels of asthma and other breathing and heart related issues.[2] Our city is also home to numerous toxin-contaminated sites, many of which are "officially" recognized as "brown fields". However, many more sites have not been adequately identified or ignored due to inadequate monitoring on the part of government as a result of insufficient resourcing. Many of the unrecognized sites are residential or are situated near residential areas or schools and pose developmental threats to our children and cancer stimulating threats in general.[3]

Our city's water management issues are becoming legendary. Not only is our water often not suitable to drink it threatens to become a consistent transmitter of communicable diseases. It must be overhauled soon in order to avert systemic health threats and its potential privatization, if we not be able to meet the consent decree deadlines imposed upon the City by the EPA.[4] It should be noted that our water issues are long-standing and directly related to intentional neglect and institutional and systemic racism. The intentional neglect of the system started when the city transitioned from being majority white to majority Black, without any corresponding transfer of the city's wealth and means of production. Then there are issues with illegal dumping[5] and the overall management of the city's waste, which is not only a problem of pollution and contamination, but also a major producer of carbon and methane gases, which are the primary contributors to climate change.

Jackson, sadly, is also one of the largest contributors to climate change in the state of Mississippi as a direct result of how it receives and consumes its energy,[6] and as result of the major industries in and around the city that are dependent on trucking, railroad, and airfreight transportation that emit tremendous amounts of hydro-carbons that are poisoning our atmosphere.

A solution: The sustainable communities initiative

To improve the quality of life in our City and for the sake of our children, grandchildren, and great-grandchildren we can and must end the overlapping environmental, climatic and human rights crises confronting us. Cooperation Jackson believes that we can solve these crises by organizing our communities to execute a comprehensive program that will protect our environment, curb our carbon emissions, stimulate employment, and democratically transfer wealth and equity.

We call this comprehensive program a Just Transition program which is premised on ending our systemic dependence on the hydro-carbon industry and the capitalist driven need for endless growth on a planet with limited resources, while creating a new, democratic economy that is centered around sustainable methods of production and distribution that are more localized and cooperatively owned and controlled. Cooperation Jackson's specific contribution to a Just Transition program is our Sustainable Communities Initiative. The Sustainable Communities Initiative has two primary components:

1. Building an eco-village

2. Just Transition policy reform

The Eco-Village component of the initiative focuses on building a sustainable live-work community in West Jackson. The Eco-Village will be situated upon and protected by a Community Land Trust (CLT) created by Cooperation Jackson and controlled by residents of West Jackson. The Eco-Village will provide affordable housing through cooperative housing and jobs through a number of integrated and interdependent cooperative enterprises that will be situated within the community, including urban farms, composting operations, childcare, solar-thermal installation and maintenance, security, arts and culture, and a grocery store. The eco- or ecological component of the community is centered on creating an integrated solar-thermal, recycling, and composting network in the community that will provide deeply affordable and sustainable energy and green jobs that will help fight ecological degradation and climate change. The exercise of collective land and home ownership and the provision of permanent affordability and tax controls will enable us to fight the encroachment of gentrification and displacement threatening the predominantly Black working class community of West Jackson.

The broader Just Transition component of the initiative focuses on instituting policies that curb ecological destruction and climate change and incentivize the creation of sustainable jobs and cooperative enterprises in our city. We are committed to helping the city realize the vision of the Lumumba administration of making Jackson the most "sustainable city" in the South (if not the country), by committing the city government to institute policies that will enable Jackson to become a Zero-emissions and Zero-waste city by 2025.

Zero-emission

Our **Zero-emissions** program calls for the following:

> 1. **Weatherization and energy efficiency retrofitting.** We want to push the City of Jackson to retrofit and weatherize all of the buildings that it owns and operates, so that they conserve heat in the winter and naturally cool the facility in the summer. We also want the City to incentivize this type of retrofitting in the private and non-profit sectors of the economy with grants, low-interest loans, tax-credits, etc.

> 2. **Solar-thermal energy production**. We want to encourage the City of Jackson to place solar panels on all of the buildings and facilities it possesses that have the capacity to host the equipment. We also want to encourage the City to install solar-thermal converters in all of the facilities it possesses that have the capacity to regulate its energy use via this technology. We also want to encourage the City to incentivize private and non- profit sector solar-thermal energy conversion and production and enable residents and businesses to supply excess energy to the main power grid to aid the energy company eliminate its dependence on fossil fuels.

3. **Zero-emissions fleet**. We want to push the City of Jackson to gradually replace its entire operating fleeting, including all police vehicles, with electric vehicles. We also want to encourage the City to incentivize the purchasing of electric cars and to create publicly owned and operated electric fueling stations throughout the city to accommodate this transition.

4. **Expanded and sustainable public transportation**. We want to push the City of Jackson to gradually acquire a fully electric public transportation fleet and to expand its public transportation vehicles, routes and hours to accommodate more efficient and accessible transportation throughout the city and metro-region.

Zero-waste

Our **Zero-waste** program calls for the following:

1. **Comprehensive recycling**. We want to encourage the City of Jackson to create a comprehensive recycling program, that includes mass public education, and a system of inducements and rewards for residents, businesses and civil institutions in the city to recycle all that can be recycled to reduce the burden on the city's landfill site(s) and to create more private and public sectors jobs in waste management and recycling.

2. **Comprehensive composting**. We want to encourage the City of Jackson to create a comprehensive composting program that gathers all of the organic refuse produced by households, businesses and civil institutions and include the requisite public education necessary to encourage individuals, families, businesses and institutions to participate and to adhere to all of the necessary sanitary standards.

2.1. **Comprehensive oil reuse**. We want to encourage the City of Jackson to create a comprehensive cooking oil gathering program that calls for all restaurants and food service businesses and institutions producing mass amounts of used cooking oils for their food production such as schools, colleges, universities, and hospitals to recycle these materials so that they may be reused for other energy and production needs and help eliminate the need for their extended production and disposal at public expense.

3. **Local food production**. We want to encourage the City of Jackson to create a Local Food and Production Charter, to encourage and incentivize local food production and distribution, to create more jobs and reduce carbon emissions by eliminating the need for extended transportation systems and refrigeration. The incentive program should focus exclusively

on supporting producers who reside in Jackson and are drawn from historically discriminated and capital deprived communities.

As these points illustrate, there are viable and attainable solutions that we can implement now that will help our city work its way out of its health, human rights, environmental, and climate change contributing crisis. We want to encourage everyone in Jackson to support us in advancing this cause by becoming a member or supporter of Cooperation Jackson, and helping us build and execute the Sustainable Communities Initiative in order to develop our collective power and advance a just transition to a new economy and social horizon.

James Farmer accurately captures the situation face the City of Jackson and the rest of humanity on the matter of ecological sustainability:

> If we do not save the environment, then whatever we do in civil rights, or in a war against poverty, then whatever we do will be of no meaning because then we will have the equality of extinction.

This article first appeared on the Cooperation Jackson website: http://www.cooperationjackson.org/blog/2015/11/10/the-jackson-just-transition-plan

Notes

1. See "Jackson Rising Statement" at https://jacksonrising.wordpress.com/local/jackson-rising-statement/.
2. See "Climate Change Health Threats in Mississippi" at http://www.nrdc.org/health/climate/ms.asp#airpollution.
3. For information on identified Brownfield sites in Jackson, MS, see http://www.homefacts.com/environmentalhazards/superfunds/Mississippi/Hinds-County/Jackson.html.
4. See one of the most critical articles on the EPA consent decree, "EPA decree will cost Jackson Big Money" http://www.jacksonfreepress.com/news/2012/sep/06/epa-decree-will-cost-jackson-big-money/.
5. See "Jackson recycling facilities close" http://www.msnewsnow.com/story/23097894/2-jackson-recycling-facilities-close.
6. See White House "Fact Sheet: What Climate Change means for Mississippi and the Southeast and the Caribbean" http://www.agprofessional.com/news/mississippi-river-mayors-send-delegation-un-climate-change-meeting.

19.

A Green Utopia in Mississippi?

Sara Bernard

Not exactly the eco-capital of the world. The city's wastewater disposal has the attention of the US EnviorONMENTAL Protection Agency (EPA), Mississippi Gov. Phil Bryant is a big fracking supporter, there's no glass recycling within city limits ... and so on. But longtime organizer Kali Akuno has a vision: He and 100-plus volunteers want to turn the hardscrabble city of roughly 170,000 into a marvel of sustainability and social justice.

Akuno is a co-founder of Cooperation Jackson, a community network that aims to solve the city's most intractable issues — poverty and unemployment, racial and economic injustice, food access and industrial pollution — through developing a series of cooperatives that radically re-imagine how people live and work. Cooperation Jackson, less than a year old, is one of the pilot communities of the Our Power Campaign, an effort launched by the Climate Justice Alliance (CJA). And its end goal, like CJA's, is to transition out of fossil fuel dependence by supporting localized economies, low-income communities of color, and the planet all at once.

Akuno has an impressive background in community justice work — he works with such coalitions as the Malcolm X Grassroots Movement and the People's Assembly, he started a school serving low-income African American and Latino youth in Oakland, Calif., and he's the former co-director of the U.S. Human Rights Network, among other things. (The city of Jackson may soon pass a Human Rights Charter that Akuno was a part of initiating, too).

But he's especially jazzed about Cooperation Jackson's mainstay, the Sustainable Communities Initiative. The plan is to buy up abandoned land and dilapidated properties and organize them into a Community Land Trust. On it, there'll be an "eco-village," or group of green homes where people can share tools and facilities, making it both planet-friendly and affordable. There'll be urban gardens (including hydroponics, aeroponics, and aquaponics), a waste management and recycling system, a child care center, and an arts center, all run by community-owned cooperatives that will provide paying jobs to local residents. One of Akuno's long-term goals is to turn Jackson into a zero-waste city.

I spoke with Akuno recently about social and environmental justice, politics, history, and building a green utopia. Here's an edited and condensed version of what he had to say:

Q: What gave rise to Cooperation Jackson?

A: It's something that's been on my radar for well over a decade, actually. It was part of some thinking and planning that the Malcolm X Grassroots Movement had been doing. And cooperatives wound up becoming a real central focus for me. How do we deal with some of the real hardships and material limitations that so many working people face? That's been a long term focus and it's just kind of taken a while to put all the social forces and pieces in place.

The real genesis of it, though, was us planning the Jackson Rising: New Economies Conference. Through that process, [Cooperation Jackson] went from a planning committee at a conference, to an organization, which was intentional.

Q: How about the zero waste idea?

A: [As part of] the environmental justice fight, we started thinking, OK, what are the things we really can do, what really can a social movement accomplish? Changes in the policy framework — *that* would be the most lasting thing that would survive into the future. So how do we change the practices of municipalities, how do we have an impact there? That's where the zero waste came from. How [do we make sure] the city goes about doing all its procurement and operations in a manner that doesn't further support the extractive economy?

Q: So you've been working on environmental justice issues for a while now?

A: Oh yeah, environmental justice is something that's been on our radar screen and agenda for a long, long time. There was a major campaign around fighting toxic dumping in Mississippi. And around all of the toxins and carcinogens and antibiotics that were used in both the chicken farms and catfish farms here in the 1990s.

[Today], in Jackson, there are some key environmental justice issues. No. 1 is water quality. The city is under consent decree already from the EPA about how bad the quality is. Jackson's pipes are extremely old and antiquated. They've burst, there's a lot of seepage, a lot of contaminants that are in there that spill off into communities. That's one problem. Another major problem is that Jackson has a lot of lead paint and asbestos buildings still that people are living in. So remediation around that stuff —that's one of the ways the eco-village comes in and why that's so critical. Beyond that, there are some air quality issues particularly in parts of south Jackson. Because of some factories there, we've got high rates of asthma concentrated in those communities. That's a big one we've been involved with and continue to be involved with.

Q: What does it mean to be an Our Power Campaign pilot site?

A: First and foremost, it puts us into a broader network of allies who are thinking the same, acting the same, planning the same. We have folks to look to: How do they build cooperatives in Black Mesa and in Detroit? And it's more muscle. We're really in the fight! We're not alone! Going up against the city council, going up against the state government—as we're waging campaigns, there are resources and allies that we can fall on to lend technical expertise, mobilization, and support that without this kind of capacity would be hard for us to do.

Q: What are some of the obstacles to getting this thing off the ground?

A: For a beginning organization, in a very poor state, in a very poor neighborhood, we are still having to raise capital, which is not very familiar to folks here— not the type of money we're talking about. So, we're in a major fundraising drive to raise every stone and rock and contact that we have to try to get some support for it. What we have, we think, is really a modest goal—we think with a minimum of $500,000 we can make a serious transformation in this community, and an impact that will last for generations.

But I think the biggest challenge for us, now and in the long term, is we're not going to be able to move and develop cooperatives as fast as the demand dictates. That's critical, just because of what real unemployment is here in Jackson. It's very, very high. Compared to other parts of Mississippi, Jackson is well off. But if you look at national averages, and people's concrete lives—it is a very poor community, very impoverished.

Q: Your hopes for the future?

A: We have an integrated plan of how to develop a new, transformative economy. It'll build our strength, and more importantly, in the long term, beat back gentrification and displacement. We want folks to come into the neighborhood and see it, and from that, expand out from there to other parts of Jackson. And then hopefully other folks will say, hey, we can do that in Seattle, in Portland, in Boise!

The typical pattern in the 20th and 21st centuries has been that [Black communities] are moved—through redlining and other practices—from one area to another. When Black people move in, the value of the neighborhood depreciates, there are less services, less stores, less amenities. Over time, the neighborhood deteriorates. Will Black communities ever find a way to beat that? Well, we're gonna try and beat it.

And there's enough capacity to actually go around. This is the first place I've ever lived in my life where I can say that. We actually have people who want to do the work, are trying to engage in the work, and are pressing it forward as best they can. We're in a really good situation as far as that's concerned. Things are picking up; we're in a good place. We're really looking forward to 2015.

This article first appeared in Grist: http://grist.org/cities/a-green-utopia-deep-in-mississippi-this-guy-has-a-game-plan/

20.

Casting Shadows: Chokwe Lumumba and the Struggle for Racial Justice and Economic Democracy in Jackson, Mississippi

Kali Akuno

In the State of Mississippi, deep down in the heart of "Dixie," a critical democratic experiment is taking place that is challenging the order of institutional white supremacy and paternalistic capitalism that form the foundations of the state's settler-colonial order.[1] This experiment in social transformation is building a radical culture of participatory democratic engagement to gain control over the authoritative functions of governance and to democratize the fundamental means of production, distribution, and financial exchange. It is being led by the New Afrikan People's Organization (NAPO) and the Malcolm X Grassroots Movement (MXGM, n.d.). We are building on nearly two hundred years of struggle for Afrikan liberation in the territories claimed by the European settler-state of Mississippi. This experiment, the Jackson-Kush Plan, is named after the state's capitol and the name given by members of the Provisional Government of the Republic of New Afrika (PG-RNA) to the eighteen contiguous majority Black counties that border the Mississippi river.

The Jackson-Kush Plan has three fundamental programmatic focuses that intend to build a mass base with political clarity, organizational capacity, and material self-sufficiency:

1. Building People's Assemblies throughout the Kush District to serve as instruments of "dual power" to counter the abusive powers of the state and of capital whether regional, national, or international.

2. Building an independent political force throughout the state, but concentrated in the Kush District, which will challenge and replace the authority of the two parties of transnational capital, the Democrats and the Republicans, which dominate the arena of electoral politics in the state of Mississippi.

3. Building a solidarity economy in Jackson and throughout the Kush district anchored by a network of cooperatives and supporting institutions

to strengthen worker power and economic democracy in the state.

This experiment is anchored in the rich history of the Black Liberation Movement in Mississippi that extends from Reconstruction to our successful 2013 campaign to elect as Mayor of Jackson a human rights attorney and long-time revolutionary organizer, Chokwe Lumumba. It draws on the practices of grassroots struggles to build consensual democracy, such as the autonomous communities led by the Zapatistas in Chiapas, Mexico, as well as solidarity economies that subordinate capital to labor, such as Mondragón in Euskadi, the Basque region of the Spanish nation-state. Our organization extensively studied these and other international movements for years via study groups, international delegations, and international exchanges. We have tried to absorb their best practices and apply them to our particular conditions.

The fundamental aim of this experiment is to attain power for Afrikan, Indigenous, and other oppressed peoples and exploited classes in order to liberate ourselves from the oppressive systems of white supremacy, capitalism, colonialism, and imperialism in the State of Mississippi.

Contextualizing the Initiative: Challenging Poverty, Prisons, and Paternalism

For most people the potential of our democratic experiment runs counter to the common perceptions about Mississippi as a historic standard-bearer for the ruthless enslavement of African people. As the demand for cotton grew worldwide in the 19th century, Mississippi became the center of the expanding domestic slave trade. Over one million enslaved Afrikans were transported to the Deep South between 1790 and 1860. The brutal conditions in the Mississippi and Ohio River regions inspired the phrase "being sold down the river." The growth of "King Cotton" also resulted in the expulsion of the Indigenous population and the marginalization of poor whites in the face of plantation economies. The failure of radical Reconstruction to dissolve the plantation system after the Civil War, along with the creation of "Black codes" to enforce segregation, created a triple "P" effect that has impacted Mississippi ever since: poverty, prisons, and paternalistic white supremacy.

This paternalist capitalism shifted how Black labor was exploited. Following the collapse of the short-lived Reconstruction government in Mississippi, Black workers were primarily confined to being sharecroppers—farm laborers who worked almost exclusively for the large landowners who were their former owners and their descendants. Wholly dependent on the large landowners for their wages, food, shelter, and medical care, sharecroppers were slaves by another name. This system lasted from the 1870s to the 1960s. It was gradually weakened by the industrialization of large portions of agricultural production, particularly the automation of cotton picking. This displaced nearly a million Black workers between the late 1940s and the early 1970s, forcing them to migrate to urban areas throughout the US.

Industrial manufacturing entered the state on a significant scale in the late 1920s. The key industries included shipbuilding, timber cutting and processing, transport and shipping, canning, and later, industrial farming of catfish, chicken, and pigs. Industrial capital created a system of super-exploitation by manipulating the existing racial order and the fragmentation of the multi-national working class. Black workers were usually relegated to menial positions and those who performed skilled labor in the factories were grossly undercompensated. Capital uses the racial divide to hinder working class consciousness and organization. Beginning in the late 1890s, regional capital, both agricultural and industrial, was able to build a solid alliance with sectors of the white settler working class to resist unionization and to use the passage of Taft-Hartley to defeat the legislative gains of the National Labor Relations Act. Furthermore, the institutionalization of "right to work" laws designed to privilege white workers became a defining feature of paternalist capitalism that governs Mississippi labor relations.

Today, Mississippi is the poorest state in the union with a median household income of $37,095. The City of Jackson is one of the poorest metropolitan cities in the US. Between 2008 and 2012 the median household income was $33,434 and the poverty rate 28.3% (Census Quickfacts, n.d.). According to the US Bureau of Labor Statistics, as of August 2013, the city's "official" unemployment rate stood at 8.0%. However, its "real" unemployment rate is estimated to be above 25% (Amadeo, 2017). Mississippi's wealth equity figures are even worse. It is estimated that people of African descent control less than 10% of the vested capital in the state. Mississippi is also one of the most repressive states in the union. It has the third highest incarceration rate in the US and the overwhelming number of those incarcerated are people of African descent [2]. It is also noted for being at or near the bottom of every major quality of life indicator, including health measures, quality of housing, transportation, worker rights and protections, and educational access and attainment.

Despite Mississippi's oppressive past and present there is tremendous potential for radical transformation. It is our argument that Mississippi constitutes a "weak link"[3] in the bourgeois-democratic capitalist system that underscores the US's settler-colonial regime. Although capitalism has thoroughly dominated social relations in Mississippi since its inception as a colonial entity, the local practice can best be described as a "contingent" expression of that system because of its overt dependency on paternalist white supremacy. The local capitalist and elite classes attempt to maintain social and political control over the state, its peoples, and its resources by tempering and distorting the profit-motive that is central to the capitalist mode of production. This severely restricts agricultural and industrial production, trade, and financial flows in and out of the state. Rather than stimulating growth and maximizing profits through increased production and trade, the local white ruling class has prioritized a strategy of containment that deliberately seeks to fetter the Black population by limiting its access to capital and decent wages, both of which constitute a critical source of labor power and strength in a capitalist society. As an old saying goes, "In Mississippi, money doesn't talk as loud as race."

This contingent form of paternalist capitalism has produced a number of deep contradictions within the state. Black populations constitute a majority in 16 western counties in Mississippi, resulting in the highest percentage of Black elected officials in the union. Furthermore, thousands of Blacks are migrating back to Mississippi every year, and, despite all of the xenophobic initiatives of the Republican Party, a growing immigrant population promises to make it a majority non-white state over the next twenty years. However, demographics are not the only determining factor. A long memory of white supremacy together with its present manifestations make the majority Black populations in the Kush District acutely aware of their interests and compel them to act upon them on every front of social life. It is this combination of favorable demographics, elevated political consciousness, and strong political mobilization that have created the pre-conditions for our political experiment. This is why we characterize Mississippi as a weak link in the chain. Although we cannot limit our activities to these weak links, it is crucial that we identify and utilize them because they provide more space to demonstrate practical alternatives that can galvanize momentum for similar projects in more difficult circumstances.

A Short History of Black Resistance in Mississippi

People of African descent have a long history of resistance against colonization, enslavement, exploitation, and white supremacy in the lands that now comprise the state of Mississippi. One of the earliest acts of resistance was the Natchez rebellion of 1729 when an alliance of enslaved Africans and Indigenous people from the Natchez nation rebelled against French colonists (Boler, 2006). This was followed by countless numbers of enslaved Africans who liberated themselves and became maroons in the backwoods of the territory during its early days as a French, Spanish, English, and American colonial possession. There were also numerous slave rebellions during the antebellum period in Mississippi.

After the Civil War, people of African descent organized several independent communities, purchased considerable portions of farm land, started countless businesses, and won a considerable number of political offices in the Reconstruction government. These efforts continued even after the defeat of Reconstruction and the imposition of the brutal Jim Crow apartheid regime established the threat of constant terror. In the three decades following the Second World War resistance grew to levels unmatched since Reconstruction.

The height of this resistance was in the 1960s during the rise of Medgar Evers and the National Association for the Advancement of Colored People (NAACP), the militant campaigns of the Student Non-Violent Coordinating Committee (SNCC), the Congress of Racial Equality (CORE), the Southern Christian Leadership Conference (SCLC), and their alliance in the Conference of Federated Organizations (COFO).

In the electoral arena, attempts by Blacks to independently challenge and change our social and political status go back to the 1964 creation of the Mississippi Freedom Democratic Party (MFDP) through COFO. The MFDP famously challenged the Democrat's "Dixiecrat" wing by attempting to seat delegates at the 1964 Democratic National Convention in Atlantic City, New Jersey. Despite its recent emergence on the scene as an organized force, the MFDP immediately carried significant weight in the Black community because of the historic struggles waged by Black activists to enter the party in the mid-1960s and then to assume majority control in the early 1970s.

Ever since, building an independent political vehicle through the MFDP or an independent political party have been points of contention. The vast majority of political activists in the Black community have argued that it is better for Black people in Mississippi to be linked with the Democratic Party and the multi-racial alliance that it has represented since the New Deal. In particular, they contend that alliances with the Democrats are necessary for promoting progressive legislation that serves the interests of the Black community and for repelling attacks from conservatives and racists. During the 1960s and '70s, the Democratic Party's tepid support for the civil rights movement as well as the policies and programs that emerged therefrom largely incorporated Mississippi's Black community into its 'hegemony,' the social processes utilized by ruling elites to consolidate, justify, and normalize their social domination. Our challenge is how to address the hegemony of "Democratic Tradition" within the Black community, particularly among its "consistent voters" throughout the state and beyond. One reason why Mississippi is a weak link is because its Democratic Party is not particularly strong. The national party leadership takes the Black vote for granted and is reluctant to invest adequate resources because of the Republican Party's firm grip on the overwhelming majority of white voters in the state.

From these struggles a tradition was born and has been nurtured over forty years. Emerging from this tradition are ongoing efforts both to revitalize the MFDP as well as to build an independent party. The work to revitalize the MFDP is the stronger of the two initiatives in large part due to its pre-existing infrastructure and credibility. More activists also view it as having greater strategic utility because it enables work to be distinct from, yet still a part of, the critical Democratic Party primary system in Jackson. Given that Jackson is over 80% Black, and that nearly 99% of the Black community in the city and the state support the Democrats, the Democratic primary constitutes the "real" election in Jackson, and it has served this purpose since at least 1993, when the split in the Black vote between Henry Kirksey and Harvey Johnson delayed the eventuality of a Black Mayor until 1997. For this reason, many activists don't want to jettison the MFDP for something wholly new. Despite this, the initiative is still relatively small and will take some time to come to full and complete resolution within the broader movement.

Our efforts to build an independent political force that could elect Chokwe Lumumba to Jackson City Council and then Mayor bridged the history of the MFDP with the radical political objectives that emerged out of the New Afrikan Independence Movement, the Provisional Government of the Republic of New Afrika, and the Revolutionary Action Movement/African People's Party, which collectively gave birth to the New Afrikan People's Organization and the Malcolm X Grassroots Movement.

The Jackson-Kush Plan was key to the rise of Mayor Lumumba, but electoral work is only one aspect. The Plan is a movement for economic, political, and cultural self-determination that emerged out of the Jackson People's Assembly in 2005 as a response to the crisis of displacement and disenfranchisement in the aftermath of Hurricane Katrina. The idea was to first build a solid base in Jackson, the center of commerce and mass media in Mississippi, which will then enable us to branch out to allies in the Kush.

There are three interlocking components of the Jackson Plan: 1) the People's Assembly; 2) an independent political vehicle that can win political office; and 3) worker cooperatives and a solidarity economy. Tremendous strides have been made in each of these initiatives, but as we will now see, they have developed unevenly.

Building and Sustaining the People's Assembly

The key to this experiment in direct democracy is building a social movement that can successfully use the favorable socio-material conditions in Jackson and throughout the Kush District to transform oppressive and exploitative social relations. The vehicle most critical to this transformative process is the People's Assembly because it allows the people of Jackson to practice democracy, by which we mean "the rule of the people, for the people, by the people," in its broadest terms. This entails making direct decisions not only in the limited realm of what is generally deemed the "political" (the contractual, electoral, and legislative aspects of the social order), but also the economic, social, and cultural operations of our community. The New Afrikan People's Organization and the Malcolm X Grassroots Movement started organizing assemblies in the late 1980s to allow Black people to exercise self-determination and exert their power.

A People's Assembly is a mass gathering of people organized and assembled to address essential social issues that are pertinent to a community. We define a body as a "mass" body when it engages at least 1/5 of the total population in a defined geographic area, whether it is a neighborhood, ward, city, or state. We have arrived at this formula after nearly 20 years of experience of what it takes to amass sufficient social forces and capacities to effectively implement the decisions made by the Assembly.

The Jackson People's Assembly is based on a "one person, one vote" principle. We emphasize that agency must be vested directly in individuals, regardless of whether the Assembly makes decisions through a voting process or some form of consensus. This aspect of direct engagement and individual empowerment distinguishes a People's Assembly from other types of mass gatherings in which a multitude of social forces are engaged. For example, alliances and united fronts tend to reinforce hierarchal structures because their leaders make the decisions on behalf of the people they claim to "represent," often without their knowledge and direct consent. On the scale of organizing millions of people, we acknowledge that it is often impossible to avoid at least some representational processes. On the population scale in Jackson, however, we can engage in more direct and participatory forms of democratic decision-making and governance.

At present, the Jackson People's Assembly operates at an oscillating mid-point between what we describe as a "constituent assembly" and a "mass assembly." A constituent assembly is a representative body that is dependent on mass outreach but it is structured, intentionally or unintentionally, to accommodate material and social obstacles to participation, such as having to work, caring for children, lacking access to information, and political and ideological differences. The challenge with this type of assembly is that it tends to become overly bureaucratic and stagnant if it doesn't continue to bring in new people, especially youth, and if it is unable to maintain the struggle on a mass-scale. A mass assembly is the purer example of a people's democracy. It normally emerges during times of acute crisis when there are profound ruptures in society. These types of assemblies are typically all-consuming, short-lived entities. Their greatest weakness is that they usually demand that participants give all of their time and energy to engaging the crisis, which is unsustainable because people eventually have to tend to their daily needs.

Due to these circumstances, the Jackson People's Assembly operates principally as a constituent assembly that engages in a number of strategic campaigns to address the material needs of our social base and to elevate its economic power. Nevertheless, during times of crisis the Assembly tends to adopt more of a mass character. This occurred, for example, amid the untimely death of Mayor Lumumba in late February 2014. This meant that the People's Assembly had to defend many of the initiatives of the Lumumba administration that were based in the "People's Platform" devised by the Assembly. Even though the current practice in Jackson tends towards the constituent model, however, the aim is to grow into a permanent mass assembly of a "new type." This more permanent mass assembly would be built by diffusing the Assembly deeper into the neighborhoods. These neighborhood Assemblies will anchor the program of the People's Assembly by addressing the specific community-level economic and social needs, such as the program of digital fabrication and 'computer numerical control manufacturing' being designed and implemented by Cooperation Jackson. These neighborhood Assemblies will form the basis of overlapping "all city" Task Force structures that would coordinate the productive and social activities of the Assembly while maintaining its coherent municipal character.

More broadly, our Assembly has two broad functions and means of exercising power. The first is to organize "autonomous" social projects not supported by the government or some variant of monopoly capital, whether financial, corporate, industrial, or mercantile. These types of projects include organizing community gardens, people's self-defense campaigns, housing occupations, as well as forming unions and worker cooperatives. On a basic scale these projects function as serve-the-people survival programs that help our community to sustain itself and acquire a degree of self-reliance. On a larger scale these projects provide enough resources and social leverage (such as flexible time to organize) to allow people to engage in essential resistance and/or offensive (typically positional) initiatives.

The second means of exercising power is to apply pressure on the government and the forces of economic exploitation in society. We exert pressure by organizing various types of campaigns including mass action protests, direct action campaigns, boycotts, non-compliance campaigns, and policy-shift campaigns that either advocate for or against existing, proposed, or pending laws.

In order to carry out these critical functions, an Assembly must produce clear demands, a coherent strategy, realistic action plans, and concrete timelines. It must also organize itself into committees or action groups that can carry them out. Our model makes clear distinctions between the Assembly as an "event," a "process," and an "institution." The Assembly as an event is where we deliberate on general questions and issues and decide what can be done to address them. The Assembly as a process is where the various committees and working groups refine the more detailed questions of goals, strategy, and timelines. The Assembly as an institution is a product of the combined social weight of the Assembly's events and processes as well as its actions and outcomes. Although the authority of the Assembly is expressed to its highest extent during the mass "events," the real work of the Assembly that enables it to exercise its power is carried out by its committees and working groups.

The coordinating committee of the Assembly is the People's Task Force. It is a body directly elected by the Assembly, serves at its will, and is subject to its immediate recall, which means that its members can be replaced, with due process, at any time. Its primary function is to facilitate the work of the committees by ensuring that they meet regularly or as often as is deemed necessary; that each body has as a facilitator, an agenda, and note-takers if these are not provided by the committees; that there is open communication between the committees; that all of the actions of the committees are communicated thoroughly to the rest of the Assembly; and that they coordinate the logistics for the Assembly gatherings.

Committees are regularly constituted bodies of the Assembly whose functions include outreach and mobilization, media and communications, fundraising and finance, intelligence gathering, trainings, and security. Working groups are campaign- or project-oriented bodies that execute the time-limited goals of the Assembly. Our working groups have successfully campaigned for the release of the Scott Sisters;[4] for the federal government to provide more housing aid to internally displaced persons from New Orleans and the Gulf Coast after Hurricane Katrina; and for an alliance between the Assembly and public transportation workers which saved Jackson's public transportation system and won its workers higher wages. All committees and working groups are comprised of volunteers who, for the most part, choose where to focus their energies on a self-selecting basis.

In various social movements throughout the world People's Assemblies wield different types of power depending on local conditions and the balance of forces. In the last five years, in places like Nepal, Greece, and Spain they have revolutionized people's daily lives and have even played significant roles in altering public discourse, shifting the balance of power within nation-states, and in a few cases have led to the toppling governments in Tunisia, Egypt, and Burkina Faso (Pandey, 2016; Moschonas, 2013; Hagberg, 2016).

What follows is a brief explanation of what People's Assemblies can accomplish in different historical circumstances and conditions.

1. During periods of stability when capitalist governments and markets can maintain the status quo, Assemblies can push for various "positional" reforms like the implementation of police control boards or local citizens' review boards, such as the Every 28 Hours Campaign (MXGM, 2013; 2014). Assemblies can also engage in projects with low-to-mid-scale autonomy like "self-reliant" worker cooperatives, such as Cooperative Jackson's Sustainable Communities Initiative, which I will describe below (SCI, n.d.).

2. During periods of radical upsurge Assemblies can push for structural reforms and engage in projects for mid-to-large-scale autonomy. For example, between 1998 and 2010, Assemblies in Venezuela were able to push the Chavez administration to make radical changes to the constitution, form numerous cooperatives, construct affordable housing, and engage in significant land transfers to poor people.

3. During pre-revolutionary periods Assemblies can become parallel institutions that assume some of the functions of the government. Over the last 10 years the revolutionary movement in Nepal organized Assemblies to act as a direct counterweight to the monarchy and the military, which

resulted in the founding of a constitutional democracy and a more "representative" legislative body. In another recent example, from 1994 until the mid-2000s, the Zapatistas in Chiapas, Mexico were able create extensive zones of "self-rule" and "autonomous production" that were governed by Assemblies.

4. During revolutionary periods, Assemblies, when buttressed by revolutionary political parties, can effectively become the government and assume control over the basic processes and mechanisms of production. In the 1980s, Assemblies commanded this much power in Haiti, the Philippines, Nicaragua, Burkina Faso, and Grenada (Roseberry-Polier, 2011; Sison, 2006; Hagberg, 2016; Boodhoo, 1984). The closest example in recent times are: Egypt in the winter of 2011 and the summer of 2013 as well as Nepal during stretches between 2003 and 2006. In the case of Burkina Faso and Grenada the Assemblies were often fostered and organized by the revolutionary political party.

5. During periods of retreat Assemblies can defend their people and leaders, fight to maintain their gains, and prepare for the next upsurge. The experiences of the Lavalas movement in Haiti in the early 1990s and mid-2000s is perhaps the best example of how Assemblies and other people's organizations can weather the storm of counter-revolutions and defeats.

The driving forces of an Assembly, and in particular, its organic intellectuals, organizers, and cultural workers, should be able to clearly distinguish between acting as a "counter-hegemonic" force during stable and pre-revolutionary periods and acting as a "hegemonic" force during revolutionary periods. This means distinguishing between, on the one hand, acts of positioning, such as building allies, assembling resources, and changing the dominant social narratives, and on the other hand, acts of maneuvering, such as open confrontation and conflict with the repressive forces of the state and capital.[5]

As for the Jackson People's Assembly, our effort to expand its scale and scope has been consistent. The greatest challenge to the Assembly has been the almost non-stop run of electoral campaigns in which our movement has been engaged since 2009. For considerable periods, significant sections of the Assembly's base have served as the organizing force driving the electoral campaigns. At times this has challenged the standard operations of the Assembly and in some moments created tensions regarding its role. On more than one occasion the strategic question has been raised, is the Assembly primarily a vehicle to build "dual power" or is it a vehicle to nurture and support progressive political candidates? The affirmative answer from the vast majority of the Assembly's base is consistently that it must be a vehicle to exercise political power outside of elected office. Nevertheless, as we will now see, the challenge to act in a manner contrary to the hegemonic sway of electoral politics is a constant struggle.

Engaging Power: the Administration of Mayor Chokwe Lumumba

To date, the most critical experience we have accumulated in the realm of engaging power is the brief administration of the late Mayor Chokwe Lumumba, which lasted almost seven months, from July 1, 2013 until his untimely death on February 25, 2014. Chokwe first moved to Mississippi in 1971 to support the project of the Provisional Government of the Republic of New Afrika to establish its capitol in the state of Mississippi. This effort was brutally suppressed by the US government in August 1971 when 11 of its leaders and activists became prisoners of war. Chokwe became a lawyer in large part to defend and free these organizers, who became known nationally and internationally as the RNA-11. After spending some years in the late 1970s and early '80s in Detroit and New York City, Chokwe returned to Mississippi permanently in the mid-1980s to build the New Afrikan People's Organization and advance the development of a mass movement through the Malcolm X Grassroots Movement, which was founded in Jackson in 1990.

The decades of base-building and forging strategic alliances among various forces in the city and state enabled us to start seriously considering Chokwe for political office in the mid-2000s. The catalyst for this consideration was our analysis of the weakening of Black people power, especially in the Gulf Coast region, following the devastation and displacement wrought by Hurricane Katrina. After careful deliberation and planning, our organizations devised the Jackson-Kush Plan and in the spring of 2009 we were able to elect Chokwe to the Jackson City Council representing Ward 2. This was followed by the successful election of Hinds County's first Black Sherriff, Tyrone Lewis in 2011. In June 2013, we were able to elect Chokwe Mayor. Although we were only able to move a mere fraction of our electoral agenda during his time in office, we did gain a tremendous amount of experience about how to better "engage state power."

We say "engaging state power" rather than "wielding state power" for two reasons. First, the capitalist and imperialist nature of the American constitutional framework limits the agency of any individual office-holder at every level of government. We often try to drive this point home to the broader movement by saying, "It should be clear that, at best, we won an election, a popularity contest. We did not win the ability to control the government, just the temporary ability to influence its tactical affairs on a municipal level."

Second, we are an organization that is part of a radical movement for New Afrikan or Black liberation whose strategic aim has historically been and continues to be the decolonization of the southeastern portion of the US. Therefore, pursuing an elected office within the US government has been viewed by many of our historic allies as a means of legitimizing the powers-that-be. In remaining consistent with the pursuit of self-determination and national liberation, our campaigns for any elected office within the US constitutional framework are assessed and conducted on a case-by-case basis according to the potential for that office to either create more democratic space or advance policies that test the limits of structural change.

Given these limitations, our electoral initiatives are "temporal," meaning short to mid-term engagements that attempt to bring to light various social contradictions by making every critical issue a mass issue. In so doing, we ask the people to demand structural solutions, what many call "transitional demands,"[6] that attempt to address the contradictions at their root. Doing this is easier said than done, but under the leadership of the New Afrikan People's Organization and the Malcolm X Grassroots Movement, our electoral work has been able to move consistently in this direction by engaging in three key strategies:

1. *Mass Education.* The key to our ability to make transitional demands on a consistent basis is to constantly engage in mass education work that makes direct causal and structural links between local realities and national and international issues. It is much easier to raise transitional demands when there is widespread understanding that our local issues are expressions of systemic issues. The People's Assembly is the primary vehicle of mass education. We use instruments such as community outreach, forums, radio, newsletters, editorials in local allied newspapers, and social media. It has taken nearly two decades of consistent mass education work to build the level and depth of social consciousness that exists presently in Jackson.

2. *Preparatory Battles.* One of the keys of our electoral success has been transferring victories from social justice struggles to the electoral arena. This requires picking key pre-electoral fights that highlight the essence of our political platform and distinguish us from other candidates and political forces. From our vantage point, these preparatory battles must not only help bring together and build broad sectors of the community. They must also have the ability to educate the masses by raising consciousness and preparing them for future struggles by building the capacity and organizational strength necessary to become transformative agents. There were two key battles in the period between 2009 and 2013 when Chokwe served as a City Councilperson.

The first issue was fighting to save Jackson's public transportation system, expand its services, and increase the wages of its workers. This was not only a fight against neoliberal austerity, but a battle to address an ongoing structural weakness in Jackson. Like a lot of midsized Southern cities, Jackson has an inadequate public transportation system. Most people must own vehicles to get around. In a city with high concentrations of poverty, transportation costs can be exorbitant for an average worker making minimum wage or less. This struggle also aided the elderly, who constitute a high percentage of the population, as well as people with disabilities. Fighting a proposed cut of a public good with a proposed expansion resonated with broad sectors of the working class and highlighted key material differences in our approach and concerns.

The second issue was putting forth and passing an anti-racial profiling ordinance. This ordinance was intentionally designed to address, on the one hand, policing strategies that would further criminalize and imprison Black people, and on the other hand, proposed xenophobic measures on a municipal and state level to detain and deport undocumented immigrants. Proposing our ordinance forced a conversation about the repressive nature of the state and the need for common unity of various communities, especially "Black and Brown Unity," in fighting the forces of white supremacy. The ordinance passed because of how it was framed. It galvanized working and professional sectors in the Black, Latino, white, and immigrant communities by demonstrating that they had common interests and common enemies.

3. *Operational Fronts.* Since the early 1990s, with the emergence of the Jackson People's Assembly, the New Afrikan People's Organization has built coalitions that are as operational as they are political. By "operational" we mean that each organization in the front plays a designated role, not just in the coalition, but in the broader arena of social struggle against white supremacy, economic exploitation, and state violence. Building a coalition in this manner helps to avoid unproductive competition within the movement and advances a division of labor that builds interdependent and vested relationships. It also enables us to develop long-term and deep political commitments to move beyond "least common denominator" platforms that are typical of coalitions. The clearest expression of the depth of these relationships is the People's Platform, which was developed in 2009 under the leadership of the People's Assembly and adopted by all of the strategic allies in our various operational fronts.

A key to our Operational Fronts approach has been the construction of three different but fundamentally inter-related bodies: the Popular Front, the United Front, and the National Liberation Front. Although these are often regarded as mutually exclusive strategies, we buck the trend. We conceive of the Popular Front as a big tent in the fight against white supremacy, fascist aggression, and other forms of economic and social reaction. It is intentionally constructed as a multi-class, multi-racial, and multi-national front that seeks to address broad social issues on the basis of the highest level of unity possible. Meanwhile, the purpose of the United

Front is to build and maintain strategic fields of engagement with various social forces with bases in the working class. It focuses on working class struggles for jobs, higher wages, better working conditions, and to counter the mass repression and incarceration of the working class. It is critical to note that in Mississippi most of these social forces are not unions or worker centers, although both are represented in the front. Rather, it is comprised primarily of churches and community organizations. Finally, the National Liberation Front is a multi-class front of New Afrikan or Black forces focusing on the broad and multi-facetted struggle for self-determination for people of African descent.

In terms of policy, since we assumed that we would occupy the Mayoral office for at least one term, we prioritized transformative policies because we thought that their impact would be the most enduring legacy of our administrative term. These policies include the following:

1. Make Jackson a sustainable city centered on the production and use of renewable energy sources and "zero waste" production and consumption methods.

2. Support cooperatives and cooperative development in the city, including but not limited to the creation of a cooperative incubator in the city's department of planning and development, as well as the creation of a cooperative start-up loan fund.

3. Mandate strict local hiring policies for city contract awards to ensure greater equity.

4. Enforce strong community benefit agreements and reinvestment requirements for corporations, commercial retailers, and developers wanting to do business in Jackson.

5. Expand and modernize public transportation systems in the city, including the support for rail projects and renewable energy fleets.

6. Expand public health services and guarantee access for residents to join the programs of the Affordable Health Care Act that have largely been rejected by the state government.

7. Expand the democratic scope of public education, and in particular, change policy to make school board positions elected rather than appointed by the Mayor.

8. Create strong community oversight of the police through a control board with the power to subpoena, indict, and fire officers for misconduct or human rights violations. We also sought to implement policies that de-criminalized the possession and use of marijuana in order to end one aspect of the "war on drugs" which has largely served as a war on the

Black working class and produced the largest carceral state on earth.

9. Create policies to institutionalize participatory budgeting in order to be fully transparent, better allocate resources, and deepen democracy on a significant scale.

10. Institutionalize a Human Rights Charter and Human Rights Commission to require the city to abide by international norms and standards of conduct and policy outcomes.

All of these policies sought to institutionalize certain aspects of the People's Platform. We believed that we could pass this entire legislative agenda because of the momentum of the People's Assembly together with the overall balance of power between the Mayor and the City Council. Jackson has seven electoral wards and seven City Councilpersons. During the Lumumba administration there were five Black Councilpersons and two white Councilpersons. Four of the Black Councilpersons were solidly aligned with the administration and the fifth generally fell in line to avoid looking obstructionist. One white Councilperson was a member of the Democratic Party and is viewed as liberal within the Jackson context. She supported and voted for our agenda as long as it didn't overtly threaten the power of developers who were key to her electoral success. The other white Councilperson was affiliated with the Tea Party faction of the Republican Party and typically voted against anything we proposed on ideological grounds. Despite Chokwe's untimely death, his short administration accomplished a number of significant things. It passed a 1% Sales Tax to raise revenues to fix the city's crumbling infrastructure and keep its water system from being regionalized or privatized, which would have diluted Black political control. It published the Jackson Rising Policy Statement, the administration's most concrete translation of the People's Platform into public policy recommendations. Finally, it introduced participatory democratic practices into Jackson's municipal government.

The Lumumba administration attempted to govern the city as an open book by allowing the City Council to engage in all departmental planning sessions, participate directly in budgeting sessions, and by having weekly one-on-one meetings with all seven Council members. These practices had never been done in Jackson and have not been followed by Chokwe's successor. We also turned all major policy decisions into "mass questions" and "mass engagements." On two major occasions the Lumumba administration organized processes for the general public to decide on a major issue: the passage of an "infrastructure repair budget" in October 2013 and the 1% Sales Tax referendum in January 2014 which passed with 94%. As part of the political project of democratizing American democracy, this process elicited mass support, built a public culture of participatory engagement, and shifted the balance of political power towards the Black working class. The more the class was engaged and actually exercised decision-making power, the less governance was an elite affair ruled by technocrats and the servants of capital.

Our administration's main constraint, which ultimately occupied much of our time in office, was a threatening consent decree forced on the city by the Environmental Protection Agency (EPA) in late 2012 to address its water quality issues. Jackson has some of the worst water quality of any midsize city in the country. The problem is Jackson's antiquated water delivery system. In the "historic section" of Jackson built before the early 1960s, most of the pipes are made of copper and lead and are over 100 years old. The EPA decree stipulates that, from 2012, the city has 17 years, with strict intermittent timelines of three, five, and ten years, to complete an entire overhaul of the water delivery system or face severe penalties and the possibility of losing control over the ownership and management of the system. It was estimated in 2013 that the overall cost of this overhaul would be at least $1 billion.

The questions this threat posed to our administration were, first, how to generate the revenue to cover this expense and retain control of the water system, and second, how to do it without sacrificing other standard expenditures and critical programs, policies, and our overall agenda. The truth is that we did not have an adequate answer to these questions. The population at large and our social base in particular were adamant about not losing control over the system. But there were divisions within and between the administration and our social base about how to save it and how to generate the resources to do so. These problems were exacerbated by members of the Tea Party in the state legislature who introduced an emergency management bill modeled on a Michigan law that would have allowed the state to take over troubled municipalities.

Our differences of opinion and lack of clarity on these issues, coupled with our general inexperience in governing, resulted in our administration enacting a set of contradictory policies. One set of policies resulted in raised water rates while another led to a 1% sales tax raise. It also compelled a faction of our administration to engage forces outside of our standard theory and framework of practice in alliance-building. On the advice of Frank Biden—brother of Vice-President Joe Biden—and the Blue Green Consultant Group—an engineering and sustainable energy consulting firm tied to Biden and to various transnational corporations—some members of our administration started to appeal to, and entertain advice and offers from, transnational corporate engineering firms to repair and finance our consent decree operations. The reasoning for this deviation was to explore creative ways to finance the water system overhaul in order to retain the city's control over it.

The end result of this confusion was that our policies and actions alienated a critical portion of our base, particularly the elderly on fixed incomes for whom the increased water rate created a degree of hardship without sufficient explanation or enough relief. This confusion and alienation proved costly for our next attempt to engage with electoral politics.

When Mayor Lumumba suddenly died, City Council followed the protocols of the city's charter by appointing an interim Mayor and scheduling a special election for the Mayor's seat in mid-April 2014, barely a month and a half after Chokwe's death. In order to continue advancing our agenda, the base of our movement compelled Chokwe's youngest son Chokwe Antar Lumumba to run for Mayor. However, the movement did not have enough time to reflect on the lessons learned from Mayor Lumumba's term, let alone collectively internalize them to refine its practice. As a result, we did not adequately address all of the contradictions that had developed during the Lumumba Administration. This led to the demobilization of a critical part of our base. Although Chokwe Antar made it to the run-off round of the special election and won a solid majority of Black voters (officially 67%), he lost the election to City Councilman Tony Yarber by nearly 2,500 votes.

In a city that is nearly 80% Black, facts generally dictate that the person who wins the Black majority vote wins the elections. The 2014 Special Election was an exceptional case in that now-Mayor Tony Yarber only won 32% of the Black vote but secured an overwhelming 90% of the city's white minority vote which turned out at a record-breaking rate of 75%. Although the historic white voter turnout was crucial, the decisive factor was actually the low Black voter turnout. Plain and simple, the base did not turn out. They sent us a clear message and we are now in the process of internalizing these lessons so that we can continue to advance our critical experiment. The key takeaways are as follows:

1. The process of mass education and instructional struggle is more important than holding office. During our brief period in office we believed that the act of governing was just as important as mass education. We now believe decisively that mass education and instructional struggle must be primary. We have to constantly engage the base on all critical questions throughout the entire process of any decision so that they understand all of the choices and their implications and can make sound collective decisions.

2. Our practice has to be as sound as our theory. Our practice of governance did not always equate to our previous work of building an independent base of political power rooted in a democratic mass movement. Capacity was our most critical challenge in this regard. Key members in the administration who had been crucial to building the mass base of our democratic experiment often did not have the capacity to fully participate in the People's Assembly or in other areas of the mass work because they were preoccupied with learning their new positions and the limits they entailed.

Since 2009, our broad efforts have developed scores of new organizers, both young and old, but our plans to systematically train and develop these new organizers have not been as intentional as we desired. Securing adequate resources to develop a school and training program we call the Amandla Project has been a challenge. Many of the organizers who have the experience, training, and skill to serve as dynamic educators and trainers have had to bottom-line other critical areas of work on our agenda that, more often than not, have taken priority. After the passing of Mayor Lumumba, the Jackson People's Assembly and the organic leadership of the Jackson-Kush Plan initiative determined that being intentional about the development of new cadres should be made a top priority. Since Chokwe's experience and skill as a leader could not be replicated and replaced, we would have to "raise hundreds of new Chokwes" to not only sustain but advance the initiative. Along with the Jackson Human Rights Institute, we are now conducting ongoing trainings at the Chokwe Lumumba Center for Economic Democracy and Development.

3. The United Front and the National Liberation Front must take precedence over the Popular Front. To pass legislative initiatives like the 1% sales tax we over-emphasized appeals to the Popular Front to the detriment of the other Fronts. The small-business faction of our base cringed at the notion of taxing corporations and the wealthy to pay for the system's redevelopment, primarily out of fear of "scaring away" the few industrial and commercial employers that remain in the city. This produced friction within the United Front because many workers felt that we were privileging middle-class interests and concerns over the concrete needs of the working class. This contributed to the demobilization experienced during the April 2014 Special Election. Even a relatively well-organized and mobilized mass movement is seriously constrained by the structural limits of capitalism, particularly in its neoliberal form. This taught us the extent to which we have to avoid the many pitfalls of neo-colonialism that are centered in unprincipled alliances among oppressed peoples as well as between the leaders of the oppressed and the forces of the oppressor.

4. We have learned the extent to which governing in the neoliberal era is a ruling class project of "accumulation by dispossession"[7] that generates private wealth by plundering public goods on all levels of government. Under present dynamics there is intense economic compulsion to govern the city as if it were a business, especially midsize cities like ours with a declining tax base and diminishing job opportunities. Rather than providing essential services, politicians ravenously search for savings like capitalists seek profits. This encourages everything from privatizing and outsourcing services, consolidating and downsizing government departments, depressing wages, and breaking unions and other forms of worker solidarity. Since there are fewer profitable ventures in the real economy, various forces of capital view the municipal state as a depository bank that they must politically capture in order to survive. This is true especially of small-business owners who are the only real faction

of capital in the Black community in Jackson. The Black elite is a driving dynamic in Jackson's politics. This poses deep challenges for a radical project ultimately trying to transform the capitalist social order on a local level, but which remains dependent in part on alliances with "petite bourgeois" or small-capital social forces in order to win elections and govern effectively. We, along with left forces engaging in similar initiatives elsewhere, have to figure out how to win elections and govern without relying on the resources and skills of these vacillating social forces.

We are now recalculating and rebuilding our Operational Fronts in the wake of the new conditions and regional alliances that have been created by the forces of capital in response to our success in 2013. The main issue is how to build a new and more reliable Popular Front in light of capital's clear aim to split our previously existing alliances over questions of economic development. In light of our mixed experiences engaging state power we are now focusing our work on revitalizing the People's Assembly and initiating economic transformation through cooperative development in the form of Cooperation Jackson. This is to better prepare us for the next round of Mayoral and City Council elections in 2017 when we intend to again run Chokwe Antar Lumumba for Mayor together with several other candidates for City Council as determined by the People's Assembly.[8]
　　We have prioritized building Cooperation Jackson during this next period to strengthen the organization of the working class, expand production in our city and region, and to build a more coherent movement for economic democracy.

Cooperation Jackson and the Struggle to Create Economic Democracy

Cooperation Jackson is an emerging vehicle for sustainable community development, economic democracy, community ownership, and resistance to gentrification. It will consist of four interdependent institutions: an emerging federation of local worker cooperatives, a developing cooperative incubator, a cooperative education and training center, and a cooperative bank or financial institution (Cooperation Jackson, n.d.). The broad mission of Cooperation Jackson is to advance economic democracy by promoting universal access to common resources. In defiance of the culture of cutthroat competition, this network of worker-owned and self-managed cooperatives will create a "solidarity economy" based in shared values of social responsibility and equity.
　　Cooperative businesses are unique from other types of commercial enterprises in that they exist to meet the needs of people, not to maximize profits. They are often formed as a way to expand economic opportunity,

promote sustainability, and build community-wealth by creating jobs with dignity, stability, living wages, and quality benefits. Rather than making working people subservient to capital, cooperatives put capital in the service of working people by:

1. Democratizing the processes of production, distribution, and consumption

2. Equitably distributing the surpluses produced or exchanged

3. Creating economies of scale

4. Increasing bargaining power

5. Sharing costs of new technology

6. Gaining access to new markets

7. Reducing individual market risks

8. Creating and obtaining new services

9. Purchasing in bulk to achieve lower prices

10. Providing credit under reasonable terms

Cooperatives and community collectives have a long history in Mississippi, particularly within the Afrikan community. In particular, Cooperation Jackson draws from Fannie Lou Hamer and her work to build the Freedom Farm Cooperative, and the Federation of Southern Cooperatives/Land Assistance Fund which helped lay the foundations for the broader initiative to build a dynamic democratic economy in Jackson (Mills, 2007).

We want to accomplish a major breakthrough for the cooperative movement in the South by becoming the first major network of predominately worker cooperatives to be established in an urban area. While it will undoubtedly take years, if not decades, we believe we possess the potential to transform the lives of working class Jacksonians by becoming the Mondragón or Emilia-Romagna of the United States (Mondragón, n.d.; People's Food Co-op, n.d.). We hope to create a model that will encourage and enable workers throughout the US to implement their own initiatives to promote economic democracy, solidarity economics, and cooperative development.

Cooperation Jackson's primary focus is the Sustainable Communities Initiative (SCI). It is a place-based strategy to transform a neighborhood in West Jackson, the working class gateway to Downtown Jackson. For more than 30 years West Jackson has suffered from rapid capital flight and divestment that are driven in large part by white flight. Since the late 1970s West Jackson has become a Black working class community with high concentrations of poverty. Since the late 1980s large parts of West Jackson have become dilapidated and abandoned. It is now estimated that there are over 1,832 vacant lots and

832 abandoned structures out of a total of 6,748 lots in the community with approximately 41% of total parcels in the community unused. The community has an estimated 13,890 people of which 92% are Black.[9]

In Municipal Ward 3, the primary focus of the SCI, there is an estimated eight thousand people, the overwhelming majority of whom are Black working class people. The community is almost exclusively a bedroom community with few employment opportunities at present. The largest employers in the community are Jackson State University and Jackson Public Schools. Vast tracts of this community are either vacant or dilapidated and abandoned. The community is also in a food desert. Residents typically have to travel 2-3 miles to access quality food.

Four major real estate and economic initiatives developing adjacent to West Jackson are driving speculative pressures on the community and confronting it with the threat of gentrification through race- and class-based displacement. The four development initiatives are the Medical Corridor being driven by the University of Mississippi and funded by the state government, the One Lake Redevelopment initiative being pushed by the Greater Jackson Chamber of Commerce and proposed in "Plan 2022," the development of a new sports stadium for Jackson State University athletics through the destruction of the old stadium in the Medical Corridor development area, and downtown real estate speculation fueled by various petrochemical companies seeking to expand their lobbying and business operations in the state capitol. Each initiative is in a different stage of development, but all have dedicated and committed funding streams and widespread support among local elites.

The primary force compelling this speculation is the Medical Corridor. Its expansion provides the economic conditions that enable the other developments. Over the course of the next decade the corridor's expansion will provide hundreds of short-term construction jobs and thousands of long-term jobs in the medical and medical support fields. All of these new doctors, nurses, technicians and other support and spin-off workers will need places to live. Many will want to avoid long suburban commutes and to have easy access to various living amenities and opportunities for entertainment. Knowing these needs and anticipating the long-term profits that can be drawn from them, speculators and developers are rapidly moving in on West Jackson due to its strategic location, accessibility, and cheap real estate values.

None of these elite-driven developments are designed to incorporate the existing population living in West Jackson. This is where Cooperation Jackson and the SCI come into the picture. Cooperation Jackson is not averse to economic development, of which West Jackson and many other Black working class communities throughout the city are in desperate need. However, we are committed to sustainable community driven and controlled development without displacement. We firmly believe that the existing community must equitably benefit from the new developments and should be able to determine and execute its own community revitalization and wealth-building initiatives.

The SCI is one of the few bottom-up development initiatives in Jackson. It is being driven by the membership of Cooperation Jackson through extensive community outreach, but its foundations were laid by the long-standing organizing efforts of the Malcolm X Grassroots Movement and the Jackson People's Assembly. The SCI's success will mitigate the displacement of the Black community of West Jackson and create an array of eco-friendly and community-owned cooperative businesses and institutions that will be accessible to both the longstanding and new residents of West Jackson.

We will accomplish this by establishing the following institutions:

1. *Community Land Trust* (CLT). Cooperation Jackson will create a nonprofit corporation that develops and stewards affordable housing, community gardens, civic buildings, commercial spaces, and other community assets. We will purchase a number of vacant lots, abandoned homes, and commercial facilities primarily in West Jackson that are currently owned by the State of Mississippi, the City of Jackson, and private owners. We will organize them into a community land trust to ensure that they are removed from the speculative market and dedicated to sustainable communal endeavors.

2. *Community Development Corporation* (CDC). Cooperation Jackson will create a community development corporation to help create new low-income housing to sustain working class communities and affordable commercial facilities to support the development of cooperative enterprises in Jackson.

3. *Housing Co-operative*. Cooperation Jackson will turn a significant portion of the land and properties acquired and held by the CLT into an "Eco-Village" housing cooperative. This will provide quality affordable housing and stable rents to help sustain and build vibrant working class communities in Jackson. It will also create a significant degree of its own energy and waste management infrastructure to ensure that it can more effectively utilize alternative sources of energy and eliminate waste by creating a comprehensive "zero-waste" recycling program.

4. *Cooperative Education and Training Center*. The Lumumba Center for Economic Democracy and Development will promote broad public understanding of economic democracy, the foundations of solidarity economics, and the principles of cooperatives, and how worker-owned and self-managed enterprises benefit workers, their families, and their communities. It will also educate and train working people to successfully start, finance, own, democratically operate, and self-manage a sustainable cooperative enterprise.

The Eco-Village seeks to radically alter the quality of life in West Jackson over the course of the next decade by increasing and improving housing that is green and permanently affordable, creating high quality living wage jobs, and servicing essential needs for energy, food, and entertainment. With the support of some of the other cooperatives in Cooperation Jackson, our housing cooperative will start by ensuring that each house in the cooperative is LEED (Leadership in Energy and Environmental Design) approved and draws 50% or more of its energy from solar energy. Each house will also have water catchment and efficiency systems and will be integrated into a zero waste resource recycling and regeneration program. We are also in the process of creating a "clean energy" division of our Construction Cooperative that will specialize in building and installing solar panels for affordable community use. The Eco-Village will also provide affordable operational space for several cooperative enterprises, which will create a mutually reinforcing and self-sustaining market ecosystem, supply chain, and network of associated worker-owners. In its broadest dimensions the Eco-Village will also be an integrated "living-systems" community based on principles of "cooperative living" whereby all of the residents of the housing cooperative will participate in the village's recycling and composting programs which will create a stable protected market for recycling and urban farming cooperatives.

Our Freedom Farms Urban Farming Cooperative plans to build a network of farming plots throughout Jackson, but primarily concentrated in West Jackson, to create a comprehensive urban farming operation that will provide and sustain dozens of living wage jobs over time. The farming operation will start with hoop house and raised bed production and hydro, aquaponic, and aeroponic farming in some of the commercial facilities held in the CLT in West Jackson. The urban farming cooperative will establish several neighborhood-based farmers' markets that supply transportation-challenged residents in low-income communities with affordable and high quality foods (vegetables, fruits, fish, and poultry). This will end our food deserts and address the chronic health issues that particularly plague Black people, such as obesity, diabetes, hypertension, and chronic heart disease. We will also become a primary supplier of quality organic produce to the Jackson public school system as well as to the grocery and convenience stores that serve low-income communities. Freedom Farms will also house our child-care cooperative and a worker and consumer grocery cooperative.

These efforts are combined with a number of campaigns that will make Jackson one of the most sustainable cities in the world and a localized attempt to transition the city away from the extractive economy. We are currently engaged in a public education campaign to get the municipal energy company, Entergy, to follow through on preliminary agreements it made with the Lumumba administration to institute a broad program of solar conversion. We are also engaged in a campaign to have the City of Jackson take the lead on the creation of clean energy by dedicating its buildings and vacant lands towards the production and distribution of solar energy. We are working with the Mississippi Association of Cooperatives (MAC) and the Federation of Southern

Cooperatives/Land Assistance Fund (FSC/LAF) on a campaign to get the numerous utility cooperatives in Mississippi to institute a broad program of solar energy conversion and production in the rural portions of the state. Furthermore, a joint study group of Cooperation Jackson and the People's Assembly are developing a strategy and campaign to challenge and end fracking in the state of Mississippi, which is being aggressively pursued by Governor Phil Bryant and a host of state-based and transnational petrochemical companies (Source Watch, n.d.). Finally, we are also engaging in joint ecosystem stewardship initiatives. In particular, we are supporting work to protect the wetlands in and around Jackson by launching a citywide campaign to end the presence of organic refuse in the city's antiquated storm drain system. Eliminating this type of dumping will help the city better clean the sledge that currently clogs and contaminates the drainage system. The leaves, grass, and organic waste that are currently dumped into the system by numerous inhabitants can be recycled and reused as organic compost to support local farmers and restore the depleted topsoil of the Mississippi Delta region.

Our anchor point for all of this is the Lumumba Center for Economic Democracy and Development, located at 939 W. Capitol Street, Jackson, MS 39203, the heart of the West Jackson community. It will serve as the organizing base for the SCI and the overall administrative operations of Cooperation Jackson. The Lumumba Center is close to 6,000 square feet, possesses a restaurant-grade kitchen, and is accompanied by a back-lot of over ¾ of an acre of land for the urban farming and recycling cooperatives. As part of our commitment to developing "new and sustainable" forms of economic activity and social living that will enable and support a Just Transition[10] from the extractive economy, the Lumumba Center will be one of the greenest buildings and business operations in Jackson. In line with our vision of sustainability, we will utilize as much of the surface area of the building as possible for the production of solar energy and will also weatherize and retrofit it to reduce energy and water consumption.

The Lumumba Center will also serve as the base of operations and production for the Nubia Lumumba Arts and Culture Cooperative, which grounds the cultural work of Cooperation Jackson, including the mass communications, issue-framing, and popular education that are key to social movements creating transformative counter-hegemonic narratives. The Arts and Cultural Cooperative conducts regular programming out of the Lumumba Center, including cultural events (public lectures, hip hop, spoken word, and art exhibits), production sessions (films, music, and visual arts), and art and wellness trainings (production classes, art trainings, physical fitness, martial arts, and yoga).

Cooperation Jackson has made some significant advances in its relatively brief history because of the foundations laid by the People's Assembly and the Lumumba Administration. Next to the People's Assembly, it is now the tip of the spear in our offensive engagements to advance the Jackson-Kush Plan.

By Way of Conclusion

We started this essay by noting that the fundamental aim of this experiment is to attain power. We have had and continue to experience small "tastes of power." In our movement's most recent victory, in early December 2014, a critical resolution was passed by the City Council to make Jackson a Human Rights City with a Human Rights Charter and Commission. Nevertheless, the road to social liberation is long and often treacherous. Following the electoral defeat of Chokwe Antar Lumumba in April 2014, we shifted towards building Cooperation Jackson and a network of cooperatives. Our major foreseeable challenge is securing enough resources, grants, and capital to build the organization and to finance our initial start-ups. Although this is a challenge for all cooperatives, it is a special one for us because our movement does not have the backing of any of the local or regional sources of finance capital. Virtually all of these sources are opposed to major aspects of our platform and avidly supported our opponent. By all indications, the harder we push and the more we advance, the more determined they become to hinder if not arrest our development.

A lot is currently riding on the success of Cooperation Jackson. Even if it only launches two or three viable cooperatives within the next two years, it will prove that our vision is attainable and worth fighting for. Should it seriously struggle or fall short it will likely reinforce the capitalist narrative that "there is no alternative." After decades of combating self-hate, individualism, consumerism, and the ethos of "get rich or die trying," we cannot afford to go one step backwards. So, the pressure is on. We are stuck between a rock and a hard place because our base doesn't have the financial resources to support multiple cooperative start-ups on its own. And we do not yet have any extensive contacts with progressive financiers and investors, either nationally or internationally, willing to support cooperative enterprises and green alternatives. So, we must be extremely innovative to survive, not to say thrive. We are looking for allies and we are encouraged by how much national and international attention our work has received.

The Jackson Rising: New Economies Conference that we organized and hosted in May 2014 has been noted as one of the most influential and inspirational conferences about solidarity economics and economic democracy in the US in decades. Our People's Assembly model, our people-centered human rights agenda, and our demand for a National Plan of Action for Racial Justice and Self-Determination have been adopted by many of the forces involved in the growing Ferguson Resistance and Black Lives Matter movements. Our challenge is to transform all of this interest and enthusiasm into a national and international network of support that will help us advance the Jackson-Kush Plan and continue to build the transformative movements of our age from Occupy to the Movement for Black Lives.

Unfortunately, we do not possess a crystal ball to indicate where we will ultimately land. Nevertheless, our collective confidence has grown through this experience as we have witnessed time and time again something that Chokwe Lumumba often stressed: "A movement that secures the love and confidence of the people has no bounds." We are still very much "making the road by walking," but we are certain that we are still headed down the right path. We believe that our experiences and contributions are worth learning from and we hope that others engaged in the struggle to liberate humanity will welcome them in the spirit of "unity and struggle" in which they are shared.

Stay tuned!

Bibliography

Amadeo, Kimberly. (2017). What Is the Real Unemployment Rate? *The Balance*. Retrieved from https://www.thebalance.com/what-is-the-real-unemployment-rate-3306198

Boler, Jaime. (2006, February). Slave Resistance in Natchez, Mississippi (1719-1861). *Mississippi History Now*. Retrieved from http://mshistorynow.mdah.state.ms.us/articles/58/slave-resistance-in-natchez-mississippi-1719-1861

Boodhoo, Ken I. (1984). Grenada: The Birth and Death of a Revolution (Dialogue #34). *LACC Occasional papers series. Dialogues (1980 – 1994). Paper 36*. Retrieved from http://digitalcommons.fiu.edu/laccopsd/36

Census Quickfacts (n.d.). Retrieved from http://quickfacts.census.gov/qfd/states/28/2836000.html

Cooperation Jackson. (n.d.). Retrieved from http://www.cooperationjackson.org/

Duvall Decker Architects. (n.d.). *West Jackson master plan*. Retrieved from http://www.duvalldecker.com/west-jackson-master-plan/

Gramsci, Antonio. (1971). *Selections from the prison notebooks*. In Quintin Hoare and Geoffrey Nowell Smith (Eds.). New York: International Publishers, pp. 229-39.

Hagberg, Sten. (2016, February). The legacy of revolution and resistance in Burkina Faso. *Stockholm International Peace Research Institute*. Retrieved from https://www.sipri.org/commentary/essay/2016/legacy-revolution-and-resistance-burkina-faso

Harvey, David. (2003). The New Imperialism: Accumulation by Dispossession. In Leo Panitch and Colin Leys (Eds.), *Socialist register 2004: the new imperial challenge*. (pp. 63-87). London: Merlin Press Ltd.

Lenin, V.I. 1963. Imperialism: the Highest Stage of Capitalism. In *Lenin's Selected Works: Volume 1* (pp. 667-766). Moscow: Progress Publishers.

Malcolm X Grassroots Movement (MXGM). (n.d.). Retrieved from https://mxgm.org/

Malcolm X Grassroots Movement (MXGM). (2013, April). Operation Ghetto Storm: 2012 Annual Report on the Extrajudicial Killing of 313 Black People. Retrieved from https://mxgm.org/operation-ghetto-storm-2012-annual-report-on-the-extrajudicial-killing-of-313-black-people/

Malcolm X Grassroots Movement (MXGM). (2014, August). The Black Nation Charges Genocide! Our survival is dependent on Self-Defense! Retrieved from https://mxgm.org/the-black-nation-charges-genocide-our-survival-is-dependent-on-self-defense/

Mills, Kay. (2007, April). Fannie Lou Hamer: Civil Rights Activist. *Mississippi History Now*. Retrieved from http://mshistorynow.mdah.state.ms.us/articles/51/fannie-lou-hamer-civil-rights-activist

Mitchell, Jerry. (2014, October). Mississippi locks up more per capita than China and Russia. *The Clarion-Ledger*. Retrieved from http://www.clarionledger.com/story/news/2014/10/18/miss-incarceration-rate-one-highest-nation/17468129/

Mondragón. **(n.d.).** *English-language page.* **Retrieved from** http://www.mondragon-corporation.com/eng/

Moschonas, Gerassimos. (2013). A new left in Greece: PASOK's fall and SYRIZA's rise. *Dissent Magazine*. Retrieved from https://www.dissentmagazine.org/article/a-new-left-in-greece-pasoks-fall-and-syrizas-rise

Our Power Campaign. (n.d.). *Our Power campaign: communities united for a just transition.* Retrieved from http://www.ourpowercampaign.org/campaign/

Pandey, Shubhanga. (2016, January). The next Nepali revolution. *Jacobin*. Retrieved from https://www.jacobinmag.com/2016/01/nepal-liberal-constitution-maoists-protests-monarchy/

People's Food Co-op. (n.d.). *People's history.* Retrieved from http://www.peoples.coop/cooperative-ownership/cooperative-history-the-co-op-difference-1

Ramos, Valeriano. (1982). The Concepts of ideology, hegemony, and organic intellectuals in Gramsci's Marxism. *Theoretical Review*, 27.

Roseberry-Polier, Alison. (2011, April). Haitians overthrow regime, 1984-1986. *Global Non-Violent Action Database*. Retrieved from http://nvdatabase.swarthmore.edu/content/haitians-overthrow-regime-1984-1986

Schaefer, Ward. (2010, November). The Tragic Case of the Scott Sisters. Jackson Free Press. Retrieved from http://www.jacksonfreepress.com/news/2010/nov/03/the-tragic-case-of-the-scott-sisters/

Sison, Jose Maria (2006, February). It was a convergence of various forces. *Philippine Daily Inquirer*. Retrieved from https://news.google.com/newspapers?nid=2479&dat=20060224&id=FFg1AAAAIBAJ&sjid=jiUMAAAAIBAJ&pg=1930,4044246

Source Watch. (n.d.). *Mississippi and fracking.* Retrieved from http://www.sourcewatch.org/index.php/Mississippi_and_fracking

Smith, Micah. (2015, August). The Scott Sisters. Jackson Free Press. Retrieved from http://www.jacksonfreepress.com/news/2015/aug/07/scott-sisters/

Sustainable Communities Initiative (SCI). (n.d.). *Cooperation Jackson.* Retrieved from http://www.cooperationjackson.org/sustainable-communities-initiative/

Trotsky, Leon. (1964). *The Age of Permanent Revolution: A Trotsky Anthology.* In Isaac Deutscher (Ed.). New York: Dell Publishing Co., Inc.

Notes

1. This is a substantially revised and updated version of a study that was originally published by the Rosa Luxemburg Stiftung—New York Office (www.rosalux-nyc.org), and is republished here with their permission.

2. 1645 blacks compared with only 399 whites per 100,000 population https://www.prisonpolicy.org/graphs/MS_incrates2001.html

3. This notion of the "weakest link in the chain" is borrowed from Lenin, 1963.

4. Jamie and Gladys Scott were convicted of armed robbery in 1994 in Scott County, Mississippi. They allegedly stole from two men in Forrest, Mississippi. The Scott Sisters were given double-life sentences. After three failed appeals over a 16-year period, the Scott Sisters were granted clemency by Governor Haley Barbour on December 29, 2010. The actual perpetrators of the robbery served no more than three years in jail. The Campaign to Free the Scott Sisters was led by the People's Assembly and adjudicated by Attorney Chokwe Lumumba. For more information on the Scott Sisters see Smith, 2015; Schaerer, 2010.

5. The concepts of the "war of position," the "war of maneuver," and "hegemony" are drawn from the work of Italian Marxist Antonio Gramsci. The term "hegemony" describes the social processes utilized by ruling elites to consolidate, justify, and normalize their social domination. For more background on these concepts see Gramsci, 1971, 229-39. See also Ramos, 1982. A free version can be accessed here: https://www.marxists.org/history/erol/periodicals/theoretical-review/1982301.htm.

6. The notion of "transitional demands" or a "transitional program" is largely adopted from the works of Leon Trotsky (1964, 254-59). For a free version, see: https://www.marxists.org/archive/trotsky/1938/tp/transprogram.pdf.

7. The notion of "accumulation by dispossession" is drawn from the work of David Harvey (2003). It describes the ongoing process of primitive accumulation or accumulation through wholesale plunder and theft. For a free version, see: http://socialistregister.com/index.php/srv/article/view/5811/2707#.WIYculNrjIU.

8. Chokwe Antar Lumumba was elected Mayor of the City of Jackson and sworn into office on July 3, 2017

9. For more information on these statistics see Duvall Decker Architects (n.d.). Please note that the section of West Jackson on which we are concentrating does not reflect

the entire region analyzed in this document.

10. The concept of a "just transition" emerged out of the labor left in the 1980s to demand that workers in the coal and petro-chemical energy be given job-training to prepare them for newer, more climate-friendly occupations in the wake of the downsizing of jobs in the industry. Cooperation Jackson uses an expanded definition of this concept drawn from the Climate Justice Alliance and the Our Power Campaign (n.d.), which it also helped to construct. According to the expanded definition, a just transition is a worker- and community-driven process of transitioning from a petro-chemical dependent economy to a restorative, carbon-neutral economy.

21.

The Socialist Experiment: A New-Society Vision in Jackson, Mississippi

Katie Gilbert

Chokwe Lumumba had been the mayor of Jackson, Mississippi, for five months when, in November 2013, he stood behind a lectern and addressed a group of out-of-towners with a curious phrase he would soon explain with a story: "Good afternoon, everybody, and free the land!"

On his tall, thin frame he wore a bright blue tie and a loosely fitting suit, extra fabric collecting around the shoulders of his jacket. Wire-rimmed glasses rested over a perpetually furrowed brow on his narrow, thoughtful, frequently smiling face. A faint white mustache grazed his upper lip.

In welcoming the attendees of the Neighborhood Funders Group Conference, a convening of grantmaking institutions, Mayor Lumumba was conversational and at ease, as he tended to be with microphone in hand. His friends had long teased him for his loquaciousness in front of a crowd.

Lumumba informed the room that on the car ride over he'd decided he would tell them a story. He explained that big things were happening in Jackson—or, were about to happen—and his story would offer some context. It was one he had recounted many times. Polished smooth, the story was like an object he kept in his pocket and worried with his thumb until it took on the sheen of something from a fable, though the people and events were real. "It was March of 1971 when I first came to the state of Mississippi," Lumumba began. "It was several months after the students at Jackson State had been murdered," he said, referring to the tragedy at the city's predominantly Black college, which left two dead and twelve injured after police opened fire on a campus dormitory in May 1970, less than two weeks after the Kent State shootings.

Lumumba had traveled to Mississippi with a group called the Provisional Government of the Republic of New Afrika. He was twenty-three at the time and was taking a break from his second year of law school in Detroit. He had put his training on hold for the work of new-society building. After the assassination of Martin Luther King Jr., Lumumba had been increasingly drawn to what he considered the radical humanism of the Provisional Government's plan to create a new, majority-Black nation in the Deep South. The PG-RNA planned to peacefully petition the United States government for the five states where the concentration of Black population was largest: Mississippi, Louisiana, Alabama, Georgia, and South Carolina. Leaders framed their demand for this transfer as a reparations payment after centuries of enslavement and degradation that Black people had experienced in America. As part of a symbolic effort to break with a painful past and announce a new way forward, the PG-RNA encouraged New Afrikans to shed names with European origins in favor of African ones. Edwin Taliaferro became Chokwe Lumumba: Chokwe, he said, for one of the last tribes to successfully resist the slave trade and Lumumba for Patrice Lumumba, who led Congo to independence and became its first democratically elected prime minister. The Republic of New Afrika's Declaration of Independence announced that its socialist society, arranged around cooperative economics, would be "better than what we now know and as perfect as man can make it."

By March of 1971, when the mayor's story began, Lumumba was an officer in the Provisional Government. The organization had made an oral agreement to buy twenty acres of land from a Black farmer in Bolton, Mississippi, a small town about twenty miles west of Jackson. They had hired a contractor to build a school and dining hall on the property. The site would be named El Malik after the name Malcolm X had taken for himself: El-Hajj Malik El-Shabazz. March 28, a Sunday, had been chosen as Land Celebration Day, when the group would inaugurate the site at El Malik.

Lumumba was in the caravan's lead vehicle as they approached Bolton that afternoon. Forty-two years later, he described to the conference attendees in Jackson how the Klan drove up and down the road in their trucks, brandishing weapons, and how state, local, and federal police formed a barricade across the road. Mississippi's attorney general, A. F. Summer, had declared that there would be no Land Celebration Day. Akinyele Omowale Umoja, an African-American Studies professor at Georgia State University, writes in his book *We Will Shoot Back: Armed Resistance in the Mississippi Freedom Movement* that the day before the scheduled event, PG-RNA leaders had seen a hand-painted sign near the property that the KKK had posted: NIGGERS, THERE WILL BE NO MEETING HERE SUNDAY. FREE SIX-FOOT HOLES.

Mayor Lumumba paused, and when he spoke again his voice had moved up a register. "This was a different day about to break," he said. "And even though sometimes we break our days somewhat recklessly, it was certainly gonna break. There were five hundred of us"—other records say there were one hundred fifty—"and we said, 'We come in peace, but we come prepared.' We had old people, we had young people, we had babies. We were praying. Hard revolutionaries, driven back to prayer!" He laughed. "Looking for God wherever we could find Him."

The day might well have combusted. What happened instead, Lumumba told the audience, was something that seemed, even as it unfolded, like a miracle best left unexamined. "I know it's hard for a lot of you to believe this—that roadblock opened up. Just like the Red Sea."

Past the barricade, the New Afrikans traveled five miles. They had arrived. Two months later, the Bolton farmer would renege on his agreement to sell, and support for the PG-RNA and its efforts would wane over the next few years, as FBI and state and local police pushed successful counterintelligence programs to undermine the group's efforts. But in looking back, Lumumba focused on the energy of that Sunday, when the people around him fell to the ground in such profound joy that they began to eat the dirt, he recalled, out of a spontaneous desire to take into their bodies the freedom they believed they'd found. "That's where that slogan came from," Lumumba said. "'Free the land.'"

In Lumumba's successful campaigns for city council in 2009 and for mayor in 2013, "Free the land" had been a common refrain of his supporters. His platform, too, echoed the vision he and his fellow New Afrikans had harbored for their new society on Land Celebration Day. He pledged that his office would support the establishment of a large network of cooperatively owned businesses in Jackson, often describing Mondragon, a Spanish town where an ecosystem of cooperatives sprouted half a century ago. In debates and interviews, he promised that Jackson, under the leadership of a Lumumba administration, would flourish as the "Mondragon of the South"—the "City of the Future."

As Mayor Lumumba neared the end of the story of Land Celebration Day, his voice faltered. He turned his head and squeezed his eyes closed to regain composure. The memory of Land Celebration Day was still a live wire running through him and through his plans as mayor of Jackson.

"The reason I started off with that little prelude," he told the Neighborhood Funders Group Conference attendees, "is that I wanted to say that what has not changed is the vision of that new society, that new way of thinking. That new way of engineering and governing a society, where everyone would be treated with dignity. Where there would be no class, no gender, or color discrimination. Even though it didn't happen in that little community which we called El Malik, now it's about to happen in Jackson, Mississippi. And would you believe it?"

As a child, Chokwe Lumumba's son Chokwe Antar sometimes wished for another name, one that sounded more like those of his friends. But Antar also trusted his parents, and he looked up to them. He knew his father's work as a civil rights–oriented lawyer was important, and he used to sneak out of his bed at night to lie on the floor of his parents' room and listen as they discussed his father's cases. He shared his father's name, and he would grow up to share his profession.

After Land Celebration Day in 1971, Chokwe Lumumba returned to Detroit and finished his law degree. In 1976, he joined the Detroit Public Defenders Office, and two years later he opened his own law firm. In 1986, Chokwe and his wife, a flight attendant born Patricia Ann Burke who changed her name to Nubia Lumumba, moved their family to Brooklyn so Chokwe could better represent his high-profile clients there, including Black nationalist Mutulu Shakur and his stepson, Tupac Shakur. Even after the PG-RNA dissolved, Lumumba had never stopped thinking about how a group of determined activists could build a new society where Black people could escape racism, racist violence, and deprivation. Lumumba cofounded two organizations to keep working toward versions of the PG-RNA goal: the New Afrikan People's Organization in 1984, and, later, the Malcolm X Grassroots Movement. According to Professor Umoja, NAPO's members still oriented themselves toward the goal of a Black nation. MXGM was slightly different—members advocated self-determination for Black communities using a variety of means, including independence, but also sought other paths that would lead toward empowerment and liberation. In 1988, when the couple's daughter, Rukia, was nine, and their son, Antar, was five, the Lumumbas relocated to Jackson, Mississippi. In the following years, Chokwe and Nubia would often tell Rukia and Antar that they'd come to the South because there was work to be done there and because they wanted to give their children the struggle.

Lumumba's work as a lawyer invited renown to the family, but also occasional vitriol. Antar and Rukia spent one afternoon hiding in a closet with a knife clutched between them after a death threat was breathed over the phone while their parents were away. In high school, on the phone with a girlfriend, Antar would wrap up by saying, "Okay, goodbye to you, too, FBI!" His parents always said that the house's phones were tapped. Years later, among the hundreds of pages of documents that emerged from a Freedom of Information Act request for FBI reports on Chokwe Lumumba, Antar saw his high school graduation photo. The sight of it there didn't unsettle him because it confirmed what he'd always been told.

After Antar's freshman year at Murrah High School, his father judged that basketball was too prominent a priority in his son's life and decided that Antar would transfer from his school and its championship team. Chokwe offered him a list of new high schools to choose from. Antar entered his sophomore year at Callaway High as a D-average student, and he went on to graduate in the top 10 percent of his class.

Antar recalls that his mother used to joke, with an edge of seriousness, that her children had better not pursue that "same old boring lawyer thing" that took so much of her husband's time without bringing in as much money as it should. She hoped her children would pursue careers that would allow them the finer things in life. She noted that Antar loved drawing street plans and hearing her talk about Benjamin Banneker's designs for Washington, D.C., and that math seemed to come easy to him. She pushed him to consider becoming an engineer or an architect. Most of all, she seemed to want to ensure that her son didn't choose a career just because it was his father's.

But once Antar entered college at Tuskegee University in Alabama, he never seriously considered anything but a path to law school. After he earned a J.D. from the Thurgood Marshall School of Law at Texas Southern University, he returned home in 2008 to help run his father's law practice. Within the year, he was watching his FBI-surveilled activist father wade into the quagmire of Jackson city politics. Chokwe had been tapped as the public face of a long-brewing effort to continue working toward the PG-RNA's vision of an egalitarian, black-led society—or at least some version of it.

In the early 2000s, MXGM's leadership formed a think tank to plot out a twenty-first-century strategy to realize the new-society dream. After some discussion, at the organization's annual Ideological Conference in 2005, MXGM's national membership determined that Mississippi was the best staging ground for the experiment in society building—the same conclusion the PG-RNA had come to in the 1970s. The eighteen contiguous counties that run along the Mississippi River on the state's western edge are all majority Black (except one, which is 47.8 percent black). The MXGM new-society drafters referred to this line of counties along the Mississippi Delta as the Kush District, as PG-RNA leadership had, named after the ancient civilization built along the banks of the Nile, in what is now Egypt and Sudan. MXGM members began moving to Jackson from all across the country. In 2012, after roughly ten years of refining their blueprint, the think tank posted a draft of its Jackson-Kush Plan to the MXGM website. The document detailed steps to build a socialist, majority-black, eco-focused model society within Mississippi's shrinking capital city, as well as initiatives to mobilize communities in the Kush district, and expand from there.

The society described in the Jackson-Kush Plan was a close descendant of the one envisioned by the PG-RNA, with some tweaks based on lessons learned and the interests of the drafters three decades after Land Celebration Day. Like the PG-RNA vision, a central pillar of the new society would be economic democracy based in cooperative ownership. Another would be the embrace of fully participatory democracy through the organization of self-governing organs called People's Assemblies, which would be the loci of real decision-making power in the communities where they operated.

The starkest difference between the PG-RNA's and the Jackson-Kush Plan's new-society visions was in the stance on engaging with the country's established system of electoral politics. The PG-RNA's leaders had based their call for a new society on the argument that the federal, state, and local governments were illegitimate, since they had long relied on broad disenfranchisement to amass their power. MXGM revised this stance: A central goal described in the Jackson-Kush Plan was the development of progressive political candidates who, if elected, could support the goals of economic democracy and self-governing People's Assemblies from that elected office.

In 2008, two of the drafters of the Jackson-Kush Plan approached Chokwe Lumumba about running as one of those candidates. They also approached Antar, then twenty-five, about running for a city council seat. Antar demurred. The idea of running for office wasn't practical in his mind or, frankly, all that appealing. He'd just returned to the city after seven years away at school; outside of family and friends, not many people knew him in Jackson, and, beyond that, he had little interest in electoral politics as a form of public service.

Antar tried to dissuade his father from running, too—Chokwe Lumumba may have been a highly respected lawyer in the community, but that didn't make for a political profile prominent enough to run a successful campaign. His father agreed; mayor would be too much just then. He'd run for city council instead. But he made it clear that he disagreed with his son on the broader point: Antar needed to consider running for office someday. Sometimes, he told his son, the movement requires that we give of ourselves and do something we didn't envision.

In 2012, as Chokwe was finishing his term on the council and shifting his attention to his run for mayor, MXGM pressed Antar to run to fill his father's vacated council seat. He declined again. Antar had just married his longtime girlfriend, Ebony, an English professor at Tougaloo College, and months later, they'd learn she was pregnant. But he dedicated himself fully to his father's campaign, serving as its official spokesperson as he helped to draft the platform on which Chokwe Lumumba would squeak into a runoff election after a second-place finish in the Democratic primary—and go on to win the mayorship. Still, Antar harbored absolutely no interest in becoming a politician himself, and he couldn't imagine what would ever change his mind.

It wouldn't be long before he'd find out.

On a Tuesday morning in late February 2014, not quite eight months into Chokwe's term, the mayor called his son complaining of chest pains. Antar left court and rushed to Chokwe's house to drive his father to the emergency room at St. Dominic's Hospital. Mayor Lumumba told the hospital staff that he thought he might be having a heart attack. According to a 2016 lawsuit filed by the family against St. Dominic's, Chokwe waited hours at the hospital before he received any treatment. According to the lawsuit, a cardiologist recommended a blood transfusion. Just before 5 p.m., Chokwe died suddenly. The cause of death was later determined to be a heart attack.

Shock and grief coursed through Jackson with the news that the mayor was dead. Many Jacksonians were still nursing the morale boost that had come with Lumumba's election. They had faith that their city was about to figure out new ways to address longstanding problems: crumbling streets and dangerously outdated water infrastructure, a depleted tax base, a lack of jobs. During his brief tenure, the late mayor had asked the city to vote on a new 1 percent sales tax to help begin to pay for the infrastructure fixes the city desperately needed. He'd helped organize People's Assemblies to provide forums to answer Jacksonians' questions about the proposal. Voters approved the new tax with 90 percent in favor.

"There was a sense of loss greater than just his passing," Antar told me later. "People said to me, 'We felt like we were on the right track. What do we do now?'"

At Chokwe's funeral, former Mississippi governor William Winter, a Democrat, admitted that during the mayoral campaign, he'd feared that as mayor Lumumba would divide the capital city. "I could not have been more wrong," he said, adding, "The strong leadership of Chokwe Lumumba has opened the door to a bright future for us."

On the night that Chokwe died, Antar was the only family member present. His mother had passed away ten years before from a brain aneurysm, and Rukia was rushing to Jackson from her home in New York. As he waited for Rukia and extended family in Detroit to arrive, Antar asked the friends who had gathered in the hospital room to give him some time alone with his just-deceased father. In that quiet moment, before the shock of Lumumba's death had spread through Jackson, Antar resolved to run for mayor. He would keep the decision to himself until he told his wife the next morning, giving himself the night to turn it over in his head. But as soon as the idea came to him in that hospital room, he knew he wouldn't separate himself from it again. He thought of his father's mandate: Sometimes the movement requires that you give of yourself and do something you didn't envision as part of your plan. A more practical concern was bearing down on him, too. The new-society vision needed a new protector, a new vessel. Who else could it be but him?

Chokwe Antar Lumumba was thirty at the time, and he looked younger. In his public appearances he shifted between a lawyerly, knitted-brow seriousness, often repeating the last few words of a sentence to underline his point, and a readiness to amiably tease a friend or fellow candidate and break into his boyish laugh. I would come to learn that with strangers and familiars alike his charisma takes the form of a warm accessibility, the sense that he has time for everyone, and doesn't begrudge anyone who asks for it.

I traveled to Jackson for the first time in March 2016, two years after Chokwe Lumumba died. In Chicago, where I live, the protracted winter still lingered, but I found Jackson was already in full leaf, deep into spring. My hotel on North State Street was across from a middle school whose grounds included space for a modest football field, faded tennis courts, and a scuffed soccer field. Across the street to the north was the sprawling campus of the University of Mississippi Medical Center, the city's largest employer after the State of Mississippi, with about ten thousand employees. Up the road was the Fondren District, the site of a dedicated revitalization effort led over the past two decades by nearby residents, where coffee shops' signs bore thoughtful fonts and a tapas restaurant and oyster bar made new use of a shuttered public school.

Antar met me in the lobby of my lodge-themed hotel on one of my first evenings in town. He strode in wearing a Black hoodie and a flat-brimmed Detroit Tigers ball cap. He had waves for the people he knew behind the front desk and a handshake for me. We sat at one of the lobby's round wooden tables and Antar told me about the last couple of years, affirming his continued dedication to the work his father had left unfinished. His wedding ring clanged against the table's glass top when he struck it to emphasize his points, which he did when he brought up cooperatives. "What we have to establish are businesses that are in the business of making money but *also* have an interest in serving the community—not in picking up and moving out," he said. He laid out an analysis of why the solutions delineated in the Jackson-Kush Plan were still necessary, quoting Malcolm X, Gandhi, and his father. He spoke of the importance of oppressed people leading self-determined lives, resurrecting the parlance of the Republic of New Afrika. But other parts of his analysis were more current, like when he talked about mass incarceration and the proliferation of prisons as a Band-Aid over the U.S.'s industrial decline and stagnant economy. "On many levels, this economic experiment that we have in this country is a *failed model*," he said with another strike to the glass. "And it's a failed model in particular for oppressed people."

Six weeks after his father's death, Antar ran in the April 2014 special election for mayor. He lost in a runoff to Tony Yarber, founder and pastor of the majority-Black Relevant Empowerment Church. As mayor, Yarber had scrapped the most notable parts of the Lumumba administration's agenda, including plans for the city-supported cooperative businesses, the People's Assemblies, and the goal to turn Jackson into a zero-waste city.

Antar's loss was another setback for the new-society goal, so the MXGM members most connected to the Jackson-Kush Plan shifted their route forward yet again. That May, members of Lumumba's former administration and MXGM went ahead with what had been planned as a city-supported event called the Jackson Rising: New Economies Conference. The three-day summit sought to provide an educational foundation for attendees in building the pieces of a democratic, cooperative economy. At the end of the conference, a few core members of MXGM announced a new organization called Cooperation Jackson to continue the co-op–building goal.

In late 2015, I had emailed Cooperation Jackson and a few days later I was on the phone with Sacajawea Hall, a cofounder of the organization who had moved to Jackson from Atlanta in December 2013. I'd been doing some traveling, guided by an interest in alternative economic models inside the United States. The prehistory of this interest might be traced to 2006 when, at twenty-two years old, I took a job as a researcher for *Institutional Investor's Alpha*, a magazine that analyzes hedge funds, which I knew next to nothing about. I was to help coax information from secretive hedge fund managers about the billions of dollars under their management. I had no idea that I'd taken the job on the eve of the strangest moment in nearly a century to be covering the financial industry. By 2008, I was reporting for *Alpha* and that year the public, U.S.-based pension funds I covered collectively lost more than one-fourth of their value after the collapse of the global financial market. Suddenly, knowing nothing became our shared national condition as we watched our economic system flail in the precise ways we were told it never would. The revoking of this system's untouchable status granted us permission to peer into our enormous, tangled economic apparatus and ask: In what ways has this system long been failing us? And, more crucially: What might we build that's better? Radical economic experiments have proliferated in the U.S. since the 2008 collapse—but then, they feel radical only if you've lived your life, as most of us have, believing that profit maximization, endless economic growth, and the individual's mandate to consume are circumstances as intrinsically human as hunger and childbirth. I count myself among those who struggle to imagine living within any other economic arrangement, but by the time I called Saki Hall I was starting to understand that other people's imaginations have granted them more leeway, and some were living out economic experiments that embody alternatives. At the end of our conversation, Saki invited me to come see for myself what Cooperation Jackson was doing.

The month before my trip, I spent a week living and working at Twin Oaks Community in Louisa, Virginia. Twin Oaks is a fifty-year-old fully egalitarian mini-society of roughly one hundred members, where labor and governance systems are modeled from the utopia described in B. F. Skinner's novel *Walden Two*. At Twin Oaks, I hauled soil on a vegetable farm, snipped strawberry bushes, and hosed down equipment in the tofu factory. I helped two affable men named Tony and Ezra prepare a Sunday dinner of split pea soup, smoked pork belly, and baguettes. I was apprised of the joys of polyamory, the necessity of requiring the group's permission for pregnancy in a community where children are supported by the whole, and the freedom in not being defined by a lifetime in a single job or role. During my week at Twin Oaks, the pebble I couldn't loose from my shoe was the place's overwhelming whiteness. It was also true that the preponderance of people at Twin Oaks came from middle- and upper-class backgrounds. Here was a vision for a drastically new way of thinking about our economic arrangement, and yet its population lacked representation from the racial minorities who had for so long been kept away from the levers of economic control in our country. I didn't know if this constituted a failure of Twin Oaks's model—but it made me less interested in the experiment being run there.

In the course of my research, I had never heard Chokwe Lumumba or any member of MXGM or Cooperation Jackson describe the Jackson-Kush Plan as a utopian vision. Still, when I arrived in Mississippi, a line from utopian scholar Ruth Levitas rattled in my head: "Utopia's strongest function, its claim to being important rather than a matter of esoteric fascination and charm, is its capacity to inspire the pursuit of a world transformed, to embody hope rather than simply desire." If I wanted to plot for myself the coordinates of the line between fantastical and real societies; between unheard-of ambitions for change and perfectly familiar ones; between a fable told for comfort and a plan for real change on the ground somewhere, I felt that I needed to better understand what was happening in Jackson. I hoped being there would offer some insight into how those lines are drawn, and how fixed they really are.

Toward the end of our conversation in the hotel lobby, Antar departed from the scholarly analysis and made a declaration that struck me as uncharacteristically dramatic: He saw Jackson, Mississippi (and he never said the city without the state), as a last chance. This was a place where long-marginalized Black communities could build a new economy for themselves, a democratic and fair society, a foundation for good lives to grow from. In his mind, this black-majority city that sat in the middle of the state with the highest concentration of Black people in our country *had* to be the staging ground for this particular experiment in moving past economic and governance systems that weren't working for so many. Antar told me he was grateful he hadn't won the special election in 2014. He wasn't ready then, he'd realized. But now he was. Though he hadn't publicly announced it, he said he would run for mayor of Jackson again in 2017.

An abundance of deep, wide potholes was my first indication that something wasn't quite working in Jackson. After an earlier rainstorm, the pockmarks dotting the capital city's streets shimmered with mock placidity. "I was trying to miss that one!" Saki exclaimed after her car lurched through a pothole pond spanning two lanes, throwing us against our seat belts and jostling the car seats embracing her five-year-old daughter and two-year-old son in the back seat. A red plastic plate dotted with the crumbs from her daughter's breakfast hopped from Saki's lap to her feet.

Saki wanted to talk about the potholes: Did I see all of them? See that one there, how deep it is? To Saki, the potholes stood for something more than a threat to her car's underbody. To Saki, and, I would soon learn, to many other Jacksonians, the proliferation of unfilled potholes was a clear sign of a downward spiral in full effect.

Saki had picked me up from my hotel on my first day in town with an offer of a driving tour of Jackson. I enthusiastically accepted. We trundled southward over the potholes until we reached downtown. Well-maintained grounds studded with magnolias and tupelos spread out around the grand, Greek Revival State Capitol, Governor's Mansion, and City Hall. These were interspersed with muted, modern, concrete and steel buildings housing government agencies like the Mississippi Gaming Commission and the Parole Board. A few local restaurants operated out of the downtown storefronts, but many of the storefronts stood tenantless. Faded signs indicated the businesses that had since departed or dissolved, imparting a feeling that the past remained cloyingly close by.

In the decades before the Civil War, the newly crowned capital city had prospered as cotton made Mississippi a wealthy state. That changed in 1863 when Union armies destroyed Jackson; its skeletal remains allegedly earned it the nickname "Chimneyville." The city has been struggling to claw back to its former economic abundance ever since.

During Mississippi's eleven years of Reconstruction, the Freedmen's Bureau established by the U.S. Congress helped lay the foundation for the state's public school system. Black citizens' participation in democracy was higher than in any other Southern state—more than two hundred Black people were elected to public office during the period. But a concerted effort to alter the trajectory of societal reshaping, called the Mississippi Plan, was devastatingly successful. Developed in 1875 by the conservative Democrats desperate to eject Reconstruction-supporting Republicans from office, the Mississippi Plan employed organized violence to intimidate and kill those working toward a society in which races were equal. Democrats had regained political power by 1876; in 1890, they passed a new state constitution that concretized the exclusion of Black citizens from the democratic process. In two years, the number of Black Mississippians registered to vote fell from 142,000 to 68,117. Generations later, Mississippi's public schools managed to delay real desegregation for sixteen years after the *Brown* v. *Board of Education* decision in 1954. According to the Mississippi Historical Society, one-third of the districts in the state had achieved no desegregation by 1967 and less than three percent of the state's Black children attended classes with white children. It took another Supreme Court decision, in 1969, to force real desegregation in Mississippi.

Jackson was 60 percent white in 1970, and by the 2010 census, 18 percent white. The city's population decreased from nearly 200,000 in 1990 to under 170,000 in 2016. As the majority-white suburbs expanded, they turned into a kind of sticky ring around the city center, pulling economic development out of Jackson. The Mississippi Department of Revenue reports that the city of Jackson brought in approximately $117 million in gross sales tax in fiscal year 1990 and $177.6 million in fiscal year 2016—worse than stagnant when accounting for inflation. And as the tax base has crumbled, so has the city's infrastructure. The *Clarion-Ledger* wrote in March 2017 that a report from an engineering firm in 2013 found that more than 60 percent of Jackson streets had four years or less of serviceable life left. In 2017, that life is about spent.

Saki steered us a few blocks west of downtown, to a silent stretch of streets lined with one- and two-story buildings. These were more like memories of buildings, with empty window frames, unkempt overgrowth outside, and encroaching wilderness inside. Saki told me we were in the middle of the Farish Street Historical District.

Farish Street was built by slaves and after emancipation it came to be used primarily by the formerly enslaved. A new business district emerged during Reconstruction, and it thrived in Jim Crow's "separate-but-equal" South as an alternative to the Capitol District blocks away, where Black Jacksonians weren't welcome. Farish Street was one of the largest African-American districts in the South; it held legal firms, doctors, dentists, jewelers, banks, retail stores, and hospitals.

In the 1950s, Black activists mobilized Black and white protestors to put pressure on white-owned businesses across the city to allow access to Black customers. A sit-in at a Jackson Woolworth's turned violent. When the Civil Rights Act passed in 1964, mandating the desegregation of public places, many African Americans in Jackson celebrated their victory by taking full advantage of it, bringing their spending to previously inaccessible white businesses. The African-American business owners on Farish Street suffered. Integration didn't work both ways; as Black people moved into previously white spaces, white spending failed to flow into Farish Street. Integration hadn't happened between two groups with equal economic footing and control, a fact for which Farish Street's slow implosion offers lingering evidence. Businesses closed like falling dominoes and new ones stayed away as the area became known as a magnet for drugs and prostitution. Revitalization efforts of various kinds were killed by infighting and funds insufficient to the area's growing needs. What I saw outside of Saki's car window in March 2016 was the result of this history: an abandoned community, a failure on the part of the city.

Saki rattled over the train tracks that bisect the capital and we passed into West Jackson, another part of the city entirely. The population here is almost completely black, and, according to the Hinds County Economic Development Authority, unemployment in West Jackson is double both the county and state averages. In 2014, Duvall Decker, a local architecture firm, worked alongside neighborhood residents and eighteen Jackson-based organizations to compile a "West Jackson Planning Guidebook" for a section of West Jackson around Jackson State University; according to their findings, residents in the area had a choice of three grocery stores in comparison to sixteen check-cashing businesses, and almost half of the properties were officially vacant. In the past year, the number of grocery stores dropped to just two. On this side of the tracks, Capitol Street—which originates in front of the Old State Capitol on the east side—is a quiet, winding road, flanked by rows of abandoned structures.

Saki's daughter announced from the backseat that she had to go to the bathroom, and Saki pulled a U-turn. We were just a few minutes from Cooperation Jackson.

In the spring of 2015, Cooperation Jackson moved into the building now dubbed the Chokwe Lumumba Center for Economic Democracy and Development. A group of volunteers set to work renovating the building, a former daycare center, to better fit its new purpose. Pastel murals were painted over and mildewed carpeting ripped out, and a fresh paint job brightened the building's exterior. The color was the deep green of the kale and collards that would soon populate a cooperatively owned farm in the backyard.

We parked in a long driveway, and I helped Saki unload the children. From the outside, the single-story structure looked like it had been snapped from a strip mall and dropped into its grassy one-acre lot. Saki pressed a doorbell and a young man wearing a lip ring and a light brown cap to hold his dreadlocks opened the door. He led us across a linoleum floor into the cool darkness of the Lumumba Center. Saki and her daughter headed for the bathroom, which had a hand-drawn sign on the door: GENDER IS A UNIVERSE.

The man who had let us in introduced himself as Brandon King. He was another cofounder of Cooperation Jackson and a member of MXGM. Brandon had moved to Jackson a little over a year ago, a month before Chokwe

Lumumba died. I would soon learn that, like Brandon and Saki, many of Cooperation Jackson's twenty cofounders had moved to Jackson from cities outside of Mississippi.

Saki had recently decorated the beige cinder-block walls of the Lumumba Center with photo collages. One featured Chokwe. She showed me the industrial kitchen where the group planned to open a cooperatively owned café called Nubia's Place. In the center's biggest room, she pointed to the areas that would eventually hold a stage for open mic nights, seating for the café, and couches. A door led to the wide backyard, where seedlings of cooperatively owned Freedom Farms were pushing upward under the soil.

Typing at a desk in a small office off the main room I recognized Kali Akuno, another founding member of Cooperation Jackson and its apparently tireless de facto spokesperson. He was also Saki's partner. I'd seen videos of him speaking about their work at conferences around the world. Kali had drafted the public version of the Jackson-Kush Plan and, I would later learn, he had been one of the first to approach Chokwe Lumumba about running for office.

A year after my first visit to the Lumumba Center, Antar would run again for the mayor's seat. As had been the case for his father's bids for office and Antar's previous run in the special election, the campaign's messaging and platform would be developed with input from members of MXGM. One of his most regularly invoked campaign slogans—"When I become mayor, you become mayor"—would be rooted in the Jackson-Kush Plan's vision of self-determination and self-governing. In his debates and speeches, Antar would regularly seize opportunities to champion cooperatives as part of the prescription for the city's economic malaise. He would also mention the Lumumba Center, a place where that work of establishing economic democracy was slowly getting started.

The Jackson-Kush Plan had reached a moment in which it had an established base in the former daycare center on Capitol Street and a charismatic young attorney seeking to offer more support for the plan from inside City Hall. But for something to come of this moment, so long in the making, Antar would need to convince voters that his vision—especially his economic vision—was the one they should vote for at a desperate moment for their city, despite the more familiar solutions competing for the role.

The first big showdown between Jackson's top mayoral candidates was in March 2017—two months before the primary election and a year after my initial trip to Jackson. (Antar had officially announced his candidacy on May 19, Malcolm X's birthday, with a press conference on the steps of Jackson's City Hall, where the assembled crowd had chanted: "Free the land! Free the land! Free the land!") Grace Inspirations Church, in West Jackson, hosted the forum on a Sunday evening and the roughly two hundred attendees who gathered in the sanctuary were still dressed in their Sunday best. I noticed men in suits with matching ties and pocket squares, and women in long dresses, a few in swooping hats.

It was a welcome occasion for civic sociability and also for indulging in some lofty plans to fix Jackson. The city's infrastructure problems continued to nose their way into the lives of every Jacksonian. Many of the forum's attendees had come from houses that were under notices to boil tap water before it was safe to drink; the next day, city officials would announce that water in a large swath of the city would be turned off for forty-eight hours the following weekend in order to replace pipes in a portion of Jackson's out-of-date water distribution system.

The church's pastor, Danny Ray Hollins, opened the forum with a word of prayer. As it turned out, it was a prayer for Jackson. "It's our home," he said. "It's a city that we love—a city with a myriad of issues. Problems. Problems not brought about as a result of any one man, or one administration. . . . We have *sent out the call!* To those who would be *mayor!* And we've invited them here—to church." His tongue delivered that last word to the room like it was wrapped in silk. "And we're here to hear them share their vision for this city."

The five most popular candidates among the sixteen running for the mayor's seat had been invited to participate in the forum. All five were Democrats, and all five were black. On Grace Inspirations' altar stage, six empty chairs were arranged in a semicircle. The moderator, Pastor CJ Rhodes, took a seat toward the center and called the candidates to the stage one by one. Along with his brief introductions, he noted each person's placement in the polls—Antar was in the lead—until a woman of grandmotherly age in one of the front pews called for him to stop it with the polls. "Yes, thank you, ma'am," Rhodes said, admonished, and followed her directive as he welcomed the last three men.

A poll released a few days after the debate would confirm that Antar stood comfortably in first place. His support was sharply racialized, and despite his overall favorable numbers, he had garnered a net negative impression among the white Jacksonians polled. But the white contingent was small enough and his favorability among Black voters was high enough that his lead in the race was a stable one. Brad Chism, a white political analyst in Jackson, declared that his own polling data indicated it was Antar's race to lose.

Antar's biggest competition was John Horhn, a veteran state senator. Horhn had run for mayor twice before, and both times he failed to garner enough support to qualify for a runoff. This year, he had refined his argument. "We're at a point in our city where we've got to make sure we get it right the next time," he said at one point during the forum. "We're only going to get one more bite at the apple in my opinion." I'd heard people speak with similar finality about Jackson in recent months (including other references to near-finished apples). They usually meant the same thing: If the city's finances didn't take a few steps back from the edge of potential bankruptcy, if crime didn't abate and the schools didn't improve their outcomes, Jackson was vulnerable to takeover from the State of Mississippi. Though Horhn presented state takeover as an implicit threat, he also positioned some level of help from the state as Jackson's last possible saving grace—and himself, with a twenty-four-year tenure in the Senate, as the one person who could broker that salvation.

Another close contender for the likely Democratic primary runoff was Robert Graham, who spent most of his speaking time on litanies of his own experience as Hinds County Supervisor and his thirty-five years as a civilian employee of the Jackson Police Department. He stressed his involvement in a deal to bring a Continental tire plant to the Jackson area, slated to open in 2018 with twenty-five hundred jobs on offer.

Ronnie Crudup Jr. was a long shot, in fourth place. He was the only candidate who didn't register particularly strong opinions among those polled, in a positive or negative direction. His father, Bishop Ronnie Crudup Sr., is senior pastor of a church serving over three thousand in South Jackson.

Incumbent mayor Tony Yarber was a distant fifth in the polls, the only candidate in the top five with a net negative favorability rating, at -39.2 percent. A perception of mismanagement along with a spate of sexual harassment cases had pulled his reputation into a sharp downward plunge over the course of his three years in office.

In one of his first questions to Antar, Rhodes bored directly into the discomfort that plenty of Jacksonians still felt about the Lumumbas, pointing to the history of the PG-RNA and the sense that Antar's platform had been born out of some sort of bigger plan—or "agenda," as the more suspicious tended to put it. "One of the concerns that came up in the last election," Rhodes said, his eyes on Antar, "was about whether or not, for lack of a better way of saying it, Antar Lumumba is going to be an anti-white mayor, and push away white folks, and gonna bring in nationalists, and it's going to be *Jafrica* and all these kinds of things." Some murmuring and laughter broke out around the room.

"I appreciate you asking that question, Pastor Rhodes," Lumumba began. In his job as a criminal defense attorney, he said, he worked with many people who don't look like him, and had plenty of success. But his voice was climbing stairs, building up to something higher. "I've been labeled as a radical," he continued. "My father was labeled as a radical. You were told that he would divide the city and what was demonstrated was something entirely different." Antar would tell me later that he and the MXGM members helping to run the campaign had made the concerted decision to embrace the loaded "radical" descriptor that had been hurled at his father and at him in his previous campaign. His pace quickened a few steps, riding on its own momentum. "Honestly, when people call me a radical, I take it as a badge of honor. Because Martin Luther King was radical." Applause spread through the room. "Medgar Evers was radical." The applause intensified, and so did Antar. "Jesus *Christ* was radical." The applause didn't break, so he spoke louder to be heard. "The reality is that we have to be prepared to be as radical as circumstances dictate we should be. If you look outside these doors and you see a need for a change, then you should all be radical." I heard shouts of "Amen!" He went on, "And the reality is that we haven't found ourselves in the condition we're in because someone has been too *radical* for us." He inflected these last few words. "I would argue we haven't been radical enough." The applause carried on like an unbroken wave.

The audience's response made me think about a question that had been posed during Chokwe Lumumba's campaign: Was it possible for a person to be both a revolutionary and a politician? Throughout the debate, the candidates piled on the Yarber administration's apparent inaction in fixing the streets, and the mayor's responses tangled into long paragraphs explaining the technical details that had complicated the solutions. I found myself wondering if the mundane, full-time job of running a city with long-neglected infrastructure could leave any room for helming a revolution. Because Chokwe Lumumba's tenure was so truncated, it remained an open question.

Still, it was true that the people in the church that afternoon became most animated when Antar shifted from the role of knowledgeable attorney into that of revolutionary. And he didn't withhold his more progressive ideas—rooted in the Jackson-Kush Plan—for reimagining how economic revitalization could happen in Jackson. "Oftentimes we find ourselves engaged in merely a discussion of how we entice businesses to come here. We have to also consider where there is a need that we can fill, where we can develop the businesses ourselves. And look at *cooperative business* models where the people who live in the community own the business, and the people who work in that business not only determine what their labor will be, but they have a say-so in what the fruits of the labor will be."

In addition to being central to the PG-RNA's new-society ideal, cooperatives had been an important part of other visions for true racial equality in the state. In 1969, in Sunflower County, Mississippi, the voting rights activist Fannie Lou Hamer helped develop the Freedom Farm Cooperative—the namesake of the beds behind Cooperation Jackson. In her 2014 book *Collective Courage: A History of African American Cooperative Economic Thought and Practice*, Jessica Gordon Nembhard, a political economist who researches African-American collective economies, argues that co-ops have existed as a necessary counterweight to this country's economic violence against Black communities from the beginning of slavery here. "There seems to be no period in U.S. history where African Americans were not involved in economic cooperation of some type," she writes. Cooperatives, though never a critical mass, have offered an alternate mindset, a means of insulating the economic participation of a group pushed out of the dominant system.

Cooperatives are a main tenet of the Jackson-Kush Plan. The framers of this new-society experiment viewed them as a way to help people unlearn the lessons their economy taught them and train them to be democratic in every aspect of their lives. They knew that the individual, foundational work of building buy-in for a whole new type of economy would be even harder than winning an election.

A few days after the mayoral forum at Grace Inspirations Church, I stopped by the Lumumba Center for a class. It was a Wednesday at noon, just in time for that week's installment of the Economic Democracy Learning Series, led by Kali Akuno. In a large room with a wall of street-facing windows, eight folding tables were arranged in a rectangle. The ten or so attendees took their seats around it with the ease of people who had done this many times before. Saki sat at the front of the room next to Kali, who clicked final preparations into his laptop. Slides lit up a projector screen on the wall behind him as students unwrapped sandwiches, flipped open Styrofoam containers of chicken wings, and forked fruit salad out of Tupperware.

In Kali's mind, Cooperation Jackson is an experiment; his hypothesis is that living and working in fully democratic communities will change the people involved. One of the experiment's first steps, he believes, is for people to realize how capitalism has shaped them and to recognize how alternatives could refresh their perspectives.

He picked up on this week's slide and began. The class was continuing its guided tour through Marx's *Capital*. Under discussion today was Marx's concept of exchange-value. Kali asked if someone would volunteer to read the first slide. After a silence, a woman wearing a green cloth headband over graying dreadlocks and strings of beads around her neck complied. She read:

The exchange value of a commodity is what one receives in exchange for this commodity.

Statement A: One chair is the exchange-value of two pairs of pants.

Statement B: Two pairs of pants are the exchange-value of one chair.

When she had finished reading, her brow didn't unfurrow and her mouth kept silently working. Kali waited. "How will we, in this new environment we're creating, fairly determine exchange-value?" the woman asked. She pointed to the woman next to her, half of a young white couple dividing their attention between the front of the classroom and their two small children playing behind them. The young woman was a skilled seamstress. If a seamstress has been developing her skill for twenty years, the woman in the green headband reasoned, a pair of pants she produces would be worth more than one chair, wouldn't it?

Kali shook his head and turned the question back to her. "Is that just profit in your thinking?"

She considered this and eventually nodded once, her brow still knitted.

Kali continued through the slides. Before moving to Jackson, Kali had worked as a high school teacher and he knew when to slow down, reword something, and expand where it might help. The overriding question he returned to again and again, in different forms, was: See how this capitalist economic system has shaped you when you weren't looking?

As the class passed its second hour, eyes fell downward. I noticed a glow of cell phones nestled in many laps. It was a clear, sunny day, but through the thick sheets of adhesive window tint lining the windows onto Capitol Street, the view of outside was abstracted, a soupy blue. After an afternoon with this view, the laborious deconstruction of exchange-value made the city outside seem blank and theoretical—like an empty place requesting something to be built in it.

Toward the end of the three-hour class, Kali paused and looked around, noting the man next to me who'd finished his chicken wings and lain his head on the table. Kali acknowledged the denseness of the material and admitted that it had taken him three passes through *Capital* before he really started to grasp it. He recited the socialist dictum stripped down to its simplest articulation: From each according to their ability, to each according to their need. "No democracy has achieved that yet," he added. It was clear that he didn't share this anecdote to caution anyone in the room against working toward the achievement. After all, he labored for three hours every Wednesday afternoon to make his lessons understood. The implicit challenge was to figure out a way to do what no one else had done.

Kali had been brought up in Los Angeles during the tumultuous 1970s and '80s. His parents were active in the Black power movement, and he grew up going to the movement's meetings and reading its literature. Most of his parents' peers ascribed to a Marxist-socialist orientation. As a young boy, Kali told his mother, in all earnestness, that he wanted to know everything. He read hungrily, and as a teenager he particularly looked forward to packages in the mail from an uncle who wrote for Black newspapers and music journals in Toronto. In these publications, he read about people like Maurice Bishop and groups like the People's Revolutionary Government of Grenada. His political education came, too, from what was happening around him in L.A. Starting from the early eighties, the crack epidemic pummeled Kali's neighborhood with a force he didn't understand. It hit most of the families in his neighborhood, and eventually his own, and its effects were devastating. When Kali saw how, in preparation for the 1984 Olympics, the city cleaned up much of the drug trade, he concluded that they could have stopped the destruction of his community much earlier and had chosen not to. He began to notice a ruthlessness in the various systems around him.

Kali joined MXGM's Oakland chapter in 1996, just six years after Lumumba had cofounded it. By the time the organization began to discuss plans to stage an experiment in Mississippi, he was MXGM's national organizer. He moved to Jackson permanently in 2013 to devote his life to the Jackson-Kush Plan. He would go on to serve in Chokwe Lumumba's administration as its Director of Special Projects and External Funding.

Talking with Kali after the Economic Democracy class, I learned that his thinking has shifted in subtle ways over the last decade, as Jackson's economic and infrastructure problems have continued to mount. He's seen that elections can, in his opinion, become a distraction from the real work of transforming society. "I'm sure Antar doesn't want to be mayor forever," he said. "So what are we setting up for beyond that? And beyond that, in my mind, is not just making sure we have someone in office for the next fifty years. If that's the best we can do, then we've failed, in my opinion.

"Because I think we're ultimately trying to get to the point where we've changed the rules of society—both formally and informally—where we've created a more democratic society, a more equitable society. And if there's a fully engaged citizenry, then the need for a city council and a mayor starts to become fairly moot."

I asked him what the movement stood to gain if Antar were indeed elected mayor in the fast-approaching election. After all, MXGM had decided as a body to run Antar as the face of the Jackson-Kush Plan. He pushed back in the metal folding chair and leaned his wide upper body onto the table. "That is a good question," he said. His head rested heavily in his hand, and his knee bobbed as he thought. "Woo. That's a good question." I realized I'd expected he'd have his thoughts on the topic crafted and close at hand, given his involvement both in the campaign and in the building of the Jackson-Kush Plan. He sighed. "Honestly," he admitted, "I'm a minority voice who didn't want Antar to run this time."

Kali's conception of a successful realization of the plan goes far beyond four years of Antar in the mayor's office. He imagines People's Assemblies—the bodies open to all citizens that drive self-government and undergird the fully democratic society described in the Jackson-Kush Plan—coming together to, for example, defy the state's orders against sanctuary cities for undocumented immigrants, and training people in Jackson to protect immigrants from ICE raids. He imagines the creation of an alternative currency in Jackson, so that the city government could use the U.S. dollar to pay off its debts and pay city workers part of their salaries in a "soft" currency to use at the corner grocery. For each part of this vision, the stakes would rise higher with Antar's election. I had figured that two subsequent electoral losses might have been a fatal blow to the current version of the Jackson-Kush Plan. But now I saw that, if Antar did win, it would be the next four years that would become the high-stakes last chance.

Kali then ticked off Jackson's problems and listed the municipal operations facing privatization or takeover by the state: the water system, the schools, the whole of downtown. "We're setting ourselves up to administer the most severe austerity the city's seen probably since the Civil War. ... We have to be clear that if we fail, that's not just MXGM failing, or Chokwe Antar failing. That's a failure for the left in this country."

Kali's fears are not without precedent. In a 1992 article, "Black Mayors: A Historical Assessment," historian Roger Biles explained a trend: Simultaneous with the changing laws and demographic shifts that finally made possible the election of Black mayors in major cities around the United States, white flight and the decline of industry were draining those cities' wealth and resources. These factors conspired to make Black mayoral victories, as Biles quotes from H. Paul Friesema, "a hollow prize." Biles writes:

As the tax base available to big city governments shrank, the same could not be said of the demand for public services. Rising costs for welfare, law enforcement, and maintenance of an aging infrastructure exacerbated the problems awaiting neophyte Black mayors. An embattled Kenneth Gibson, mayor of Newark, concluded resignedly: "Progress is maintaining the status quo."

Biles, who is completing a book on Harold Washington, the first Black mayor of Chicago, told me that the hollow-prize problem persists to this day. The problem is most pointedly felt, he observed, by leaders who come into the mayor's office on a wave of expectations that are, perhaps, "unrealistically high."

During Chokwe Lumumba's truncated term, the combination of Jackson's tight municipal resources and massively expensive problems created rifts within his administration. The Environmental Protection Agency had served the city with a consent decree in 2012 to force it to fix the antiquated sewage system that was spilling into the Pearl River. A 2013 estimate put the cost of the infrastructure fix at around $1 billion. Infighting festered over how to raise the revenue. Eventually, the city increased water rates and passed a 1 percent sales tax—a regressive tax, in that it could burden low-income Jacksonians more than high-income earners. In a report reflecting on Chokwe's eight-month tenure, Kali wrote: "The most critical lesson we learned is that our practice has to be as sound as our theory. While in office, our practice of governance did not always equate to our previous work of building an alternative base of political power rooted in a democratic mass movement." The very real problem of insufficient resources highlighted a central rub inherent in the Lumumba administration: Were they aiming to capably govern a city, or to altogether reimagine it? Insiders didn't agree on the answer.

In the week leading up to the primary election on Tuesday, May 2, Jackson was crackling with the full focus of the competing campaigns. Yard signs bearing the faces of the main candidates—Lumumba, Horhn, Graham, and Yarber—clustered in abandoned lots like weeds competing for sunlight. It was the primary, not the general election in early June, that came freighted with the suspense of determining the city's next mayor. In the thoroughly blue city, a Democratic candidate was guaranteed to win the final race, and the only serious contenders fell on that side of the ballot. Antar ran in a crowded field of nine Democratic candidates, and pollster Brad Chism was certain that their support would be too divided for any one person to earn more than 50 percent of the vote. A runoff between the two top Democratic candidates was all but inevitable. By the weekend the local papers had unveiled their endorsements like the sharing of long-guarded secrets. All three publications endorsed Lumumba, even the long-running, conservative-leaning daily the *Clarion-Ledger*.

On Saturday morning, I stopped by Cooperation Jackson, where I found Brandon King in the backyard, working on Freedom Farms. From the gate, I saw him near the far edge of the fence, plunging a hoe into the ground, alone. When he noticed me approaching, he rested his hoe in the soil and smiled a hello. He was dressed like a farmer, but one who had gone to art school. Layers of necklaces strung on leather bands rested their shells and stones above his sternum, and a solid tattoo band wrapped around his left arm, opening into the shape of a star on his elbow.

The day hadn't yet unleashed its full heat, but Brandon was sweating from the work of turning a grassy patch into a new bed. He indicated another fifteen feet along the fence and told me it would be a bed for sweet peas. In the grass beside us lay a coil of chain-link fencing that he planned to install against the wooden fence so the pea shoots could climb and curl their way up toward the sun.

"How's it going?" I asked, lifting my hands to indicate, how's it *all* going—the farming, but also the mounting of the new society experiment which had brought him here to Jackson. Brandon grabbed the hoe, lifted it high, and drove it down into the soil. He knew what I meant, and he answered for all of it. "Oh, you know me!" He let out a laugh, tinged with exasperation. "I'm impatient."

In our conversations over the previous year, Brandon had never struck me as impatient. His voice had a soft edge of something like shyness, and he always revealed a willingness to be deeply introspective and an ability to rest in the contradictions he noticed in himself, in other people, and in circumstances.

Brandon had lived in New York before moving south, and he had moved to Jackson to live in the City of the Future that Chokwe Lumumba had described. He'd never stopped wanting to live in that place. Here in the backyard, perspiring as he lifted and pulled his hoe, he was still working toward it.

Brandon's mother was one of the first Black women to work as a machinist in the Norfolk Naval Shipyard near Chesapeake, Virginia, the town where Brandon and his brothers had grown up. She frequently confronted racism and sexism on the job. At home, she introduced her children to radical Black thinkers like Malcolm X and Marcus Garvey. When Brandon was sixteen, she put down those books in favor of a Bible and became a devout Christian. He picked up her books and fell deeper into them. He respected his mother, but he didn't want her life. The nine-to-five grind was anathema to him. In every conversation I had with Brandon, he repeated his insistence that he hopes to never become a "status quo manager," like an incantation that can keep that life away. He fears the numbness, the existential stuckness—and the resigned acceptance of society the way it is

During college—Brandon studied sociology and art at Hampton University in Virginia—he took two trips to New Orleans to provide support for the survivors of Hurricane Katrina. While there, he met members of the Malcolm X Grassroots Movement. After graduating, he moved to New York to work as a union organizer and DJ, and he joined the local MXGM chapter. In the three years since Brandon had moved to Mississippi, the Jackson-Kush Plan had seen some progress—in the founding of Cooperation Jackson, for example, and the securing of the land on which we stood—but it had also slammed up against obstacles. Nubia's Place had struggled to obtain the food license necessary to serve food out of its space in the former daycare center, though it had been catering for local organizations and events for two years. City worker furloughs, instituted under Mayor Yarber to save the city from bankruptcy, have made for a lean city staff and the resulting interminable wait times for securing business licenses.

In December 2016, Brandon, Kali, Saki, Antar, and Rukia traveled to Barcelona to observe, in a more fully developed form, elements of the society they were working toward in Jackson. Barcelona's deputy mayor took them on a tour of the city's cooperatives, including stops at a cooperatively owned bar and a cooperatively owned bookstore. They also visited the Green Fab Lab, a place to tinker and research new ways to produce renewable energy and use 3-D printers, laser cutters, and other machines to make all manner of stuff. It was a chance for Brandon and the others to see an on-the-ground, functioning version of some of the plans struggling to move past dream-stage in Jackson.

A boarded-up building across the street from the Lumumba Center was meant to be the location of Jackson's own Fabrication Laboratory, where collectively owned 3-D printers and other machines would turn out items the community needs: everything from car chassis, piping, copper wire, and insulation for houses, to dishware and utensils for Nubia's Place. But Cooperation Jackson's purchase of the building was being held back by legal snafus, and the organization was struggling to raise the money for the 3-D printer and other technology. A fifteen-minute walk away on Ewing Street, Cooperation Jackson owned a grassy lot where Brandon pictured an affordable eco-village, with housing built in the Fab Lab and a collection of cooperatively tended farms. The first step was establishing the urban farm that would provide food to residents. But that work had been held back, too. The empty lot had long been used as a dumping ground, and the soil was poisoned with the old paint, garbage, and construction debris of the society Brandon is trying to move away from.

On the eve of Jackson's mayoral primary, Brandon was suffering these various mundane hindrances pointedly. It was all just moving so slowly, and the new society they were building wasn't feeling sufficiently set apart from the old one. "I didn't move here to help build a bunch of big cooperative businesses," he said. "When are we going to break off and do our own thing?" He leaned on his hoe, and the dreams tumbled from him: When will we be making and distributing products from the Fab Lab? When will we have a self-feeding network of cooperatives? When will we have an alternative currency mediating our new economy?

I told Brandon I'd help with the farming while we talked, and he grabbed another hoe. I asked if he'd been helping with Antar's campaign. A bit, he said. "But I'm not going to vote," he added. When I didn't hide my surprise, he explained that he didn't want to participate in what he considered to be an "illegitimate system." While Kali was anxious about the pressure the election could impose, Brandon was skeptical of the entire enterprise. A system relying on People's Assemblies to select the next mayor, he offered, would do a better job of bringing more voices and perspectives into the democratic process.

A few hours later, we put away the gardening equipment and shifted to loading subwoofers, folding tables, and eight crates full of records into Brandon's pickup truck. He had been asked to DJ a community cookout at Antar's campaign headquarters that afternoon. The parking lot in front of the A&D Tax Services office that housed the campaign's daily operations was taken over by a bouncy castle, grills, and tables of food. Antar and Ebony moved among their friends and supporters, laughing and teasing. They seemed eager and excited about the potential that the next few days would usher in. Under fast-moving clouds, dozens of Jacksonians mingled in the lot, holding their plates of grilled meat and fresh fruit, or they sat in folding chairs along the building's front windows. I watched people form lines to do the Cha Cha Slide in front of the table where Brandon stood, lining up his tracks. It wasn't the work of new-society building, but it might turn out to be related.

Three days later, Chokwe Antar won ten thousand more votes in the primary than his father had. His 55 percent support in the Democratic primary meant there was no need for a runoff in a Jackson mayoral race for the first time in twelve years. In the general election the next month, he secured 93 percent of voters' support.

Around the country, pockets of attention snapped toward this decisive win of the young mayoral candidate running on a plan to establish a society with socialist roots in the Deep South. Antar's landslide primary win came on the heels of President Trump's one-hundred-day mark. A post-election analysis released by Millsaps College and Chism Strategies noted that the "Trump Factor" might have helped mushroom support for Antar late in the race: "To the extent undecided voters wanted to express a protest vote against the status quo, Lumumba was that vessel."

Antar indicated on a national stage a willingness to accept the role when, in early June, he appeared as a speaker at the People's Summit in Chicago alongside Bernie Sanders, author Naomi Klein, and environmental activist Bill McKibben. With his speech, Antar made headlines in Jackson and in a smattering of national publications by declaring that his administration would make the capital of Mississippi "the most radical city on the planet." He called for other cities to join him, name-checking Washington, D.C.; Gary, Indiana; and Chicago.

Inauguration Day was July 3, a hot and sunny Monday in Jackson. Museums and city offices were closed for Independence Day. The people who streamed into one of downtown's newest structures, the hulking Jackson Convention Complex, for the swearing-in ceremony wore lumumba-for-mayor t-shirts, suits, dashikis, and sundresses. After he had lain his hand on a Bible and sworn to protect the constitutions of the United States and Mississippi, Chokwe Antar Lumumba took to the podium and asked the hundreds of Jacksonians present to look past the inevitability of the present society with him.

"This is the building of the *new* society," he said, adding later: "For so long Mississippi has been known as the symbol of limits. It has been known as a haven for oppression, for some of the most horrible suffering in the history of the world. So it is only fitting that we should become the leaders of that change."

The inaugural address was an opportunity to posit a possible future, and Antar embraced it. What would happen next with Jackson's roads and water systems, with the People's Assemblies, with the cooperatives and the Fab Lab, wasn't certain. But on this Inauguration Day just before Independence Day, Antar was helping a city and a country to see past the present, and that, in itself, was radical.

"Free the land!" he called out three times as he concluded his address, raising his right fist high above the rose boutonniere pinned to his lapel.

"Free the land!" the city of Jackson called back to him.

This article was originally published the Fall 2017 issue of the Oxford American, *with support from the Economic Hardship Reporting Project.*

VI

AFTERWORD

22.

Home Isn't Always Where the Hatred Is: There is Hope in Mississippi

Ajamu Baraka

> *You don't have to live next to me*
> *Just give me my equality*
> *Everybody knows about Mississippi*
> *Everybody knows about Alabama*
> *Everybody knows about Mississippi Goddam*
> — Nina Simone

Mississippi, the poorest state in the U.S. with the highest percentage of Black people, a history of vicious racial terror and concurrent Black resistance is the backdrop and context for the drama captured in the collection of essays that is *Jackson Rising: The Struggle for Economic Democracy and Self-Determination in Jackson Mississippi.*

Undeterred by the uncertainty, anxiety and fear brought about by the steady deterioration of the neoliberal order over the last few years, the response from Black activists of Jackson, Mississippi has been to organize. Inspired by the rich history of struggle and resistance in Mississippi and committed to the vision of the Jackson-Kush Plan, these activists are building institutions rooted in community power that combine politics and economic development into an alternative model for change, while addressing real, immediate needs of the people.

The experiences and analyses in this compelling collection reflect the creative power that is unleashed when political struggle is grounded by a worldview freed from the inherent contradictions and limitations of reform liberalism.

As such, *Jackson Rising* is ultimately a story about a process that is organized and controlled by Black people who are openly declaring that their political project is committed to decolonization and socialism. And within those broad strategic and ethical objectives, Jackson Rising is also a project unapologetically committed to self-determination for people of African descent in Mississippi and the South.

And while the end of this story is not yet written, the documentation of the social, political, and economic context and players involved in this ambitious drama is required as part of our collective learning. It is a form of bearing witness to a process of collective self-empowerment and reversing the silencing imposed on our communities by oppressors who want us to believe that "there is no alternative" to the existing order.

What we see in *Jackson Rising* is the historic task of building the new within the context of the already existing. Instead of abstract theorizing, or worse yet, despondent passivity and even collaboration that we have witnessed from some progressives and radicals in the West over the last few decades, Black activists in Mississippi are exercising agency as historical subjects.

But what is this Jackson-Kush Plan that guides *Jackson Rising*?

I will not attempt to comment on all the plan's intricacies here because that will be done elsewhere in the book. But also, because for me what is valuable about the plan is not its intimate details but what it represents broadly as the very embodiment of a de-colonial project.

This audacious plan for Black empowerment and self-determination was written by Kali Akuno one of our leading intellectuals and revolutionary theorists. But brother Kali is not just an intellectual and theoretician, as important as that is for a broad-based, mature movement, he is also a long-time practitioner whose work reflects the dialectic of theory and practice that informs praxis. So while the plan is imprinted by Kali's unique contributions, its essence was collectively formed by the broader context and congealed experiences of the Black liberation movement in general and specifically by the work of the Malcom X Grassroots Movement (MXGM) and its "parent" organization the New African People's Organization in the South.

These activists defined what they refer to as the Kush district as the areas that link Jackson within and as part of contiguous Black majority counties along the Mississippi River in the states of Mississippi, Louisiana, Arkansas, and Tennessee.

It is therefore, a project to build Black political, social, and economic power within the heart of the Black-Belt South, re-centering the issue of land, Black culture and Black "peoplehood." It says without any equivocation that it is a project committed to building socialism unrestrained by the fear of Trumpism and in the most bourgeois society on the planet.

The plan and work represent an ethical, de-colonial break with the constraints of "Northern" radical theory and practice and its myopia related to colonialism and U.S. "domestic colonialism."

The work is informed by the base-line position that the struggle for self-determination and the liberation of Black people in the U.S. has been undermined, not just as a result of the repression from the state, but the reluctance of many Black activists to come to terms with the fact that for there to be authentic liberation there has to be a "critical break with capitalism and the dismantling of the American settler colonial project."

However, the value of Jackson-Kush Plan is not just in its material/ structural analysis, but the alternative ethical framework that it asserts as being fundamental to revolutionary practice and a consistent world-view that links their work to the work/struggles of people globally against neoliberal capitalism.

For me, the plan reflects an alternative ethical framework that rejects capitalist market fundamentalism in which everything, including nature itself, becomes a commodity to be bought and sold for profit.

It even rejects the left "economism" that sees production and productive relations in ways that mirror capitalist production with its emphasis on mass production and notions of "growth."

Building on that idea the ideas of economic development is rooted in the needs of the people, the Jackson-Kush Plan for economic development is rooted in its commitment to people and not objects. It is committed to community power and community based economics that closes gap between spaces of production and consumption

The economy should serve the people, not the reverse. And the notion that economic activity is legitimate that rationalizes production in which a small group of private individuals are allowed to own and thus steal the value of what is produced by the majority for their own private use, is rejected as absurd and irrational.

Politically, the Jackson-Kush plan and the work it informs represents an unalterable commitment to the principles of democracy. Not bourgeois democracy that is reflected in five minutes of voting but democratic participation and accountability in every aspect of social life.

The Jackson-Kush Plan reflects an understanding that Authentic liberation cannot be achieved without creating independent structures but it does not automatically reject engagement with bourgeois electoral processes and state structures. However, it recognizes the absolute necessity of relating to those structures from an organized and independent base.

The popular base that grounds their relationship to those structures are the Peoples Assemblies. From that base the Jackson organizers believe that "engaging electoral politics on a limited scale with the express intent of building radical voting blocs and electing candidates drawn from the ranks of the Assemblies themselves is important. As we have learned through our own experiences and a summation of the experiences of others, we ignore the power of the state at our own peril."

Understanding the complex and delicate line that must be walked when participating in bourgeois processes from a radical base with the intention of exploiting these spaces to alter power relations, the analysis represented in the plan demonstrates that the activists are aware of how easily these kinds of engagements can be co-opted by the state and used to prop-up the hegemony of the state and system. The plan states that:

"... it should be clear that we do not engage the electoral system of the settler colony that is the state of Mississippi because we aim to legitimize its existence or its claims to being a democratic institution ... we struggle to engage it as a means to create political openings that provide a broader platform for the struggles to restore the "commons", create more public utilities (i.e. universal health care and comprehensive public transportation), and the democratic transformation of the economy to be waged. As we are struggling against a state apparatus that is an edifice of white colonial supremacy and neo-liberal in its orientation of governance, we are clear that this combination of defensive and offensive struggles must be given equal attention. If this perspective of critical struggle against the state is not maintained, our initiatives could easily turn opportunist and fall victim to becoming the latest Black-faced trend in the neo-liberal administration of austerity."

What these activists are engaged in is important not only to the people of Jackson, Mississippi or the territory that is at the foundation of the Jackson-Kush Plan for self-determination, but also for peoples throughout the world still caught in the rapacious grip of the 524 year-long racialized, predatory colonial capitalist experience.

By situating its struggle for self-determination and socialism within the context of the dynamics of global struggle against neoliberal capitalism but informed by the specificities of Mississippi, it is a project that has a transnational relevance for Black people in the U.S. and across the "Americas."

Like the innovative work of the "Black Community Process" in Colombia that integrates culture, territoriality, people-centered development that they refer to as "Buen Vivir" (the good life), mass direct democracy, and the right to be recognized as a people, *Jackson Rising* de-centers U.S./Eurocentric assumptions as the foundation and source of knowledge production and revolutionary praxis.

Jackson *IS* rising and emerging as a model for resistance and visioning beyond the challenges of the present. It stands as the dynamic counter to economic redundancy, political marginalization, and systematic state violence.

23.

Resist and Fight!

Hakima Abbas

In 1601, African freedom fighters established the village of Palenque de San Basilio in what is now Colombia and in so doing broke the imperial logic of enslavement. From this village, African people established their own cultural, social and political systems in the Americas, including their own language, in counterposition but also independently from the genocidal hegemony of the rapidly expanding European colonialism of the territories. For decades, the growing community of people of Palenque de San Basilio launched attacks on the nearby port of Cartagena where ships arrived carrying kidnapped African people, vowing to free all enslaved Africans arriving there. The Palenquenos at once resisted and built.

Between 1959 and 1974 the African Party for the Independence of Guinea and Cape Verde (the PAIGC) created liberated zones on the territory it had taken back from Portuguese colonial forces. By the end of colonial rule in 1974, this liberated area constituted two thirds of the territory of Guinea-Bissau which half of the population lived on. On this territory, during the bloody war of independence, the PAIGC and the peoples of Guinea-Bissau and Cape Verde began to construct the decolonized society they were seeking to create. They formed village committees, to deepen direct democracy in each cantonment, elected from and by the people with at least two of the five positions on the committee being held by women. They also established people's courts, health clinics, and schools and began to develop the basis for solidarity economics through People's Stores in which an exchange, rather than purchase, system was established for goods and products. In these liberated zones, the PAIGC and people of Guinea-Bissau were able to build counter-hegemonic realities despite being faced with the direct assault and wrath of fascist colonial forces. They resisted and built.

The world in 2017 is marked by a global fascist surge: from the reactionary religious or ethnically based southern fundamentalisms, to white supremacist populism in the North. These right wing forces are gaining traction out of the systemic collapse of liberal democracy and neo-liberal capitalism. Often couched in anti-globalization or even anti-imperialist language, these fascisms are led by classed elites uninterested in shifting the super-exploitation of the last decades of capitalist voracity but cementing divisions amongst the working classes. In the global Black world, colonial patronage and an internal comprador class have been maintained in the economic relationships established by globalized capitalism. Ecocide has given an ever more desperate twist to the struggle of peoples to protect land and territory.

Black people across Africa and the diaspora live outside of hegemonic imperialist logic because our very survival counterposes our disposability in the system. Our cultural expressions are by their nature thus counter-hegemonic, but like Benkos Biohó and the Palenqueros, we are surrounded, impacted and affected by the imperatives of globalization's engulfment. Without counter hegemonic intention, we become mere pawns to use, dismiss and discard at the will and necessity of colonized interests: Black communities pose little threat as territories of resistance and militarized murderous police are established to ensure even the menace of Blackness is quelled. But when Black territories are organized, when we call to action our collective survival, when we split with the crumbs of the state, end our collaboration, resist and build—then our territories become liberated zones: epicenters of rebellion, posing clear and present threat to the logic of patriarchy, capitalism and white supremacy. If effectively engaged to build Black futures outside of the logic of domination, we can begin to realize radical queered, decolonial, crip, feminist, Black realities: liberation practice.

Autonomous or liberated Black territory is space where the relationship of people to land, exchange, life, value is torn away from the logic of capitalism, white supremacy, patriarchy and domination, and where self-determination and direct democracy mean that people are able to shape realities in the image of their freedom dreams. Cooperation Jackson attempts to create economic democracy and self-determination within the oppressed Black nation inside the belly of the imperial beast itself. It is a star in a constellation of African Autonomous Zones throughout the Black world, with self-determining communities being built across Africa and the diaspora.

As you have read, Jackson Rising is an attempt to document the theoretical foundations, practical applications and hard lessons learned from this emerging African liberated zone. What the success of the Jackson-Kush Plan demonstrates is that we, as our ancestors, can develop and execute effective liberation strategies through organizations of struggle like the Malcolm X Grassroots Movement and Cooperation Jackson and democratic experiments like the People's Assembly. But, one Palenque or Kilombo or Autonomous Zone is not enough. We need thousands of Autonomous Zones and we need them to link on the basis of mutual aid and solidarity to break the back of imperialism and move us towards collective liberation and eco-regeneration.

In this moment, the lessons of this book are essential reading to all people interested in saving this earth from the devastation of capitalism and building a world free from oppression where many worlds are possible. So, wherever we are, wherever we are situated, let us develop our plans to resist and build!

About the Contributors

Hakima Abbas is a revolutionary. When she closes her eyes, she can see, taste and feel the warmth of liberation in the breeze. She aspires to tending the land, dancing with the ocean and be surrounded by the laughter of children.

Kali Akuno is a co-founder and co-director of Cooperation Jackson. He is co-editor of this volume along with Ajamu Nangwaya.

Kate Aronoff is a Brooklyn-based freelance writer, the Communications Coordinator for the New Economy Coalition, and a co-founder of the Fossil Fuel Divestment Student Network. Her writing has appeared in The Nation, The American Prospect, Dissent and The New York Times.

Ajamu Baraka is an internationally recognized leader of the emerging human rights movement in the US and has been at the forefront of efforts to apply the international human rights framework to social justice advocacy in the US for more than 25 years. Baraka was the Founding Executive Director of the US Human Rights Network (USHRN) from July 2004 until June 2011. Ajamu served as the Green Party's nominee for Vice President of the United States in the 2016 election. He is currently an editor and contributing columnist for the Black Agenda Report and a writer for Counterpunch.

Sara Bernard is a former Grist fellow, wilderness junkie, and globetrotter.

Thandisizwe Chimurenga is a Los Angeles-based writer who is the author of *No Doubt: The Murder(s) of Oscar Grant* (2014) and *Reparations...Not Yet: A Case for Reparations and Why We Must Wait* (2015). Thandisizwe is committed to infusing radical Black feminist/womanist politics within revolutionary nationalism, which she believes is key to destroying capitalism patriarchy and white supremacy, has been informed by the political thoughts and/or practice of Aminata Umoja, Assata Shakur, Pearl Cleage, bell hooks, Angela Davis, Queen Mother Moore, Gloria Richardson, Fannie Lou Hamer, Ella Baker, Claudia Jones, Ida B Wells and the "Amazons" of Dahomey.

Carl Davidson is a national co-chair of the Committees of Correspondence for Democracy and Socialism and a national board member of Solidarity Economy Network, advocating a mixture of market socialism and worker ownership.

Bruce A Dixon is managing editor at Black Agenda Report, and a state committee member of the Georgia Green Party. He served seven years on the board of a 480 unit housing cooperative in Chicago, and now lives and works near Marietta GA. He can be reached via this site's contact page, or at bruce.dixon(at)blackagendareport.com.

Laura Flanders is an English broadcast journalist living in the United States, who presents the weekly, long-form interview show *The Laura Flanders Show*.

Kamau Franklin has worked as a community activist for over fifteen years in New York City and is now based in the US American south. In addition to his work as an activist attorney, he is a leading member of the Malcolm X Grassroots Movement, an organization dedicated to human rights advocacy and building grassroots institutions in the Black community. The organization works on various issues including youth development, fighting police misconduct, and creating sustainable urban communities. Kamau has helped develop community cop-watch programs, freedom school programs for youth and alternatives to incarceration programs.

Katie Gilbert lives in Chicago. She has written for *Al Jazeera America*, the *Atlantic, Pacific Standard*, and others.

Sacajawea "saki" Hall is a radical Black feminist activist, mother, birth-worker, educator and journalist who loves crafting. She sees her life's work as engaging in the collective struggle for African liberation, human rights and social transformation. She is a native Lower East Side New Yorker who migrated to Jackson, Mississippi, in December 2013 to help advance the Jackson—Kush Plan. She is a founding member of Cooperation Jackson.

Chokwe Lumumba (August 2, 1947—February 25, 2014) was an attorney and politician, affiliated with the Republic of New Afrika and serving as its second vice president. He served as a human rights lawyer in Michigan and Mississippi. In 2013, after serving on the City Council, he was elected as Mayor of Jackson, Mississippi. He was born in Detroit, Michigan, as Edwin Finley Taliaferro, and was raised there, attending local schools.

Rukia Lumumba is Founder of the People's Advocacy Institute and campaign manager for the successful Committee to Elect Chokwe Antar Lumumba for Mayor of Jackson, Mississippi. Rukia Lumumba is a transformative justice strategist and community organizer. Named a "New Activist" by *Essence Magazine* and an "Emerging Leader" by the Congressional Black Caucus, the daughter of community justice icon the late Mayor Chokwe Lumumba and Nubia Lumumba, Rukia continues the Lumumba family's rich history of advancing issues and
initiatives that elevate the legal, economical, health and educational rights of individuals, families and communities.

Ajamu Nangwaya, PhD., is an educator, organizer and writer. He is a lecturer in the Institute of Caribbean Studies at the University of the West Indies, Mona Campus. Ajamu is co-editor with Dr. Michael Truscello of the recently published anthology *Why Don't The Poor Rise Up? Organizing the Twenty-First Century Resistance*. He is co-editor of this volume along with Kali Akuno.

Jessica Gordon Nembhard, PhD is Professor of Community Justice and Social Economic Development in the Department of Africana Studies, John Jay

College, City University of New York, and author of *Collective Courage: A History of African American Cooperative Economic Thought and Practice*, Penn State University Press, 2014.

Max Rameau is a Haitian born Pan-African theorist, campaign strategist, organizer and author. He works at the Center for Pan-African Development, Positive Action Center

Michael Siegel is a civil and human rights lawyer who lives in Austin, Texas.

Bhaskar Sunkara is the founding editor and publisher of *Jacobin Magazine*.

Makani Themba-Nixon is executive director of the Praxis Project, a media and policy advocacy center based in Washington, DC.

Jazmine Walker is from Jackson, Mississippi, and currently lives in Washington, D.C. As a native southerner, she is committed to strengthening southern leadership and organizational capacities. Jazmine is committed to strengthening leadership and organizational capacities to increase communities' effectiveness and deepen the impact of their work. Her vision is to build resources across social justice movements and develop alternative economies that dismantle systematic oppression that harms and excludes communities of color.

Elandria Williams is on the Education team at the Highlander Research and Education Center, a social justice and movement leadership, strategy and cultural center, where she has worked since 2007. Elandria helps co-coordinate the Economics and Governance program at Highlander and is a co-editor of *Beautiful Solutions*. Beautiful Solutions is a project that is gathering some of the most promising and contagious stories, solutions, strategies and big questions for building a more just, democratic, and resilient world. Elandria also serves on the boards of the Southern Reparations Loan Fund (SRLF), US Solidarity Economy Network, Appalachian Studies Association, is a founding member of the Black Immigration Network and on the Movement for Black Lives Policy Table. Highlander also is an anchor for the Media Grassroots Network (MAG-Net) and doing some work around Movement Technologists.

Additional Readings and Documentation

The Lumumba Administration

- Jackson, Mississippi, Mayor-elect Chokwe Lumumba on economic democracy http://sfbayview.com/2013/06/jackson-mississippi-mayor-elect-chokwe-lumumba-on-economic-democracy/
- Mayor looking for radical change in the Deep South http://www.belfasttelegraph.co.uk/opinion/news-analysis/mayor-looking-for-radical-change-in-the-deep-south-29384680.html
- The political, historical significance of Chokwe Lumumba mayoral win in Jackson, MS http://www.workers.org/2013/06/25/the-political-historical-significance-of-chokwe-lumumba-mayoral-win-in-jackson-miss/

Mayor Lumumba and His Legacy

- Chokwe Lumumba, radical mayor of Jackson, MS dies at 66 http://america.aljazeera.com/articles/2014/2/26/chokwe-lumumba-radicalmayorofjacksonmsdiesat66.html
- A New Kind of Southern Strategy http://www.thenation.com/article/162694/new-kind-southern-strategy
- Chokwe Lumumba: A Revolutionary to the End http://www.thenation.com/article/178546/chokwe-lumumba-revolutionary-end#
- The Legacy of Chokwe Lumumba Must Not Be Buried with the Man http://www.thenation.com/blog/178538/mayor-who-brought-economic-democracy-vision-mississippi
- Waltz for Lumumba http://www.thenation.com/article/178691/waltz-lumumba
- Remembering Chokwe Lumumba http://www.yesmagazine.org/commonomics/remembering-lumumba
- Jackson Mourns Mayor with Militant Past Who Won Over Skeptics http://www.nytimes.com/2014/03/10/us/jackson-mourns-mayor-with-militant-past-who-won-over-skeptics.html

- Remembering Chokwe Lumumba: A Revolutionary Politician http://www.theroot.com/articles/culture/2014/03/chokwe_lumumba_remembering_a_revolutionary_politician.html

- Chokwe Lumumba (1947 – 2014): Activist and Revolutionary Mayor of Jackson, MS http://www.commondreams.org/news/2014/02/26/chokwe-lumumba-1947-2014-activist-and-revolutionary-mayor-jackson-miss

- Honor Chokwe Lumumba http://www.workers.org/articles/2014/03/11/honor-chokwe-lumumba/

- Mayor Chokwe Lumumba: A life of Struggle, A Legacy of Progress http://www.truthdig.com/report/item/mayor_chokwe_lumumba_a_life_of_struggle_a_legacy_of_progress_20140226

- Chokwe Lumumba: A Legal Biography http://www.ncbl.org/chokwe-lumumba-a-legal-biography/

- Chokwe Lumumba: Long Distance Runner http://drgregcarr.squarespace.com/blog/2014/2/26/chokwe-lumumba-1947-2014-long-distance-runner

- After Chokwe Lumumba's Death, Mississippi Auto Workers Mourn Ally http://inthesetimes.com/working/entry/16363/with_chokwe_lumumbas_death_mississippi_auto_workers_lose_a_union_ally

- Chokwe Lumumba Be Like Him: Dare to Struggle, Dare to Win http://blackworkersforjustice.org/chokwe-lumumba-be-like-him-dare-to-struggle-dare-to-win/

- A Tribute to Chokwe Lumumba http://www.theblackscholar.org/a-tribute-to-chokwe-lumumba/

- The Election Victory of Chokwe Lumumba http://www.socialistalternative.org/2013/12/12/the-election-victory-of-chokwe-lumumba-part-one-of-two/

- Freeing the Land, Rebuilding our Movements: Reflections on the Legacies of Chokwe Lumumba and Luis Nieves Falcon http://www.tandfonline.com/doi/pdf/10.1080/10455752.2014.916954

Jackson Rising Conference Mobilization

- After Jackson Loses its Radical Mayor, a Movement Spreads in the South http://www.thenation.com/article/179878/after-jackson-loses-its-radical-mayor-movement-spreads-south

- Jackson Rising: The Bold Agenda of Mayor Chokwe Lumumba for 2014 http://hiphopandpolitics.com/2014/01/16/jackson-rising-bold-agenda-mayor-chokwe-lumumba-2014/
- Why We All Should Care about the Mayoral Race in Jackson, MS http://www.huffingtonpost.com/asha-bandele-/jackson-mississippi-mayor-election_b_5086812.html
- Realizing Mayor Lumumba's Promise http://www.huffingtonpost.com/aaron-bartley/realizing-mayor-lumumbas-sustainability_b_5185933.html
- Building Jackson Strong, One Person at a Time http://www.jacksonfreepress.com/news/2014/apr/30/building-jackson-strong-one-person-time/
- After Death of Radical Mayor, Mississippi's Capitol Wrestles with His Economic Vision http://www.yesmagazine.org/commonomics/mississippi-capital-jackson-wrestles-economic-vision

Jackson Rising Conference Reports

- Free the Land! Jackson Rising http://www.theselc.org/jackson_rising
- Will Co-Op's Spark a New Civil Rights Movement? http://rooflines.org/3714/will_co-ops_spark_a_new_civil_rights_movement/
- Jackson Rising, Black Mutual Aid, Cooperatives, Mondragon, and All That http://oreaddaily.blogspot.com/2014/05/jackson-rising-black-mutual-aid.html
- Up South, Down South: A Detroit Delegates Recap of Jackson Rising http://www.orchestratedpulse.com/2014/05/jackson-rising-detroit/
- Jackson Rises to Face New Challenges http://www.solidarity-us.org/site/node/4175
- Mississippi Rising http://www.progressive.org/news/2014/05/187692/mississippi-rising
- A Radical See Grows in Jackson, MS http://wagingnonviolence.org/feature/radical-seed-grows-jackson-miss/
- After Jackson Loses its Radical Mayor, a Movement Spreads in the South http://www.thenation.com/article/179878/after-jackson-loses-its-radical-mayor-movement-spreads-south#
- The Dream that Lives in our Hearts: Reflections from Jackson Rising 2014 http://blackorganizingproject.org/dream-lives-hearts/
- Jackson Rising: People Power and the New Cooperative Movement

http://www.commondreams.org/views/2014/05/30/jackson-rising-people-power-and-new-cooperative-movement

The Struggle Continues: Cooperation Jackson and the Road Forward

- Chokwe Antar Lumumba doesn't need City Hall to lead Jackson, MS into a new Era http://www.ebony.com/news-views/chokwe-antar-lumumba-294#axzz3TdfQqD5K
- After Death of Radical Mayor, Mississippi's Capital Wrestles with His Economic Vision http://www.yesmagazine.org/commonomics/mississippi-capital-jackson-wrestles-economic-vision
- Chokwe Lumumba Center Opens with Ferguson Talk http://www.jacksonfreepress.com/news/2014/nov/20/chokwe-lumumba-center-opens-ferguson-talk/
- How Cooperation Jackson is transforming the Poorest State in the Union http://www.shareable.net/blog/how-cooperation-jackson-is-transforming-the-poorest-state-in-the-us
- Bringing Solutions to COP21 http://www.truth-out.org/opinion/item/33948-bringing-solutions-to-cop21-a-conversation-with-cooperation-jackson-s-brandon-king
- COP21: What Paris can learn from a Mississippi Coop http://www.yesmagazine.org/new-economy/cop21-what-paris-can-learn-from-a-mississippi-co-op-20151203
- Lessons and Attempts: http://thresholdmag.org/2015/02/09/kali-akuno-speaks-from-jackson/
- The Revolutionary Life and Strange Death of a Radical Black Mayor https://www.vice.com/en_us/article/5gj7da/free-the-land-v23n2
- Building Power in a Frontline Community: The Cooperation Jackson Model http://www.tandfonline.com/doi/full/10.1080/08854300.2016.1195180

CPSIA information can be obtained
at www.ICGtesting.com
Printed in the USA
LVHW080313251020
669609LV00003B/39